# VILLAGE TALES

# VILLAGE TALES

Henry Williamson

BRESLICH & FOSS

with ROBINSON PUBLISHING

LONDON

Breslich & Foss
with Robinson Publishing
Middlesex House
34 Cleveland Street
London W1P 5FB


First published as *Tales of a Devon Village* by Faber & Faber 1945
Published by Robinson Publishing 1984
© The Estate of Henry Williamson
Series Design: Lawrence & Gerry Design Group

British Library Cataloguing
in Publication Data

Williamson, Henry
    [Tales of a Devon village]. Village tales.
    I. Title      II. Village tales
    823'.912[F]         PR6045.I55


ISBN 1-85004-019-2 Pbk


Printed in Great Britain by
Richard Clay (The Chaucer Press) Ltd,
Bungay, Suffolk

# CONTENTS

TALES OF A DEVON VILLAGE, with its companion volume LIFE IN A DEVON VILLAGE, is compiled with material gathered together originally in two books I wrote some years ago and called *The Village Book* and *The Labouring Life*. Both dealt with an observed and authenticated period that has now passed away—the first decade between the two industrial wars of the twentieth century.

I was never fully satisfied with them; they were a collection of varying fragments rather than unified books. Now, after an interval of several years of hard physical work, as labourer and farmer, I have set about giving each its own unity, based on what spirit of truth accompanies my life.

1944                                    H. W.

## Chapter One

# THE BADGER DIG

I was a young ex-officer who had got through the war, and later had escaped from a distasteful job in London to a cottage in North Devon. I was filled with excitement and ambition to write about the things I heard and saw about me in the village, on the hills, and by the sea. To be sure, not many of the stories I wrote were published, but I knew they would be read and esteemed, one day. When I first went to Devon, it had not become a national holiday ground. Cottages by the sea could be rented furnished for fifteen shillings a week. Few motor cars were to be seen on the red iron-stone roads. I found the village, where I had settled, to be full of petty jealousies and conflicts, the inevitable condition of a remote living where every other man was a small owner of property, where the old squire had departed, and only a few went to church on Sunday morning, or to Chapel on Sunday afternoon. This book is a record of village life of those times—the decade following the Armistice of 1919.

I lived in a thatched cottage with a spaniel dog and a small black and white cat; and one morning in February, 1922—it was St. Valentine's Day I remember—I closed my door behind me and set out to walk across the hills to a distant coombe or valley where a badger was to be dug out, accompanied by what I imagined to be the rites of the chase. I did not like badger-digging, or the idea of any bird or animal suffering or dying; even so, occasionally I got on my racing motor-cycle and went to a town twenty miles away, and hired a hunter, to follow the foxhounds. I was only an amateur sportsman: I did not like to think of the death of a fox, although in the country of the Stevenstone Hunt few foxes were killed, they were so numerous, and the woods were thick, with much covert or holding; and as in all North

Devon, there were many "hedges" of stone and earth, topped by ash, thorn, beech, and other scrub growth.

A local publican, whom I disliked—though later we were to become the best of friends—had told me of the badger dig. He was taking his famous terrier, the Mad Mullah, to try it for courage against other terriers. He said he was going by car, but I preferred to walk there by myself. Fancy riding in a car when one could walk across four miles of hilly fields!

On this St. Valentine's Day I set out with my spaniel, to walk north up the lane to Windwhistle Spinney and onwards to the valley running down to Woolcombe Bay. From the high ground of the down I could see the Atlantic Ocean, grey and troubled. Lundy arose vaguely out of the mist of the night's storm. I could see the headland over my shoulder, in the line of the wind, its brown and green fields divided by dark lines that were stone-ditched banks, topped with ragged furze and thorns, some cut and laid under sods. The distant headland was like a dead animal lying on its side, the green flanks sunken on the hidden frame.

Along the uneven line of dark cliffs below the headland fields rose white bursts of waves along its length, recalling to my mind a preliminary bombardment of the Siegfried Stellung seen from the high ground of St. Leger five springtimes since. Over the westward point, called Bag Leap, I saw a flock of wheeling sea-gulls; probably a trapper was at work along one of the hedges, and they were crying out against his presence. I could well imagine the wild wailing and cries as of insanity that these birds made in early spring, when they had chosen their nesting sites; but now the wind thrumming in my ears was the only sound.

Suddenly my spaniel, who had been hunting rabbits in a patch of brake fern in a corner of the stony field, began to yelp in distress. The yelp changed to an agony of howling; I could see him rolling and leaping in the bracken. He had put his foot on the iron plate of a rabbit gin, and the steel serrated jaws had snapped up, and now held his paw. He would not keep still while I tried to release him. He twisted and leapt, biting the iron spring, and the chain fastening it to the ground. I shouted encouragement

8

to him, and he lay down for a moment, but the pain and the fear, the frenzy of being held by something he could not understand, were stronger than the voice of his master. The spring was too strong to be depressed by my hand, so I stood on it; while he snapped at my hands, each snap ending abruptly in but a graze of my fingers; he would not bite me. Putting all my weight on one foot I pressed down the spring, the jaws loosened, and he was free, barking and gurgling with delight, jumping up and licking the hand he had almost bitten.

His voice was low, with numberless subtle inflexions. He had many thoughts, which he could not express; he was incoherent and hysterical. He looked at me, straining to speak with his lips and tongue; but his mouth was large and slobbery, his tongue only fit to lap with, and to perspire through; his teeth were too primitive for conversation. A fine head for holding a rabbit, with its long jaws and white ivory teeth: and I thought as the gentle creature told his love for me that one day in the future his descendants would be able to talk. The thoughts were there, some of them inherited from generations of ancestors faithful to men; others taken in from impressions of myself, a further layer stored in the remote mind-cupboard. For man may pass on to others the fine traits that are the heritage of his long and struggling evolution: this was true of his fellows especially, and, I thought as I walked along the high down, it was true in various degrees throughout the realms of all life where intelligence and reasoning had been alchemized from instinct—which was made by habit founded on adaptation.

The wind rushed past us, shaking the dry skeletons of the thistles in the stony field, trembling the carlines—so loved by the goldfinches—the dry grasses, the white and brittle charlock frames. From each it drew a sound: a whistle, a sibilance, a sigh, a keening noise. On the ground, where during the past summer the charlock had risen in legions with the oaten stems, small fern-like leaves were grey and shrivelled: these were the dead silverweeds, whose yellow sensitive flowers had throbbed to the sun, and closed in shadow. I looked for a blossom, a sign of

9

growing plant life, but there was nothing. I must wait: the time was not yet. For the time of year before the early spring had been hard and sunless, with frosts at night and icy ocean winds. Some years it is a mild period, with hot sunshine and warm rain, when stray burnet roses bloom on the sandy terraces below, primroses and celandines open under the thorns on the hedges, and larks sing with April fervours.

There were great rainclouds in the sky, seeming from the top of the down to be hanging lower than myself; they drifted above the scores of strip-like fields which lay behind me. Where the plough was at work the fields were dark brown, and seabirds were grey specks in the new hair-like furrows. Miles behind me, to the south, and now dim in the mist, an expanse of sand dunes and grazing marsh stretched flat to the estuary; and across the estuary the spray of the high-tide breakers rose like smoke off the Pebble Ridge. The sun was shining there in the gold, breaker-blown vapour. Nearer, as I watched, the headland fields glowed with a beautiful luminous green; and then were shut off from my sight as by a grey lattice blind, where the rain was falling.

I walked onwards in a northerly direction, so that the rain-wind from the south-west cut over my left shoulder. Beside one of the stone hedges, on which bent thorns grew with grey lichens fastened on them, a man was standing, knocking iron with a hammer. He was a trapper, who rented the trapping rights from the farmer, paying for them by a number of weeks' labouring in the summer. He had a sack containing gins and pegs. Talking with him, I learned that the badger holt or earth was just over the brow of the hill. I left him to his gin-tilling, and walked with the wind behind me to the higher hill in front. Suddenly the valley opened before me. Fields seen across the valley, small under the sky, were square, three-sided, and in long strips cut up by dark lines of bank and hedge. Down one field, moving slowly in the distance, was a trickle of black specks and tinier white specks—the men and terriers of the Badger Digging Club walking down the hillside.

Very slowly the trickling party crossed the valley, and climbed the hill. When they came near I saw that some of the men **carried** picks and shovels; one, with a nose once broken and re-set irregularly, carried a large basket of sandwiches and a gallon earthenware jar of whiskey. About twelve terriers, some of the rough-haired kind, were trotting on single and double leashes. In front walked a tall man in old fawn riding breeches, cloth leggings, a red waistcoat, tweed coat, white stock fastened by a pin made from a badger's penis bone. It resembled a two-inch length of quill. He wore a grey bowler hat. He was, as I soon learned, the Master of the Club. Just behind him walked a shorter man, the huntsman, dressed in the same style, but with a cloth cap. He wore pince-nez glasses, and had a fat, pale face. He looked what he was, as I learned later, an urban shopkeeper. He and the Master were friends. Like the Master, the huntsman wore a red waistcoat with brass buttons engraved with the Club initials.

The party, when first I had viewed it, was moving to the badger's earth, about fifty yards from where I was standing with my excited spaniel. It was tunnelled in a small brake of black-thorn, elderberry, gorse and bramble. Here the peaceful badgers had lived for many years, slowly digging their corridors and relining their sleeping chambers with moss, grass and bracken. By day they slept, coming out at night to seek food, usually following the same tracks or paths down hedge and ditch.

The badger does little, if any, harm to the countryman. In the Middle Ages he may have been a nuisance, for records exist in some parish churches of sums of 4*d*. being paid for his death. Sometimes in a field of corn his passing or playful rolling will press down many stalks; but no one in the village inns, when I asked, had heard of any harm being done by a badger. Brock, as he is called, goes his peaceful way, digging roots and taking berries, worms, slugs, beetles and mice; if he scents a nest of young rabbits in a bury he will dig them out and eat them. Wasp grubs he likes, and will soon discover the comb with scrapings of curved, black, bear-like claws. When, lumbering down a hedge at night, he finds a rabbit in a gin, he will eat it or take it away. Gins and wires have been found in his earths; the badger is a strong digger, and soon digs up the iron peg that has been hammered into the ground.

Just before the brake the master and huntsman stopped. The innkeeper who had carried the food and drink put the basket on the grass and removed his cap to scratch his head. Terriers strained at the leash, yapping and howling. Some were shivering. The others walked up the hill, and stopped: a farmer and two labourers with digging tools; three small boys; an adolescent schoolgirl with flaxen hair, ruddy face, always smiling; her father, a small, nattily-dressed, red-faced, long-nosed man who reminded me, vaguely, of a badger; and his wife, a brown-faced woman in tweeds. The master and huntsman, in their red waistcoats, scrambled up a mossy bank, and examined the entrance holes to the badgers' home.

My spaniel by this time was extremely excited, leaping up at me and telling me about the strange dogs and men. Fearing that the sportsmen would be annoyed by his presence, I took him fifty yards away and tied him to a stump of furze bush, and went to the badgers' earth. His howling mingled with the terriers' whining and the wild cries of gulls soaring over the hill.

The master was kneeling before a heap of earth outside a round tunnel about fourteen inches across, and slanting down in darkness. He was looking for the marks of pads. He found a hair about two inches long. Twiddling it between forefinger and thumb, it was felt to be flat. He held it out for me to twiddle. It was silver for a quarter inch at the tapered end, then brown, in three shades scarcely discernible.

A yard outside the tunnel entrance two shallow pits had been scratched. The master stooped to examine them. They were the latrines. There were many beetle wing-covers. It was obvious that the earth was being used. He stood up, and said "They're home. All right." The spectators came up and crowded round. A terrier was slipped from leash, and crept down the pipe. On his knees the master kneeled and listened. He drew a copper horn from between the second and third button of his red waist-coat, pressed it against the side of his mouth, and blew three faint toots.

He heard a terrier snarl come from the darkness, and the thud of feet. Tally ho!

The huntsman cut a long bramble, stripped one end of thorns —the end he would handle—and when the terrier returned with red-frothed jaws he poked it down the pipe to find which way it was tunnelled. It ran west. The master ordered digging into the hill about two yards from the entrance. A ragged hairy man seized a pick and drove it into the turf. The master commanded everyone to get back as he lit a cigarette, and with three toots of the copper horn encouraged a second terrier to enter the hole.

The terriers tied to various trees continued to howl into the cold wind, and men began to swing their arms to get warmth into them. Almost fiercely the strong, hairy labourer tore at the grass. For an hour the dog remained by the unseen badger, then it crept out, bitten on the shoulder and in the lower jaw. The wind blew a flake of bloody froth on the grey bowler of the master simultaneously with the ash of a man's cigarette. These marks, I noticed, remained to the end of the dig.

A terrier bitch was sent down, and the digging went on. I went to see my spaniel, and found him frantic with misery and joy. He implored to be released. Petting made him more frantic so I left him yelling to the dull clouds his utter misery of being tied while some sport, immense and unknown, was going on without him.

The badger holes were on the slope of the hill, above a thorn brake. The blackthorns were spiny and leafless, but their buds were bound tight from the winter's cold. A magpie's nest, with the thorn-cover fallen in, was derelict in the centre of the brake. A mouse-like squeaking came from the tree as the wind swayed a stiff bough and rubbed it against a dry branch. Underneath, curving slightly, a path about nine inches wide was pressed through the scanty dead weeds and past the thin blackthorn stems. It was the exit path of the badgers, down which they had bundled in the dusk; had it been the return route, the effort of climbing up would have worn a more distinct path. A gorse bush near had two gold specks among its green prickles. I thought as they dug that it was eager for the sun to send the green south wind of spring, when its blossoms could multiply, even as the thoughts of man. The sow badger would have her little ones; and perhaps a bright-eyed kestrel would come to the old pie's nest in the thorns and lay her eggs. Swaling fires for the gorse, tongs and hunting knife for the badgers, gamekeeper's shot for the kestrel, loneliness for man; these were the ways of life, I thought. Yet endeavour went on; all things aspired to the sun and the sky.

My habit of unfocusing my senses from the present made me forget the cold as I noticed blossom, nest, and badger path; but a hoarse burring voice over my shoulder asking me if I would care for a drink made me aware that the broken-nosed innkeeper was by my side. I went with him to the basket a few yards away, and in a thick glass he poured me nearly half a pint of brown whiskey.

The raw spirit was like sunlight on my throat. Soon the badger dig took on a jovial aspect. It was a survival of one of the oldest sports in Britain, going back to the time of the Normans, when the terriers, the earth-dogs, came over in the wooden galleys. The master came for a drink; he told me with rage that someone recently had shot a badger near Lynton. Such a thing, he declared, was monstrous, when a postcard would have brought himself and terriers and diggers. He insisted, and he was sincere, that badgers would soon be exterminated were it not for the clubs; for where a club was in existence, generally no badgers were killed except by the club, and therefore a certain number would be left alive. I knew this was true of the wild red deer on Exmoor, which in summer did much damage to corn and root crops; but I did not know it was so with the badger. Also, declared the master, badger-digging improved the strain of terriers; the bravest dogs were sought after for breeding. Feeling the kick of the whiskey, I asked him if it improved the strain of badgers. He stared at me, and left me. He thought me silly, I imagined.

Noon came; and they were still digging with spade, two-bill, bar, pick and mattock. The hours rushed away with the wind into space. We ate our sandwiches, and various men took turns at digging. A terrier was below, the very fierce dog belonging to the innkeeper of the Lower House in the village, a rough-haired fox terrier that was a perfect badger dog: the Mad Mullah. He was so fierce that whenever he saw the stuffed masks, or heads of badgers, on the walls of the Lower House bar, he snarled and leapt up at them. It was not safe to take my emotional spaniel near him when a badger mask was held out to the Mad Mullah. Once he flung him on his back, and straddled him with teeth bared at his quick-swallowing throat.

I could hear the Mad Mullah's ceaseless barks below, with the grunts of badgers, and scraping noises. Very shortly the shouts of the diggers caused everyone to crowd round, the master to implore more room, and the tethered dogs to whimper and yelp more furiously. A pick had broken into the "pipe", and the tail of the Mad Mullah was seen. Picks were thrown down, and shovels taken in hand. Quickly the hole was enlarged. Suddenly the terrier backed out. The onlookers crushed back in panic, for a flat head shaped like a bear's, but no larger than that of a terrier, had appeared at the hole. It had black patches on its cheeks and through its eyes, and a white broad arrow running from nose to forehead and along both sides of its neck. It disappeared, and the terrier, with earthy hackles raised, dashed after it.

Very soon the hole was widened. The master, after many demands for space, all made in tones of the greatest exasperation, knelt down with a pair of tongs in his hands. His pallid brow was sweating. The tongs were made of iron, the handles being three feet long, and when closed round brock's neck the pincers formed a collar, or iron circle, which pinned him down. The terrier was pulled off by his master, struggling and snarling. It is the custom of some clubs, I learned, to allow terriers, especially untried dogs, to face the badgers held in the tongs. The bites, if any, are said not to harm it, as the hide of the back and shoulders is tough and nearly half an inch thick.

Handing the long tongs to the huntsman, the pale-faced master grasped the badger by its stumpy yellowish tail, and held it at arm's length. The captive made no attempt to bite or struggle. Its tiny pig-like eyes were fixed, its short legs spread, showing the squat body and yellowish-white underparts. With his knife the master scraped at a part of the suspended animal's body; and suddenly thrusting the knife under my nose, he explained that it was the scenting gland of the badger.

Someone held open the mouth of a potato sack, a little fearfully, lest the animal writhe sideways and bite him; but swung by its tail, the badger appeared to be helpless. Had a man's wrist been near its jaws, it might have bitten it through, making to meet the front and canine teeth of upper and lower jaw, and cracking, in the same bite, the bone with its hind teeth. The master, who addressed most of his remarks to me, then continued his lecture: the badger, he said, "in proportion to its weight, has the most powerful neck and jaw muscle of any of the carnivora. It belongs to the same family as the stoat, the weasel, the otter, the ferret, and the rare polecat." I thought it must have had very powerful jaws, for when I was a boy a ferret accidentally caught in a gin one day bit through the knuckle bone of one of my fingers, making its teeth meet four times in the space of two seconds or less; and the ferret did not weigh two pounds. The spring balance gave the badger's weight—it was the boar—as thirty and a half pounds, or more than fifteen times the weight of the ferret. I thought the master's lecture unknowledgeable, but said nothing. He looked extremely unfit for a sportsman.

The badger in the sack having been weighed, it was tied and thrown down. The hidden, curled-up shape was quiet. The fierce terrier was in the pipe again, engaging the sow badger. After a few minutes' digging she was seen. The Mullah's muzzle was pink with blood and froth. The sow, heavy with young, was swift in her sudden lunges—much swifter than the dog. Round her neck the curved iron forceps met in a circle, and she was held. The master tailed her, and dropped her into another sack. He pushed back his hat, with its dirty brilliantine stain spread through the grey felt and the band, and lit a cigarette with a shaky hand. Then he began to yell *Leu-leu-leu! Gar-gar-garn!* He and his huntsmen made other bloodthirsty cries. Then they drank more whiskey. Terriers howled and yelled. The badgers lay still in the sacks. Everyone seemed pleased with the sport. I went away to release the spaniel, who leapt up at me, distraught with joy. He sniffed the destroyed holt, the bitten fern, grass, and moss in the broken cavern that had been the badgers' kitchen. He seemed not to like the scent, and ran away. I called him to heel, and seizing him by the collar, put his nose to one of the sacks. He gave a gurgle of fear and struggled in terror. He would not go near the sacks again.

Master and huntsmen had another drink of whiskey, and received congratulations from the short man, his daughter and wife, and the innkeeper. As the master was praising the Mad Mullah's goodness to its owner, that dog pulled the leash out of the innkeeper's hand and dashed at the nearest bag, biting the bulge of jute. It was secured, however, and given a kick in the ribs by its embarrassed owner. The crooked-nosed man lifted the jar again, and filled up the master's mug with the brown spirit. More cigarettes were lit, and questions asked about the fate of the badgers. The farmer was consulted, and said that he would let the master decide. "I'll be satisfied, gennulmen, with whatever you gennulmen may care to decide." So it was decided to kill the boar and to release the sow.

One of the bags was opened. The greyish animal lay quiet and subdued at the bottom. It made no effort to escape or to bite as the jute was rolled back. Someone held its tail. Underneath, the gland containing the musk-like scent—which the master again informed us was for sexual attraction—was again pointed out. It was the boar. Both sacks were taken to the grassy field below,

17

while the terriers howled and the wind flapped overcoats and made a squeaky sighing in the blackthorns.

In the middle of the field they stopped.

"All terriers to be leashed, please," ordered the master. "Everyone to stand behind me."

The mouth of the bag was untied, and the sow badger tumbled out. Immediately she set off for home: a grey animal, low and wide and heavy, her short pointed tail yellow like an old tallow candle. She bounded along, heavy with the unborn, seeming to move slowly, and yet covering the ground quickly. The master shouted *Leu-leu-leu! Aa-ee-i-oo-yah!* and blew the horn. The terriers set up a frenzied yelping chorus. Somebody cheered. Suddenly the Mad Mullah got loose, and raced after the sow. The master swore. The dog overtook the sow a few yards before the brake of blackthorn. I saw the white flash of her head many times. The dog would not go near her. Every time he rushed she turned and snapped, and the white arrow showed against the grass. Through the brake she bundled, getting safely into her ruined home. The innkeeper went for his dog, gave it several kicks in the ribs and returned with flushed face, muttering.

The second bag was held up. A sharp spade blow on the nose stunned the still boar badger inside. The inert body was rolled out, with half closed eyes and stumpy paws held up limply. From his pocket the master took a knife with a dagger blade. Putting his foot on the boar's chest, he leaned down, and pressed the blade into its throat, turning the blade with a scooping movement in order to enlarge the hole. When withdrawn, purple-red blood gushed. The grey hairy body was held up by its scut. The thick flow drained out and fouled some early daisies. The animal gave two feeble kicks as the life broke out of its body.

I heard the first lark of the new year singing at that moment, the shrill silver-shavings of music coming in a lull of the wind. High against the rain clouds it fluttered, a dark speck. Just before me on the ground the master was kneeling, hacking at the neck of the dead badger. The sharp blade severed skin and red-brown muscles. It was a thick neck, and the head had to be twisted off.

Rising with it in his hand, the master presented it to the smiling schoolgirl, whose smile, I fancied, was only on her lips, not in her eyes. Her dislike of the scene was probably not my fancy, for I learned afterwards that she was the daughter of the long-nosed little man who had been standing by quietly during the dig. His resemblance to a badger had been remarked by others before me. I learned from the broken-nosed man that his friends called him Brock. He told me he had dug out a thousand badgers in Kent and Sussex, and had released all but fifteen, which the farmers had insisted were hen-takers. The fifteen he had killed reluctantly, he said.

Next a pad was cut and twisted off. Then the Mad Mullah got loose again, flinging itself with a snarl on the carcase, fixing its teeth into the neck and shaking it. The master, who had been straddling the trunk, went white in the face with rage, and raising himself on his knees, he flourished the bloody knife and screamed, with froth at the corners of his lips,

"If you don't hold your flaming dog in, I'll cut his blazing head off."

"He's too strong for me," yelled the angry innkeeper. "He broke his lead."

"I'll cut his flickering neck off next time!"

The innkeeper's face grew lilac with anger, and shaking his fist he bawled that "if his flickering dog's head was cut off, then he would cut off the master's bloody head," and other things as well. Our eyes brightened; this was much better than the business with shovels, picks, tongs, and knives. But unfortunately the master, after going a putty colour in the face, which blended well with that part of his grey hat not stained with hair-oil, did not reply. His mouth was frothed along every part of his lips; those lips moved, but no words came; he pushed his grey bowler further back on his head, while a big vein slowly subsided on his temple. Then he went on with the severing of the pads.

These four trophies being removed, the trunk was opened and the liver ripped out. A small boy came forward to be blooded, and on forehead and cheeks the gore of the slain was dabbled.

The same thing was due to myself, since it was the first time I had remained to see the death of a badger. I submitted; after all, I was a guest. I was given a pad—covered with short black hairs, with five black digging claws, three of them broken. I murmured thanks, and tried not to look unpleasant, as I wondered if the boar had broken them as he dug for the safety of his mate and himself. His labour availed nothing, for pick and spade and harrying terriers working along a tunnel are more speedy than ten claws scratching on hard stone and earth. Now he was a lump without head and paws, and his blood was on my brow and cheek. I felt I had been false to myself, and yet another thought told me such feelings flourished only in nervous weakness. Why worry? And yet, only ten claws.

The lump was thrown into the air with yells of *Tear 'im, tear 'im*. The terriers having been released—except that of the innkeeper which was being dragged, howling and looking back, up the hill—the master blew his horn. Snarling, worrying, snapping, shaking, the mob of dogs pulled the grey lump down the sloping field, leaving behind on the mossy grass a long red smudge like the track of a giant ruddled slug. The little copper horn was examined, and the score of graven names of former meets read by the curious. I released the spaniel, who leapt to the worry, barking his excitement, but giving no more than the gentlest touch with his nose. He kills nothing; he will retrieve an egg; not the smallest dent is made. With the dried blood stiff on my temples I climbed the hill, cursing the satanic ways of men, yet knowing myself vile, for they had not known what they were doing, but I had betrayed an innocent; and all the tears—weak, whiskey tears—would not bring the badger back to life again.

## Chapter Two

# THE DARKENING OF THE DOORWAY

### I

One morning as I was sitting at the table with the wheels and pins of a grandfather clock spread before me on a newspaper, the only door in the cottage being open to admit light to the dim and ancient kitchen, the space was darkened, and looking up I saw a man in a picturesque get-up standing there. He was big and burly, with arrogant dark eyes and long curly coal-black ringlets. He wore a suit of rough greenish material, with bell-bottom trousers. As I looked up he said:

"Have you any old jewelry, gold, silver, rings, brooches, precious stones such as diamonds, opals, pearls, emeralds, rubies, articles of ivory, jade, or old false teeth in any broken condition? I buy particularly in the smallest quantities, old watches and everything of the slightest value. Don't be afraid to show me even one tooth if you have it."

"Do you mean that?" I said, a sudden thought coming to enliven me.

He looked uncertain.

"Have you any old jewelry, gold, silver, rings—" he began.

"I heard you the first time," I replied, trying to be funny; and certainly not meaning to insult him, I added, "Wait, I have the very thing you are after," and going to the dresser, I picked up a wisdom tooth which Mr. Sunncott, the dentist, had wrenched out of my jaw the previous afternoon. The visitor stared at it. His chin was blue with uncut bristles.

"Are you asking for a sock on the jaw?" he asked, appearing to crouch a little, and drawing back his formidable chin.

"I asked for nothing," I replied, as easily as I could. "I thought you asked me for a false tooth."

# THE DARKENING OF THE DOORWAY

"Because you'll get it, quick, if you ain't careful!"

"I shall certainly try to be careful, then," I replied. "And I assure you that this is the only precious metal, jewel, or false tooth in this cottage."

The other stared at me, then at the tooth, then at me again.

"Don't you know no difference between real and false?"

"Not always. This is an alleged wisdom tooth. It did little, if any, work; it has played me false as a molar—"

I picked myself up from the floor, as I heard him saying to Mrs. Revvy next door, "Have you any old jewelry, gold, silver, rings, brooches, precious stones—", and when he had finished, he moved on to Mrs. "Thunderbolt's" door beyond, and then to other doors in the village. As he went down the walled passage before the cottages I called out, "Did you get any emeralds or old false teeth?" but he replied with an expression which was a command to achieve the supernatural, since Man is not hermaphrodisaical.

I returned to the wheels and pins of the clock, which recently I had bought at an auction. It was a grand old clock, with supernatural flowers and birds painted on its face, some of them almost obliterated by the touch of the index-fingers of previous owners turning round the iron-scrolled minute hand, for how many corrections during the past two hundred years? I was trying to discover why the clock sometimes struck twenty-seven times at one o'clock, and anything from three to about three thousand at midnight, when my doorway was darkened again.

An entrancing figure stood there, surely a sight for sore eyes, or, to adapt the literary phrase, for sore jaws. What a beautiful gipsy girl, to visit a lonely young author! Her purple hat was perched on coils of fair burnished hair. Her eyes were sea-gray. Her face and neck and the upper part of her shoulders, and her rounded arms, bared to the elbows, were a clear golden brown. High tan boots were laced half-way up the calves of her shapely legs. She carried a wicker basket of feather dusters, mats, tea-cosies, small brushes, and some china cups and teapots. Did she look at me with an expression of intellectual, of even poetic eagerness, tinged with sorrow, as she spoke in a low voice,

"Oh, do buy a duster or a mat, my dear. Your floor needs a broom to sweep it clean. Have you a teapot? I have a beautiful cosy for it."

"I make my tea in the kettle," I stammered.

"Buy a teapot," she wheedled, stepping over the threshold. She was about eighteen years old. Her ears under the bright thick coils of hair were small and pink as coral. "Look, my gentleman, a teapot of the best quality. Only five shillings and sixpence. With a cosy to keep your tea warm, ten shillings. I'll tell you what, nine shillings. Only nine shillings. Eight and sixpence, my gentleman, don't be hard on a poor girl trying to get enough for some bread and cheese."

"I've got some bread and cheese," I managed to reply. "Onions, too. Would you care—?"

"There, I knew you had a kind heart, sir. Eight shillings the teapot and cosy. With this brush, only ten shillings. Come now, don't be so hard. Although it is good for a man to get value for his money. What, be the old clock valled abroad? Look here, seven shillings and sixpence. I can't go no lower, wish I could, but times be hard."

Once more the doorway-light was partly occluded. A neighbour of mine stood there, called Uncle Joe. Taking his pipe from his gums, he paused, then said slowly, "Begging your pardon, neighbour, but if you'll take my opinion about thaccy clock—"

"Thanks," I called out, hastily, "I'll be able to see you in a moment. Thanks for coming. In a few minutes—"

"Thank you, sir," said Uncle Joe, and after solemnly spitting on my step, he shuffled back the way he had come.

"Really, you know, the kettle is sufficient, really—" I began, hoping thereby to prolong the visit of the beautiful feline creature. She seemed to like me, too. Perhaps—

"Seven shillings. That's the cheapest I dare sell them. They cost me more than that. Times be hard. They'll look proper on the chimney piece over there. What, be mending th' ould clock?

Come, six and sixpence, and it's getting blood out of stone."

Slowly I got on my feet, and went to the seal's skull on the dresser where I kept my loose change for housekeeping.

"Six shillings," I said, feeling mean and hard-hearted under the candid gaze of her gray eyes.

"Thank you, sir," she said, and quickly put a broom of the kind I had seen in Woolworth's marked sixpence, and a teapot ditto, together with a tea-cosy of thick wool, red, green, yellow and black, on the table.

"Please don't call me 'sir'," I replied, astounded at my own boldness. My jaw had ceased to ache. Perhaps I could make her a cup of tea? But I said instead, while despising myself for my cowardice, "Did you make this cosy?"

Perhaps she would divine that I was trying to reveal how the thought of her handiwork was inspiring a lonely artist dedicated to beauty?

Before she could reply, another shadow fell across the threshold. It was a very small shadow. An individual peered round the door-post. The greater part of one hand was in its mouth. It was the fattest baby, nearly naked. Its skin was as golden-brown as the half-exposed bosom of the girl whose gray eyes, I had been thinking, were the colour of sea-trout leaping through the waves in summer. With relief I noticed that the thick curly hair of the monstrous baby was black as coal, that its eyes were dark as an Exmoor peat-pool.

"Your little brother?" I asked, just as the baby, without removing hand from mouth, emitted a lusty bellow of "Momma!"

"Momma's just coming," she crooned. "No, sir, the cosy was made by my husband."

"Oh?" I said. "He must be very clever."

Then, as a monstrous shadow completely darkened the sun, I perceived in my doorway the figure of the man who had called about precious stones and old false teeth. As she followed the burly giant, who was slouching away with the baby in his arms, I called out,

"Oh, that's your husband, is it. Then tell him to go and—" Only my knowledge of physiology prevented me from continuing.

"Tell him yourself," she retorted over her shoulder. "But don't blame me if he snouts you again."

While I was fumbling with the wheels and pins of my clock, in the peace of solitude once more, I heard Uncle Joe shuffling along, and once more my light was absorbed.

"I only wanted vor tell 'ee, begging your pardon," he said. "That if you was to boil your glock in soda water, it might well cure thaccy extra striking you was telling about. I boiled my glock when others said it were gone in, and it goeth yet, although it ain't particular about half an hour or so every day. I thought I'd tell 'ee that's all."

"Thank you," I replied, looking at the dozens of parts hopelessly mixed up on the table. "Your advice comes just in time to prevent me taking it to pieces. Here's a brush for you. Brush your glock every day with it, and it might recover its old form."

Uncle Joe thanked me, spat in friendly fashion on my doorstone, and went away. Yet once again the shadow in the doorway.

"Yurr," he whispered, glancing over his shoulder, "did 'ee buy it from they rogues and vagabonds? Did 'ee, surenuff? What did they get out of 'ee?"

"A sock on the jaw," I told him.

## 2

The foregoing was an attempt to write lightly and humorously, in desperate response to the negative criticisms of these village tales by the Editors of popular magazines in England and America during the 'twenties.

Most of the stories passed from editorial desk to desk, vainly seeking a home. *The London Mercury* in England and *The Atlantic Monthly* in New England housed a few, thus earning the gratitude of the author; but the majority of Editors considered them dull, uninteresting, altogether unsuitable. The Editors of most magazines declared that they needed sure-fire stuff for their readers in the depressing period when circulations were not always being maintained.

Now for what really happened. The original dull but factual title of this chapter was

### VILLAGE TRADERS

One morning as I was sitting at my table, indolently trying to make up my mind to repair the grandfather clock, which struck at the wrong time, a man in a seedy blue serge suit suddenly appeared in the doorway, and delivered a set-piece request for old gold, old silver, and old false teeth. He made no mention of rubies, sapphires, pearls, or the like. He was not a gipsy, but probably a Jew; he looked like any poor Jew to be seen in any European city or on Broadway. He was unshaven, and looked dirty with it, in his nervous, townee eagerness. "Sorry," I said, "I have nothing." He was persistent, and I repeated curtly that I had nothing. His appearance annoyed me; but in retrospect I was sorry I was so curt, for blank refusal must have been his usual lot in the village through which this poor man walked— for only a poor man would have been forced to do such work. He went away. It is true that a tooth had recently been extracted; but only when he had gone did I think of a joke with the tooth which was still in my pocket. Later, however, I may have told my neighbour that I had offered it to the visiting trader.

As for the gipsies, they came periodically to the village, usually a group about a high two-wheeled cart drawn by a shaggy pony, one probably captured from the wild herds on Exmoor. The pony looked as though it were biding its time while awaiting a chance to escape to the heather hills, to the wind and rain of its wild life again.

Brushes, pans, brooms, mats, rugs, dusters, these are the stock-in-trade of the gipsies, who are disliked and suspected by the villagers. Their prices are high; they are persistent, and hard to get rid of once you have ceased firmly to say that you do not want anything. The women are fine-looking creatures, and usually carry a baby in their arms, to which they make reference, inferring that the baby wants a meal. How they manage to live I do not know, for never have I seen a gipsy selling anything. The gipsy girl described in Part I was to be seen with brooms, etc. for many years; she was certainly good-looking; but I never dared to speak to her.

Another type of regular visitor hoping to leave with more money than he arrived with was the earnest beggar who offered scissors, bootlaces, cotton reels, and such things, and then showed a letter from someone usually unknown expressing the hope that his daughter, or his son, would be enabled to get into the Home or Hospital for his or her sad disability. One man, whose home was twenty miles away, visited the village once a year; and for at least seven years he had shown the same letter, or a copy, from a woman novelist declaring that he was working to maintain an epileptic daughter.

Another old man, with long white hair and beard scrupulously combed, and threadbare clothes without stain, and worn boots always brushed but never shining, used to arrive at my cottage twice every spring and summer. He was mild-voiced and grateful if I bought only a penny stud. He appeared to be serene and happy; the walking kept him in health; and possibly he made three or four shillings a week to add to his Old Age Pension.

Then there was the tall thin man who got into a small boat made by himself out of herring-boxes, and rowed down with the ebb-tide from Barum, past the swift-receding gravel ridge called Shrarshook and its spinning red buoy, past the lighthouse and the chequer buoy by the rocks called the Hurleyburlies, and out over one of the worst sand-bars in English waters. In the boat, which was flat and only about 8 feet long, he carried lengths of deal wood, an old tent, and a grey-faced dog. Sometimes he travelled by night, down the river and over the bar, five miles across the sea to the swirling waters hiding the sunken rocks called Bag Leap, and down under the North Side of the headland to Vention Sands. There among the grey boulders above the tide-line he pitched his tent, first making his herring-box

27

flat-bottomed craft fast by mooring her fore and aft with anchors. By day he carved deal hulls and masts for toy boats. Sometimes he walked slowly—a lank grey man, followed by his thin, ancient, narrow-headed, thin-nosed terrier on very tall thin legs—to the village, trying to sell his toys for eighteen pence. Among summer visitors he found an occasional purchaser. The village boys admired and coveted the lovely white ships, but eighteen pence, O sir, only they visitors' children have such a lot of money!

One summer the old man was driven off by rats, which swarmed into his tent, ate his food, and so scared him and his dog that they went home by the next tide and never returned.

These were honest traders; but petty crooks and chisellers also came to the village. Once in a while an old motorcar stopped in the village street, and two men dressed in cheap clothes and carrying large hand-cases called at every cottage. The car had appeared in the village a couple of days previously, and a handbill with an alluring lay-out had been handed in at, or slipped under, every door.

Such a notice—to be called for—gave a ready entrance into every cottage, except that owned by Miss Sleet, the aged body who like a black bat lived alone in the house on the rock. Ladies' Silk Hose, 6d. per pair! Large Bath Towels, 4d. each! Very few of the cottagers ever had a bath—Tom Physick or Fissik, aged 76, once declared that he never had one since he was a baby, if then—but bath towels at 4d.! Dusters 1½d.! Even an umbrella, silk, perfect condition, at 2/-, might be managed.

Prompt cash on delivery only; so scores of orders were taken. "No money until goods are delivered." It must be all right, then. Mary dreams of half a dozen Lawn Handkerchiefs, of using one in church next Sunday. Will they arrive by then? Mrs. Clib thinks of the Striped Shirting Flannel she has ordered for her man Clib, the gravedigger. Since the Rectory has changed hands, Clib misses the lovely shirts he used to be given; and he sweats a lot when digging a grave nowadays. Alice of Hole Farm has ordered half a dozen yards of scarlet flannel, only 3s., for new nightshirts for her father, who always wears red next to

28

# THE DARKENING OF THE DOORWAY

Notice—to be called for

## GREAT CLEARANCE SALE!
### OF UNCLAIMED GOODS AND
### SALVAGE STOCK, FROM
## MESSRS. X. Y. Z. & Co.
### Commission Salesmen,
## LONDON and LIVERPOOL,

Having an ENORMOUS STOCK OF GENERAL MERCHANDISE thrown on the Company's hands through delay and other causes, beg to invite your attention to a short Catalogue of some of the principal items therein

---

### The Stock consists of

LARGE BATH TOWELS, 4/- per dozen
JAP SILK, 6/- dozen yards, 36 inches wide
GLASS CLOTHS, 2/6 per doz.   DUSTERS (large) 1/6 per doz.

We respectfully call the attention of Professional and Business Gentlemen and the Trade, to a large Quantity of Patent Scotch Saxony and other Tweeds, Serges and Worsted Suitings, worth 6/6/0, to be sold at 3/3/0; also Ladies' Costumes, worth 5/5/0, now selling at 50/-. Gentlemen's Flannel Shirts, worth 7/6 each, to be sold at 2/6.

White Calico, 3/- dozen yards, worth 2/- per yard

Oxford Shirting, 3/- doz. yards

Serviettes, 2/- per dozen double damask

500 doz. Lawn Handkerchiefs, 5/- per dozen, worth 18/-

Flannelette, 3/- dozen yards

White and Scarlet Flannel, 6/- doz. yards

50 Gross Ladies' and Gent.'s Silk Umbrellas (perfect Condition), 2/- each

Ladies' Silk Hose, 6d. per pair

LARGE QUANTITY OF FOREIGN SKIN RUGS
LADIES' HANDSOME FUR SETS at a Quarter their Value

One of our travellers will call, when samples can be seen and purchases made

---

### TERMS OF SALE

All Goods warranted equal to sample. Prompt cash on delivery only. On no account shall goods be paid for until delivered.

Prices herein mentioned are quotations only without any engagement whatever, and are subject to being in stock and unsold.

### PLEASE RETAIN CIRCULAR UNTIL AGENT CALLS

#### Orders to be delivered within 21 Days

his skin, as he declares red keeps away colds. Everybody has bought something. Don't pay if you don't like them on delivery!

One man entered the cottage of a neighbour, a young married couple. Carefully his wife looked over the samples. She ordered bath towels, glass cloths, dusters, white calico, Oxford shirting, a gent's silk umbrella. Her husband was working in the garden. The Jew salesman retired to bring in rolls of tweed cloth. He tried to persuade her to buy some. She said no; but he was persistent. Thereupon he began to try and break down her resistance. After five minutes, with red cheeks and tears in her eyes (she was going to have a baby) she implored her husband to come into the house.

Even then, the salesman would not go. He talked, he urged, he gesticulated. He became nasty. He was surly because he could not sell his suitings. He stood there, refusing to go, in the hope of getting an order by causing embarrassment. The cloth was inferior cloth; the suitings were commonplace. Later I learned that he had behaved like that at all the places he had visited where he had dealt with women.

None of the things ordered in the villáge were delivered. They were but lures to get the shoddy cloth-salesmen past the threshold. Such merchants do not return.

*B. R.*

I was standing outside my house when a man with a round clean-shaven face and big horn-rimmed spectacles came up to me, and putting a piece of paper in my hand, he said, with extreme politeness, "Pardon me speaking to you, but do you want the price of a pint?"

"Yes," I replied.

"Well then, am I right in assuming that there is a nice little lot of old stuff in your master's house?"

"There is," I said, "almost nothing else."

"Well then, look me out a few old suits, as well as the other stuff, and a bob's yours for every ten bob I pay out. I'll be back tomorrow. Look, instructions on the bottom. Don't forget."

# THE DARKENING OF THE DOORWAY

## THE WEST COUNTRY PAPER MILLS
### BOBBY ROBERTS
#### WHOLESALE AND RETAIL
## RAG, BONE AND METAL MERCHANT,
*Dealer in Ladies' and Gentlemen's Wardrobes*

In submitting this bill for your inspection, B.R. assures you that there is a great demand for White and Coloured Rags of all sorts for the better supply of Paper Mills.

B.R. is authorized to buy such white and coloured rags, old stocking feet, bits of stuff, bombazines, fustians, velveteen, cotton worsted, cord, bed ticking, old smock frocking, dusting rags, or any kind of rubbish made of linen, hemp or worsted—even if they are as rotten as tinder, and only a pound or half-pound. Please to look them up, and B.R. will call for them next day.

Please do not forget that every piece of rag helps to make a sheet of paper. Please to look up out of your coal holes and back places all bits of rags which you have thrown out of your back doors, dirty or clean, a great quantity of rubbish being wanted at the present time for the better supply of the Paper Mills, for which B.R. will give the best price.

White rags, coloured fustians and bed ticking, old cloth stuff, horse hair, old brass stuff, lead, hare and rabbit skins.

B.R. buys horse and cow hair, brass, broken spoons, brass taps, old warming pans, copper kettles, and tea urns, brass candlesticks, metal teapots, stew pans and boilers.

B.R. also deals in Ladies' and Gentlemen's wearing apparel, such as coats and waistcoats, and every description of Ladies' Wardrobes.

B.R. will collect such as above in the neighbourhood, and he gives a regular market price without attempting to impose on anyone.

B.R. will be very thankful to all persons who will look up any of the above articles, FOR READY MONEY, if only a handful, and he will call for them next day.

RABBIT SKINS, etc.

Then I read the instructions on the bottom, which he had asked me not to forget.

**PLEASE SHOW THIS BILL TO YOUR MASTER OR MISTRESS AND RETURN IT ONLY TO B.R. WHEN HE CALLS.**

*Chapter Three*

## THE WELL

### I

Under the elm avenue of Higher Ham, where the rooks
caw in the tops of the tall trees, there stood the home-
stead of Jonathan Furze, the richest man in the parish.
He was a keen, energetic farmer, with an eye to cattle: his Devon
reds were always deep-chested, heavy, tranquil beasts, eating the
good grass of his higher fields, on which they grew fat, in prime
condition, without any linseed "cake" or other rich food. Grass
only. Jonathan Furze was disliked in the village: he was a man
apart: a Chapel goer: a sound farmer: he worked while other
men talked.

The lane under the dry-ditched stone wall enclosing his garden was shady in summer, cooled by the green ferns hanging
above the runlet of water. At the bend of the lane the curve of
the wall held a well, which was protected by a wooden door.
The well-house was not so tall as a man; the water within, which
renewed itself eternally, was scarcely deeper than a pitcher, and
in volume less than half a cubic yard.

A dry-ditched wall is one built of stone and earth, standing by
its own weight. The corners, or coigns as the stone-ditchers call
them, are bound by heavy flat stones, or slabs of rock, placed one
on top of the other; but the stones of the wall proper stand like
books in a shelf. Usually the stones are upright; sometimes the
rows alternate in a herring-bone pattern. The ditched wall ending Mr. Furze's garden at the roadway was a plain one; but the
well-house, small as it was, abutted from the curve of the garden.
The well was enclosed by a mason's wall—the stones were held
by mortar. Who paid for the mortar? It was a subject which
caused periodical argument and mental heat in the village—

THE WELL

every fifteen years, said Jonathan Furze. There the well was, the
spring welling imperceptibly out of the rock which showed so
clearly in the little square of water, under the wraith of its inner
walls. Ferns like lizards uncurled out of the chinks of the mortar,
and sometimes in the hot summer a lizard looking like a fern
basked there, ready to whisk away to its chink if a shadow fell
athwart the dream which was its life. Mosses grew there, with
their seeds upheld on hair-like stalks, amidst the dragon-yellow
and silver-curd lichens spread over the stones.

In frost and heat, ice-winter and droughty summer, the water
flowed, welling up into the cool cavern, rising cold from the
rock which had lain inert and dark since the last wan flames of
star-chaos had dwindled and lost themselves in spaces of after-
creation, leaving the shocked and immingled elements to their
travail of resurrection with the sun into forms of man, tree,
lichen, and the myriad swarming struggles of life, travail wherein star-memory was transmuted and resurrected. . .

Words, words, vain indications of what arose in dim thought
one day as I peered into the innocent water of the well, a mental
glimpse of the past shut off by footfalls and the clank of a pail.
I looked over my shoulder, and saw Charlie Tucker, rate-col-
lector, Parish Councillor, one-man farmer, one-man master-
builder. He carried a pail. Charlie Tucker was tall and strong, a
rapid solitary worker for whom no other carpenter or mason in
the village would work. He was married, but without children.
He lived in one of the several pink-roofed houses he had built.
His wife kept his house extraordinarily clean, and resented, if
she did not forbid, others entering upon her scrubbed and
polished floors. It was known that she and Charlie did not get
on well together. Usually she looked grim, but occasionally she
bloomed with tender feeling for children. "Wish your little boy
belonged to me, proper little boy," both she and Charlie Tucker
had said to me several times; but never in the hearing of the
other. "If I undertook any job, I'd do it just as required, I
would," Charlie Tucker was wont to say, "I'd till tetties upsy-
down if you asked me to." As a fact, he could only work his own

33

way; he could neither work under anyone nor give workable instructions to anyone; he lost his temper easily, but had a sense of humour, and was entirely honest about what time he charged for work done as carpenter or mason. Now he dipped the five-gallon bucket in the well, and hauled it up as easily as if it had been a kettle.

"Thirsty weather," he remarked to me.

"Going to drink all that today?" I asked.

"There's no telling," he replied, as he walked back the way he had come.

A simple action, a non-committal conversation; but just as fire-abandoned elements resolve themselves into the legion forms of planetary life, so the simple acts of men resolve themselves into the complications known as human life. The village is as the nation, as the continent, as the world.

## 2

As it became known soon afterwards, Charlie Tucker had taken the water from the wayside well for the purpose of flushing the closet in one of his houses. Owing to the drought, the well in the garden of this modern brick and tiled structure was dry. Well-sinkers charged fifteen shillings a foot for the first fifteen feet, twenty shillings for the next twenty feet, and twenty-five shillings per foot thereunder to the maximum of about fifty-five feet, when the air became bad. These prices were for digging into rock, which had to be bored and blasted all the way. Charlie Tucker's well was about fifteen feet deep; it went dry quickly, to the distress of his tenants, who were forced to make various requests to him on account of other things—the kitchen stove, which would not heat water, the veranda which leaked or was unbuilt or uncompleted, and other demands which landlords receive in varying measure from tenants. So busy was Charlie that he made promises which he had not always the time to fulfil: he would see about it tomorrow, tomorrow, tomorrow; until those to whom he had promised attention were forced to realize

that his word was unreliable; one villager said, "A useless vibra-
tion upon the ear-drum".

As a fact, Charlie had built seven houses in the village, by
himself: he had too much for one man to do. His only life was in
work: his wife's only emotional outlet was in keeping her house
so clean that Charlie was forbidden to enter her best sitting, or
rather non-sitting, room.

Eventually Charlie Tucker kept his promises; eventually the
over-busy man would begin the job; he seldom if ever refused
an offer of work, and so trouble arose all around him; but when
he started a job, he did it rapidly and cheerfully. One day he
would have the well deepened: he would dig it himself, save
money and do it in half the time: one day he would see about it.
Meanwhile, the flush-tank was dry; and dragged by worried
words of his tenant from clipping his sheep and disinfecting
where the flies were blowing eggs, Charlie Tucker drew a
bucketful of water from Jonathan Furze's well. Jonathan Furze's
well? Noomye! (The equivalent of the New World, "No—
sir!") That well belonged to the parish. Anyone could draw
water from that well, if they'd a mind to! So declared Charlie
Tucker.

Harry Zeale the carpenter—Charlie Tucker and his brothers
were carpenters too—hearing of what had happened, immediately went to Jonathan Furze and told him. Mr. Furze was an
elderly man with a nice expression, a cheery hard-working yeo-
man, whose fortune, as has been remarked, was based on in-
dustry and judgment. He had slowly acquired the best grazing
fields in the parish; and had made most of his money by buying
yearlings at various markets, keeping them as "stores", and
selling the not-so-good bullocks to others who hoped to "finish
them off for the butchers". He had an eye for a young beast,
seeming to know which would grow into the heaviest animals
in the quickest time. He was the chief of the Chapel brethren, he
neither smoked nor drank, he never interfered in other people's
business. *Furze by name and furze by nature* ran the village expression. Furze, or gorse, is a hardy tree or shrub which is prickly,

which endures the criticism of salt-wind, frost, and drought, which puts forth its yellow blossoms throughout the year, responsive to the sun. It remains where others do not succeed. Jonathan Furze was not popular, an elderly man with a rolling unsteady gait, almost slopping along to his work; a nice face, open and kind, yet reserved; a type which used to be called materialist by those writers of an earlier generation who dreamed —for the purpose of asserting themselves—of the regeneration of Man. Jonathan Furze, hearing of what Charlie Tucker had done, went to the well with a padlock.

## 3

All who could walk went to the Parish Meeting in the School-room a few weeks later, many with the mood in which they would have hastened at the news of a dog-fight. Farmer John Brown of Crowcombe was Chairman. Charlie Tucker was there, with his wife, both quiet, as though grim; "Stroyle" George in his torn leather jerkin looking like a gigantic sparrow; Colonel Ponde, one of the councillors, one of the ex-managers of the Church School who had resigned owing to disagreement with the Rector; Tom Gammon the owner of lurcher dogs; Mr. Alford the deaf old District Councillor, who had been saying the same things in the same rigid way during most of his years of retirement from the secretaryship of a Miners' Union in South Wales; the schoolmaster withdrawn into the neutral background, near the faded wall-map of the World (British Possessions coloured pink); Tim Pin the husband of red-haired Zilla. These were some of the speakers. The schoolroom was filled with people, over a hundred.

After the Chairman had declared the meeting open, he said the Parish Council was prepared to hear any opinions or require-ments among those present concerning parish matters. After a pause Harry Zeale the carpenter got up and said he would like the question of the well up to Higher Ham decided once and for all.

Several faces turned to Charlie Tucker, who remained still, his eyes downcast, but his hands moved about as though seeking a hammer or a trowel. He was biding his time.

Then Farmer Furze held up a letter which he said decided the matter of the ownership of the well. He flapped it about in the air, and sat down. The letter was moved about in his restless hands.

After a pause, there were whispers among some of the labourers, the little men who always resented the farmer who had more money than they had. The whispers encouraged other whispers, then audible fragments of sentences; a voice spoke out, then other voices grew louder until cries of "Read the letter!" were raised.

"Have you seen this letter?" asked Mr. Furze of Mr. Alford, the elderly District Councillor. "It should interest you. It proves that your father, who was, as you know, a tenant of the previous owner of the property I now own, paid the owner a nominal fee of sixpence a year to draw water from the well."

Mr. Alford arose to speak, shaking his bald head emphatically. "We have seen no letter bearing on the subject in the District Council. But I'll give you the law on the subject. The well water in the parish is free to the parish, except those wells are on, which ARE ON—" Mr. Alford's voice became louder, overriding a suggested interruption from Mr. Furze; he was partly deaf, and for years in the Lower House he had in this manner overridden interruptions, for years he had worked the same ideas with his stringy vocal chords: "which are on, I said, which are on private property, as opposed to those, as OPPOSED TO THOSE, I said, which abut on rights of way or parish roads to which the public, I SAID TO WHICH the public have access. That's what I said, gennulmen, and I challenge anyone, I CHALLENGE ANYONE to say otherwise."

Mr. Furze jumped up and waved the letter again. "Read it, that's all I asked!" he smiled.

Mr. Alford went on, "Public denied access to parish water, I declare it unlawful. I have seen I HAVE SEEN—"

"Your father, living in the cottage which is now my property, paid the previous owner of Inclefell for the right to draw water," interrupted Mr. Furze, calmly.

"I have seen, I said, I HAVE SEEN no letter bearing on the subject—"

Jonathan Furze waved his letter again, an amiable expression on his face. "Read it!"

"I have something written before you were born!" cried Mr. Alford, abandoning the set speech he had prepared in his mind. He patted importantly a thick book held up in one hand. "In this book, containing the minutes of Parish Council Meetings during the period referred to by Mr. Furze, there is no reference to any payment made by the Parish to the previous owner of Inclefell. Not a reference!" He stared round the faces, before resuming with a mechanical dramatic manner, "The letter is no evidence. This is the evidence, I SAID THIS IS THE evidence. No such letter was ever written by my father, my father, I say, never wrote such a letter. Noomye!" He sat down abruptly, shaking his head. He was breathing heavily.

"I didn't say your father wrote the letter!" remarked Mr. Furze. "Why not read it?"

"I have seen no such letter, I said NO SUCH LETTER!" declared Mr. Alford, getting up and sitting down again.

"Well, see it now," retorted Mr. Furze.

At this point there was a stir amidst the group in semi-darkness round the doorway, where the buttons of Mr. Bullcornworthy the policeman's uniform gleamed subduedly. Tom Gammon the owner of poaching dogs, pushed his way through, and sat down, his decayed mortar-splashed hat remaining on his head. He tried to light the burnt end of a self-made cigarette. Immediately there were cries of "No smoking! Put it out! This ban't th' Higher House!"

"Whose money pays for the meeting?" muttered Tom.

"No smoking!"

"I've as much right here as anyone in th' parish."

"No smoking!"

# THE WELL

"I pay rates, don't I?" His moustache ends were damp with beer. He puffed at his fag end. It was out.

"No smoking!"

"I ban't smoking!" shouted Tom Gammon. He inspected it, then stuck it behind his ear.

"Order, gentlemen," spoke the Chairman quietly. "Perhaps Mr. Furze might want to read the letter?"

Harry Zeale, the informant carpenter and agent of Jonathan Furze, got up nervously on his thin legs, and said in his thin voice, "Tidden right that the letter should be read before the Parish Council sees 'n," and sat down again, looking like a scared child who has said its piece in a Sunday School inspection.

Charlie Tucker, who was sitting silent, smiled grimly at the ceiling.

The Chairman asked Mr. Furze if he had any objection to the letter being read, "which reading might shed some light on the controversial nature of the subject now under discussion."

"As you wish," said Mr. Furze, "I've no objection to the letter being read, if it be of any interest to anyone."

The Chairman was given the letter. He put on his steel-rimmed spectacles, held the letter to the light of the oil-lamp swung over the meeting from one of the beams, and appeared to be in difficulties about it.

"The writing be a bit screwed up," he said.

"What's the date of 'n?" demanded Mr. Alford.

"Dated September 1917, so far as I can see, gennulmen."

"No such letter, no such letter," said Mr. Alford. "No such letter. No." He shook his head many times. "Out of horder. I said hout of order. My old books show no trace of parish money paid for the water. No trace at all. None."

Slowly the Chairman deciphered the letter, which declared that the writer remembered that Mr. Alford had paid sixpence annually to the Inclefell estate for the right to draw water from the well.

Mr. Alford jumped up and shouted, "No such thing. No such thing. I said NO SUCH thing. My father paid no money. The

39

letter is no evidence, I said NO HEVIDENCE. Out of order, no such letter, no sir!"

A voice cried "Where be envelope?"

"Well, there you are, you wanted it read," said Mr. Furze.

"Who wrote 'n? Where did the letter come from?"

"An old emigrant from the village," replied Mr. Furze.

"What be the name?" asked a voice from the back.

Mr. Furze hesitated. "I am not at liberty to disclose the writer's name, but I may tell you it is from an old emigrant."

"What be his name?" cried another voice from the back.

Tom Gammon, who had removed his hat, called out in a sepulchral voice, "Charlie Chaplin!"

Amidst laughter, Mr. Alford said:

"No such person!" He had never seen a Movie. "No evidence, no evidence. Public water! Disgraceful!"

Colonel Ponde then got up and said, "Mr. Chairman and gentlemen, I suggest to the meeting that this matter does not concern the Parish Council. It is a matter which the District Council has to decide. All this talk is therefore void, vain, and ineffectual."

"Yes!" cried Charlie Tucker, like a spring uncoiling. "The District Council be the proper authority to deal with the illegal closing of parish wells! All this be clitter-clatter, nothing legal about it, noomye! Yes, you can laugh! Furze by name, and furze by nature."

"I've been pestered every five years by this well business!" declared Mr. Furze, flushing, as he sprang to his feet. "Why should I bother about your flim-flam? It be my well, and there be an end to 'n." He clapped his hat on his head, and left the meeting.

A small tousled man then got up, and cried in a high voice, pitched higher with nervousness, "There ought to be protection on the culvert down to Zeales. I demand compensation, the li'l old place I lives in ban't fit for pigs to live in, I shall come on the Council, I will, I ban't gwin' vor keep on fishing my child out of the culvert."

# THE WELL

This little squeaky parishioner, by name of Pin, cried his grievance periodically at every Parish Meeting, for periodically the stream flooded his cottage. He blamed Mr. Furze, the owner of the cottage, for this.

"Aiy, and what be sense in us paying rates for the rummage cart if th' bissley bigger (beastly beggar) be late every time?" cried Tom Gammon. "Tidden no sense."

"You never use it, anyway!" said someone, amidst laughter.

The rubbish cart, by which old tins and broken glass, ashes, and other refuse was periodically collected, was paid for out of a penny rate by the Parish Council. It was a recent institution, resented by many.

"Wull, good evening," said Tom, putting his hat on his head, and walking out. It was, by the schoolroom clock, ten minutes to ten. The Higher and Lower Houses closed at 10 p.m.

"Have a pint for me," said a voice.

"Aiy," replied Tom. "If you pay for 'n!"

"Never!" declared Mr. Alford, who appeared to come out of an ivory trance. "Never! Never did I hear the like of it. The well be parish property! No one has a right to deny the public access—" His pale bald head shone dull as his leather leggings.

Outside my cottage at 10.15 p.m. I heard "Stroyle" George declaring to Tom Gammon, "To my way of thinking, there should be either a vote of censure or a vote of confidence proposed by you about thaccy rubbish cart, the subject of which you 'm always reeving up. Us has to pay for 'n—"

"Aw, gitoom! (get home). You farmers don't pay rates no longer," shouted Tom.

"But I be same as you, a parishioner, I be, ban't I?" went on the earnest voice of Stroyle George. "It be the concern of all i' th' parish. Yesmye! You be wrong, you know, only you'm bittle-'eaded, and won't listen to reason. A vote of confidence, or a vote of censure—" Farmer George was an assiduous reader of the *News of the World*. "That's your trouble, Tom Gammon, you'm bittle-'eaded!"

41

A bittle or beetle was a large wooden mallet, for driving spars into the thatch.

"You bliddy fule!" cried Tom, and shambled down the lane, his lurcher silent at his heels.

From the pulpit the following Sunday was preached a sermon with the text *Love ye One Another*. They were all good children of God, said the parson, who had been at the meeting.

# 4

Three men met in the village shortly after the Parish Meeting. They were the Committee appointed by the Rural District Council. Two arrived from the town eight miles distant. The train fares to Crosstree Station and the three-mile taxi-cab ride thence to Ham, would be charged eventually to the ratepayers, which included that careful critic of public administration, the mason, Tom Gammon. The third man, Rear-Admiral Bamfylde, D.S.O., R.N. (retired) walked from Pidickswell Manor, a mile distant among trees shorn by sea-winds. The Admiral, like the other two, was a District Councillor. The Committee was to investigate the ownership of the well.

Mr. Furze met the Committee by appointment outside his gate, and together the four gentlemen went to inspect the well. There was the clear water, the wooden door, the hand-forged hinges, the lichened masoned walls. The unlocked padlock hung from the rusty staple. Mr. Furze opened the door, and stood back.

"Nothing very complicated about that, gentlemen. Pure spring water, never fails. But it is drinking water: not water for other purposes."

"Quite right," said the Admiral, a red-faced man who had a jovial word for everyone. He had lived in the manor house for about three years. He was so unaffected and friendly that some village people thought he was not quite right in the head; but the majority liked him. All knew that he was "a proper gennul-man", which meant that he was generous, he provided work, he was rich, he was courteous to all. He got up concerts in the village, and stage-managed revues and farces, taking the principal parts himself. "Nice ferns," said the Admiral. "Well, gentlemen, about the well. Sorry, no pun intended. Ha-ha!"

This eased the others. Mr. Furze, locking the well-door again, stood aside, but the Admiral said, "It seems a very trifling matter, Mr. Furze. Here is the well. For drinking water. The nearest common pump is down behind the rectory. The parish claims the well. But that only means free access to draw water. I understand that the Council is prepared to keep the well clean and in repair. This will relieve you of any obligation in the matter. Frankly, do you ever draw water from the well for your own household purposes?"

"I understand what you mean, sir, and I'm grateful for your kind help in the matter; but the well is clean, and the door is sound. I can keep my own property in good order and repair, without the assistance of any council, intending no disrespect to you, gentlemen, for your well-meaning efforts."

"But you have no objection, Mr. Furze, to the public drawing water from the well?"

" Drinking water, no."

"But the well has been locked during the past fortnight, during which the public have been denied access to the drinking water."

"I consider, Admiral, that I am within my rights in using my own discretion in that matter."

"Certainly, Mr. Furze, certainly," said the Chairman. "We, as the Committee appointed to meet you here, have only one purpose: to try and conciliate the various conflicting thoughts about this little matter, and also to try and come to some arrangement by which water, for domestic purposes, can be drawn in future without let or hindrance."

"Without anyone being bothered, including of course, the owner," smiled the Admiral.

"I'm sure I'm with you in your purpose, gentlemen."

"Good man," said the Admiral. "As far as we are concerned, the well is your own property; but don't you agree that if something were placed on record which would assure free access, say in a hundred years' time, when we're all dead and gone, it would clinch the matter effectively?"

Another of the committee spoke, to ease the silence. "If you agree that the parish may draw water in fee, Mr. Furze, will you put that in writing, if we, at our cost, draw up a simple agreement to that effect?"

The Chairman said, after a glance at Mr. Furze's face, "It seems simple. You, as owner of the well, make a gift in fee of free-water-drawing, for domestic purposes."

"But the parish always has had, so long as I've owned the well, free access to the well, for drinking water. But not for other purposes."

"In that case, wouldn't you prefer having the well off your hands? Why should you pay for the upkeep if others are to benefit? Mason's walls sometimes need repair and that means $1s. 5\frac{1}{2}d.$ an hour labour. It seems hard that you should have to pay for other people's convenience."

"I don't see it that way, gentlemen. I am used to the idea of maintaining my own property in good repair. But I thank you for your kind suggestions."

"Well, I think we agree that the well is the property of Mr. Furze?" said the Admiral.

Mr. Furze smiled.

"And we may report that you, Mr. Furze, agree to access to it by the parish, for domestic purposes?"

"I have always allowed the parish to draw drinking water, gentlemen."

The Admiral's eyebrows lifted perceptibly. He sighed audibly. The rooks cawed cautiously in the trees; the birds had been shot at by Mr. Furze during the previous afternoon, and many of the fledgelings had fallen. The Admiral did not shoot; he felt ironical about the mass slaughter of young rooks which could not fly. The Admiral had been awarded the Distinguished Service Order for torpedoing and sinking a Turkish troopship during the War. The water trickled under the cool green ferns.

"A lovely day," said the Admiral.

"Yes," replied Mr. Furze, breaking a bright yellow dandelion with the iron tip of his boot. Why must he do that, thought the Admiral.

"Well, that appears to be all," said the second committee man. "You will receive a copy of our report, of course, Mr. Furze."

"Thank you," replied Mr. Furze. "And now, gentlemen, if you will excuse me——"

"It seems clear. Mr. Furze, the owner of the well, is prepared to let water to be drawn in fee by the parishioners of Ham?"

"As before," said Mr. Furze, "I am willing to allow the drawing of water for domestic purposes."

"Well, gentlemen, it seems as clear as the water in the well. How's the hay, Mr. Furze?"

"A middling shear, I fancy, Admiral, thank you."

"Splendid. Good day, Mr. Furze."

"Good day to you, gentlemen."

The door of the well remained locked.

5

Little is known by the unofficial historian of Devon village life in the 'twenties of that body of elected men called the Rural District Council. Whether the halls in which it sat and directed its business were marbled or oak panelled; whether or not there was mace-bearer or toast-master for its functions—of these and similar things the historian must confess his ignorance. All he knows is that periodically a man with jackdaw's eyes and a long nose appeared in the Higher and Lower Houses of Ham—these and similar places of refreshment were the unacknowledged parliaments of Great Britain—and offered all a pint of beer at his expense: then he knew that the Rural District Council Election was once more imminent.

It must be confessed that the historian was also ignorant of the powers and territory of the Rural District Council as opposed to that of the Parish Council; but from casual observation it had been assumed that the roads tended by the Parish Council were narrow, muddy, and chains of plashes in wet weather; the District Council roads were somewhat less narrow, with surfaces partly or wholly covered with tar and/or bitumen and granite chips from Dartmoor; the County Council roads were in places considerably better than Brooklands Racing Track, with a concrete surface, and in other places were often under what appeared to be permanent repair and/or enlargement. Of what body hung over the County Council no man in the village pubs knew or cared, unless it were Mr. Alford, but no man sober dared to ask him, for Mr. Alford knew so much that he contradicted everyone, and everyone contradicted him. Mr. Alford was a spare, elderly man, with kind eyes and, like Mr. Furze, he attended to his own business, except to correct wrong-headedness and violation of the public rights. He was never rude to anyone deliberately, but most younger men were rude to him; he bore this with the tolerance of age and partial deafness.

The members of the Rural District Council were elected by the parishioners of many parishes; two or three from each parish. A few days after Jackdaw-Eyes appeared in the pubs of Ham, one saw motorcars moving about the lanes and roads and speed-

| | |
|---|---|
| V O T E<br>FOR<br>B U N N | JACKDAW-EYES<br>ONCE<br>M O R E |
| DUCKINGHAM<br>FOR<br>NORTH DEVON | PLUMP<br>FOR<br>BAMFYLDE |

ways of North Devon bearing placards and bills on radiator and windscreen. You paid your taxes and took your choice.

In addition to this excitement, a week or so before election day the observant reader of the local weekly papers might notice advertisements on the front pages in the forms of flattering letters to Electors, full of thanks and promises for past and future services. The advertisers declared in effect that they were industrious, careful, well-meaning, efficient, sober, lynx-eyed, idealistic, and the very men to be trusted with the responsibilities of acquiring and using the money of the intelligent rate-payers. Mr. Furze had sat on the District Council in his time; so had Mr. Charles Tucker. Men of all classes sat under the marbled and/or panelled walls of the Rural District Council Chamber.

The important question of the well was first on the list of agenda when the Rural District Council assembled for its next meeting following the appointment of the Well Committee.

The Clerk, a solicitor, who was the legal adviser of the Council, reported that the following letter had been received from Mr. Jonathan Furze:

"I thank you for your letter of the 5th inst. with proposed agreement in regard to the well. Your council now admit that the well is private property, and part of the Inclefell estate. Therefore, I am quite willing to allow anyone to take water for domestic purposes at any time at my discretion. As to 'preventing the water from being fouled and maintaining doors', naturally I shall see that my property is looked after without signing any agreement. Your committee report that I agreed to the water being taken 'on fee', which I understood to mean a payment in fee or acknowledgement, but I would rather not take any fee."

The Clerk, having read the letter, added that the proposed agreement had been returned unsigned. He held it up: lowered it; and sat down.

Councillor Bunn, J.P., said, "I was Chairman of the Committee recently appointed to investigate the ownership of the well, and I state definitely that no mention was made by Mr. Furze at the time of the public having water 'at his discretion'. We came to our decision entirely on the lines that Mr. Furze's solicitor, the late Mr. Buydon, prepared and offered when there was a dispute about this very well seventeen years ago between Mr. Furze and the Parish Council. There was an agreement drawn up then, but it was not signed owing to a question of cost, but, I believe I am right in saying, the spirit of the agreement has been kept until this year, when Mr. Furze locked the door of the well. I think there was some excuse for Mr. Furze locking that door, although not for the whole time. I am under the impression that a gentleman came for water, not for domestic purposes, but for building purposes. I still think Mr. Furze will sign the agreement on the lines we suggested, for it is entirely on the lines of his late solicitor's letter. I am certain that Mr. Buydon would not have offered those terms unless he had thoroughly investigated the matter. When we came across the letter, we felt we could not do better than adopt Mr. Furze's former agreement. There is only a question of interpreting *in fee*, which means, of course, *in perpetuity*. I still hope in the interests of peace that Mr. Furze will sign the agreement. Personally, I have had no intimation from Mr. Furze of his objection to signing the agreement."

Another councillor arose, and after a deliberate pause, said: "Well, Mr. Furze's answer is the answer a good many of us expected would result when we heard the report of the committee at the last meeting. The committee no doubt have done useful work in their investigations, in that they have confirmed what was found by a previous committee, namely, that the well was in private ownership. That being so, I personally am astounded at the committee's conceiving that any individual would sign the conditions imposed in the later part of the report."

"A point of order, I rise to a point of order!" cried Councillor Bunn, J.P., "I contend that no previous committee from this council has ever been to Ham to investigate the ownership of this well!"

At this, Councillor Duckingham, J.P., jumped up and said, "I stated that, and I restate it!" He sat down firmly.

Councillor Bunn, J.P., went on: "I say again categorically that no committee has ever been appointed from this council to investigate the ownership of this well! The dispute at that time was entirely between the parish council and Mr. Jonathan Furze, and I state emphatically that the parish council never referred the matter to the district council. Never! I know that the gentleman who just now interrupted me has been doing his best to prove me wrong!"

"Mr. Chairman, I rise on a point of order!" cried Councillor Duckingham, J.P., springing up again. "I beg leave to ask if it is in order for another member to impute motives to another member. I further ask if it is in order to dispute those other members' bona fides. I appeal to the Chair—I have a duly authenticated letter proving my contention right up to the hilt —I ask the Chair to endorse my statement that a former committee of three did go to investigate the question of the ownership of the well!"

"I cannot say that my memory is as good as another's," said the Chairman of the District Council mildly as he fluffed out his moustache slowly. "But I distinctly remember going to Ham to investigate this same question, and to the best of my memory we were satisfied at the time that the well was private property."

The Admiral then rose up and said, with eyebrows raised blandly, "Well, you know, I happened to be there the other day when some of the, er, discussion took place, and I do not think that the agreement put forward by the Chairman would ever have been brought before the council if Mr. Furze had not openly agreed to sign it. He left no doubt in my mind that he would do so, and was quite glad to do so, otherwise we should not have recommended that the agreement be drawn up, don't you know."

The third committeeman then spoke, "Perhaps it would

49

interest the meeting to know that there exists in the parish council minute book a minute that definitely states that an agreement was drawn up for Mr. Furze by the late Mr. Buydon and forwarded to the parish council, who unanimously decided not to sign it as it was not in accordance with the proposals set out by them. In other words, they flipped back the same shuttlecock then as they do now!"

Councillor Alford, one of the elect of Ham, then arose and said, "I should like to clear up one thing regarding the visit of the gentleman who said he was in Ham on this same question in June or July 1908. Let me tell you that there was no dispute there then. It was in 1909 or 1910 before any dispute over this well ever came about."

"I said 1909!" cried Councillor Duckingham.

"Well, the Press is wrong!" retorted Councillor Alford.

Councillor Alford got a laugh; he sat down, looking happy.

The moustache-stroking Chairman said, "The Press is not necessarily infallible, gentlemen."

"Nor am I," confessed Councillor Duckingham.

Mr. Alford resumed his feet and said, more easily, "I say that it was in 1909 before the Parish Council put up a frame or door and repaired it. I say the Parish Council did the work, or paid for it. The Parish Council never referred the matter to the District Council. Noomye! I'm telling you, there is nothing on the minutes, nothing at all, that it was ever discussed by the District Council at all! Then why was a committee there in 1909? Can anyone answer me? I'm asking if anyone can answer me?"

"Well," said the Chairman, conversationally, "It may not appear on the minutes, but I distinctly remember going there as a member of the District Council with Mr. Duckingham and another. I should not have gone there for pleasure—although Ham is a most delightful place."

Jackdaw Eyes then said, "Isn't it a waste of time, all this? Two committees have decided that it is private property. Mr. Furze has said water can be taken any time for domestic purposes. No good could come of forcing a man's hand. Let it rest there."

# THE WELL

"Mr. Chairman and gentlemen," cried Councillor Alford, "I rise as a native and resident of Ham. This is a most important question, involving principles and rights. To my knowledge, the public has had access to that well for sixty years. I say that without fear of contradiction. Why has it cropped up at this time of day? The well is abutting the highway. We have nine parish wells, and some are 10, 15, 20 feet from the highway. The public go through other people's property to reach them, but they always have access to them. What will happen, I said WHAT WOULD happen if owners of private property erected barriers and said the public should not go there?"

"A good deal of this is a legal question," declared the Chairman, "I will ask the Clerk to give his advice on the matter."

The Chairman of the Well Committee arose and said, "The present trouble, in my opinion, is entirely due to the fault of Mr. Duckingham, who is a well-known friend of Mr. Furze!"

Cries of: "An uncalled for remark!" "Withdraw!" "Order, order!"

The Chairman of the District Council: "A very undesirable remark, sir!"

"Another thing I'd like to say. Mr. Duckingham, from the very first my committee was appointed, tried to influence my committee. He tried to undermine it all the time! I say that without fear of contradiction!"

When the cries of contradiction had subsided, the Clerk, a thin, stooping man with a weary appearance, who looked as though life for him were mere endurance, said quietly that his advice was to acknowledge Mr. Furze's letter and add "the council trust that his discretion will be exercised only·sufficiently to preserve his right, and that the parishioners will not be denied water when they want it."

"But we are quite agreed to that!" expostulated the Chairman of the Well Committee, "That's already agreed!"

Mr. Alford, doggedly, his bald head looking like solid ivory, "Have we then to ask permission every time we want a drink of water?"

"No, not ask: Mr. Furze says you may *take* water," said the Chairman, in a tone of voice that suggested he would like to add, "You may go with your little buckets and pitchers and draw it, and drink it."

"That is all we want; but if the door is locked, what can we do? The door is still locked."

"Drink beer."

"At sixpence a pint!"

"Well, who's to blame but the public for buying beer at that price?"

"Even the pub doors are locked nowadays."

"Blame Jonathan Furze."

"He's teetotal, anyhow."

"Order, gentlemen, order!"

The stooping Clerk, wearily: "I advise you to try and avoid friction."

The Chairman: "A sensible solution."

Mr. Alford: "Yes, but—"

Here the ink in the historian's pen runs out.


*Chapter Four*

# THE MYSTERY OF A DAMP COTTAGE

## I

After awhile it was a common thing for one man to stop another in the village street and say to him, "Have 'ee heard anything about they strangers down to Sam Pidler's cottage yet?" and the answer was always, No.

The cottage was adjacent to the row of three cottages occupied by myself, Revvy the labourer, and the retired dairy farmer nicknamed "Thunderbolt". For many years the cottage had been occupied by Uncle Joe, an old pensioned railway porter. Uncle Joe had died, and the cottage had been sold to a hairdresser in the town eight miles away. The hairdresser's idea was to furnish it and let it to summer visitors; but the place was dark, the sanitation crude, water had to be drawn by hand from a well sixty paces away; and so it remained empty. Meanwhile the value of cottage property had fallen, owing to a lot of jerry-building in the district, and when the speculating hairdresser sold it a few years later, he had to drop about a quarter of his money. The village knew this; the village knew everything—sometimes the wrong thing; but the village knew that Mr. Pidler, the retired coastguard, had bought it from the hairdresser for just under two hundred and fifty pounds.

Mr. Pidler had put his unwanted furniture, and other people's unwanted furniture which he had bought cheaply at various auctions, into the place, and had advertised an old-world picturesque furnished cottage in the *Devon and Exeter Gazette*, to be let at a low rent.

Soon afterwards two strangers had alighted from the bus, an elderly man leaning heavily on a stick, and a thick-set youth wearing boots laced to his knees. The boots resembled the type of boots worn by horse-transport drivers of the British Expeditionary Force during the Great War; boots which were at this time being advertised and sold as Surplus Government Ordnance Stock, but by their poor quality it was obvious that they were cheap imitations. That was what I thought, anyway; but I was wrong, as later events showed: the boots had recently been Government property. To Mr. Pidler, they looked very good boots on that misty winter day, when the youth alighted from the bus, carrying a pressed-paper suitcase in one hand, and an old-fashioned phonograph in the other. He wore an army pack on his back.

He was followed by the elderly man who limped, and who was immediately noticeable for a moustache or moustaches with long waxed points extending wider than his face. Mr. Pidler met them, and led the way to the cottage. After the slightest inspection of the four rooms, the stranger said he was prepared to take the cottage for three months. His name was Cannon, he explained —Joseph Cannon—er, Captain Joseph Cannon. He wanted rest and quiet, and since the Sinn Fein trouble in Ireland, when his home had been burned down, he had been moving about England with his batman, trying to find a place which would benefit his gout. He explained that his belongings had perished in the destruction of his old family place, which accounted for the smallness of his luggage.

"My man and I will be very comfortable, thank you," said the Captain, screwing up one end of his moustache. "I will take your house from to-day, and pay you a month's rent in advance. Please don't bother about a receipt. Between gentlemen—" He twirled his moustache.

Sam Pidler went away satisfied, with six pounds in his pocket.

Very soon everything that was to be known about the strangers had been repeated in the village: their clothes, appearance, luggage, and such fragments of autobiography as the Captain had told Sam Pidler. It was even remarked that the young man had not said a word from the time of meeting Sam to when Sam left with a month's rent-in-advance in his pocket. The bus conductor, in the Lower House that evening, reported that the young man had not spoken during the journey from Town to Ham, but had kept his gaze on the floor, never once looking out of the window.

Sometimes the two were seen going for walks in the lanes, the young man either following the other or walking in front of him, his hands in his breeches pockets. He always wore the same boots and breeches, and coat of thick dark material, with a woollen scarf round his neck and tucked under the lapels of his coat. When calling at the village shop for food, he bought bread, margarine, jam, and tinned stuff; the amount of cooking done was apparently small. Neither Thunderbolt Willy's wife nor her cousin Mrs. Revvy could find out much about what cooking was done, for the door was always shut and the windows closed, with the blinds half-drawn.

No letters came for them. Often the phonograph was heard

screeching at a great speed. And so the first month went by. Only once the older man had spoken to Mrs. Revvy, and then the subject was the young bearded man living near them.

"Calls himself a captain does he? Captain of the Salvation Army perhaps, but even they don't have boys with their mother's milk still inside them! Bah, he was no captain, unless it was the Boy Scouts!"

Mrs. Revvy hastened to tell this to Mrs. Thunderbolt Willy, to Mrs. Brown, to Alice of Hole Farm, to Mrs. Tigg, and to Mrs. Willy Gammon, and lastly, to myself.

Mr. Pidler, the landlord, came for his rent promptly at the beginning of the second month, and went away with no more than he arrived with. The Government apparently had not yet decided what compensation should be paid to the Captain for the destruction of his property in Ireland.

Mr. Pidler got a job as a chauffeur about this time, and as his duties took him to another part of England, he asked Mr. Ridd to collect the rent for him, and to keep an eye on the place. Mr. Ridd had been in service with a gentleman for many years, and his wife with a lady; the two were spending their grey-haired retirement tranquilly in a cottage in Lower Ham. Mr. and Mrs. Ridd had perfect manners; they never commented on their neighbours. Mr. Ridd would see Captain Cannon, certainly; the money would be sent to Mr. Pidler.

After ten days or so Mr. Ridd went down to call on Captain Cannon, and found the door locked. He went back to his own house, and continued his two hundred and fifty seventh attempt to win £1,000 or £2 a week for life, by forecasting how many times football goals would be kicked, and in what direction, by any or all of several hundred teams playing any or all of each other in various parts of England during the next seven days.

Less frequently the untalkative young batman or servant or companion of the Captain was seen in the village shop. Mr. Ridd paid several visits to the cottage, and on each occasion he found the door locked. When the third month came round, and he went down to see about it, as it were officially, Mr. Ridd found that the door was not only locked, but that the blinds of the downstairs windows were also pulled down.

Mrs. Revvy, waiting just inside her open door, welcomed Mr. Ridd with eager eyes and whispered voice. Safely within the midday gloom of her kitchen she told Mr. Ridd that neither the old man nor the young chap had been seen by her, nor by Cousin Bessie or Cousin Willy's wife next door, or by anyone else, for three days. Didn't Mr. Ridd think something ought to be done about it? At this moment Cousin Willy's wife trotted in from the back door, and breathlessly passing her hand over her bodice as though the strain were too much for her, she whispered rapidly that the old man had just that moment opened the door and had peered out.

"Thank you, Mrs. Carter, thank you ma'm," said Mr. Ridd, "Just a little matter between us—excuse me, Mrs. Carter," and he went out of the kitchen, just as the rusty lock in the door of the cottage scraped back again. After knocking, Mr. Ridd prepared to wait until the door should be opened. He waited with the polite patience of one who for more than forty years had waited on and sympathized silently with every mood and whim of a being whom he considered in every way superior to himself. At length, after several discreet knocks on the door, Mr. Ridd found himself regarded through three inches of space by a pair of small eyes set close together above a thin nose and a pair of moustaches that drooped raggedly to their owner's shabby, food-stained coat-lapels.

"Er," said Mr. Ridd, clearing his throat. "Good morning to you, er, Captain. I've called on behalf of Mr. Pidler in connection with a little matter of rent, if you please."

The door was opened wider.

"Sorry, old man," replied the Captain. "Fact is, those deuced authorities in Ireland haven't yet coughed up the dough. I'm expecting it at any moment."

"Er, thank you, Captain. I'm sorry to bother you, but Mr. Pidler appointed me—"

"Quite, old man, quite. As a matter of fact, I was coming round to see you about it. My man is cleaning my boots at this moment. Unfortunately my health don't permit me to get about as I'd like to. Never been the same since the dysentery and starvation in Mafeking."

Mr. Ridd sympathized with the Captain, who then asked him inside.

Mr. Ridd was used to stuffy interiors, but he said to himself that this place was a bit nifty. In fact, it was unhealthy. Through the jamb on the kitchen door he saw the other occupant stretched before the fire, muffler round neck, boots on the rusty stove. Mr. Ridd left a few moments later, after half a crown had been transferred from his pocket to the Captain's unwashed hand. Nothing of this borrowing was said at the time, for the Captain had asked Mr. Ridd to "keep it confidential, as between one gentleman to another."

Soon afterwards the servant, or batman, was seen in the village shop, buying the cheapest cigarettes, a tin of bully-beef, a loaf, some margarine, and candles. He took them away, not replying to the good morning of the girl behind the counter.

## 2

It was about this time that Mr. Jaggers, a newcomer who had built himself and family a shack above the sea—later to become a large asbestos edifice called *Casa del Mare*—on returning home one night discovered that his pair of Angora rabbits were partly gone from their hutch beside his shack. The wire-netting doors were fastened; but inside were only the remains of cabbage stalks and the intestines of the animals.

P.C. Bullcornworthy was informed the next day; and most of the next evening was spent by P.C. Bullcornworthy watching the approaches to "Orange Boxes", as Tom Gammon rudely described Mr. Jaggers' recent attempt at building. The following morning P.C. Bullcornworthy discovered that someone had cut two of his cauliflowers, while he had been in execution of his duty.

Then Thunderbolt, Revvy's cousin, missed a box tray of seed potatoes from his outhouse and wood-chopping shed. The loss of the vegetables, however, was not immediately connected with the missing exteriors of two Angora rabbits; nor was the part loss of the rabbits connected with the screeching of the phonograph, which had been silent for nearly a week now, behind the subdued opaque glow of the drawn blinds of the cottage.

The next day, as Revvy was digging up part of his garden, it being Saturday afternoon, the door of the cottage opened and the younger man walked out, dressed as usual, but with a towel on his arm. He went to the stream, where he bent down and began to wash his neck and face. The Captain appeared at the door, and Revvy was surprised to hear him say:

"Well, old boy, how goes the garden?"

"'Tes lookin' a lot better lately, I fancy, thank you, sir," replied Revvy.

"Musical?" enquired the Captain.

"Beg pardon, sir?"

"I said, Do you like music?"

"I do, sir, but don't often get a chance vor hear it."

The Captain beckoned. His moustaches were like twin skewers again. Revvy went to the low wall which divided his garden from the drang or passage way before the cottage.

"Would you like to buy a gramophone, a jolly good one, going cheap?"

"Thank you all the same, Captain, but I haven't got the money vor buy one."

"Cheap, old boy, really cheap. With a dozen records, dam good comic songs, sentimental ones too, and band pieces. Plenty of needles thrown in. Look, just a minute, wait there, don't go. Fact is a dam lawyer of mine is away in Switzerland for winter sports, and until I get his signature to a cheque that's owing, I can't do a thing. I'm a stranger here, as you know:

and the village people aren't too friendly. I have my pride as a gentleman, you'll understand. Look here, yours for a quid."

The upshot of it was that Revvy and Mrs. Revvy had an excited, almost agitated, discussion in their kitchen, behind closed doors, while Ernie and Madge listened with eyes alternately round and shining. At last Mrs. Revvy knocked at my door, and importantly beckoned me into her cottage. Would I look at the gramophone for them? Certainly, I would look at it. We all went into the stranger's cottage, and I was introduced. The Captain was stand-offish, eyeing me guardedly, as I looked at surely one of the first His Master's Voice phonographs to be made.

"Very good too," said the Captain, as the trial record screeched to silence. His haughtiness was lessening as though it had occurred to him that here was an alternative buyer.

"Very good," I agreed, listening to *Sailors Don't Care.*

"Ay, it be!" cried Revvy, his eyes shining. "I like a bit o' music, I do!"

After the trial we three returned to Revvy's kitchen, where the conference was continued. I suggested that the gramophone was very old, but Mrs. Revvy said it worked all right. The records, too, were very old, and mostly comic or sloppy songs, *Out went the Gas; I do like to be Beside the Seaside; Don't Go Down the Mine, Daddy,* and such stuff. Revvy said he liked a good comic, and Mrs. Revvy said it would help make the place a bit more lively.

I had come to that remote village in order to find peace and quiet, but seeing that they wanted the thing I suggested that they offered ten shillings for the lot, and not to pay a penny more. Mrs. Revvy had ten shillings saved up in the cracked teapot on the chimneypiece, and so the phonograph screamed two cottages nearer me every night, as I paced my kitchen floor muttering and groaning and writing realistic notes in my book.

For a few days the newcomers were occasionally visible, then the cottage became silent again. It was as if the occupants slept during the daylight, and awoke with the sunset. The nights became frosty with rime. Smoke went straight up from chimney pots, scarcely tarnishing the stars; and drifting down, mingled with the chill vapour lying low over the gardens. The lower windows of the stranger's cottage were wanly opaque long after midnight; having no object in life now that I was not writing, I often sat up till 1 a.m., and the blinds were always alight when I went to bed. One night, or early morning, I heard the door being opened, and slipping out of bed, I thrust my head through the small open window and listened to the sound of footfalls decreasing cautiously up the road. About two hours later I awoke, with an unpleasant smell of burning in the room. The lights were still going behind the blinds of the cottage, and smoke was ascending from the kitchen chimney. The smell was of burning feathers.

The next evening I mentioned this to Revvy. Mrs. Revvy, who had developed sympathy for the "poor old chap", was mending some of his socks, after washing them. They were "darned to shreds," she declared. When the young chap came for the socks, she mentioned that burning feathers had been smelt in the early morning by her neighbour.

A few moments after the young chap had gone, the Captain came round to ask how the gramophone was working. He said he had come to tell her that he had some more records for sale; and in course of conversation mentioned that during the night, just as he was at last able to get the first wink of sleep for four days and nights, owing to his disability gotten in the War, he had been awakened by sharp stings in his neck, and to his horror and disgust, he found that the pillow of his bed was a nest of bugs. Immediately he had ordered his man to light a fire and burn the pillow then and there. Of course, he trusted to their honour not to impart this confidence to anyone else, for he did not want to hurt his landlord's feelings, and he proposed to replace the defective pillow with a new one of the best quality as soon as his lawyer came back from winter sports in Switzerland.

Mrs. Revvy was so sorry for him that she bought the rest of the records, some twenty in number, for sixpence each, paying three shillings down and promising the rest in two instalments, on the following Saturdays, when her husband would bring home his weekly wages of thirty-two shillings and sixpence.

Ernie arrived home with news that put the Captain out of their minds for the time being. During the night, said Ernie, a fox had raided the henroost of Farmer Gammon, taking three chickens, and leaving their heads on the ground. Else 'twas a badger, declared Ernie, for Farmer Gammon said the heads looked as though they had been pulled off; and Farmer Gammon said a badger often skinned a rabbit caught in a gin, so was capable of pulling the heads of a chicken. Coo, he was going to till gins, was Farmer Gammon, said Ernie.

Mr. Ridd called periodically for the rent, but was not successful in getting it. On his fifth call the Captain, who was smoking a cigar, gave him a tennis racquet and a handful of cheroots, saying a friend had called the previous evening and given the racquet in exchange for one borrowed and not returned years before in India. He insisted on Mr. Ridd's accepting the racquet, and the cheroots. Holding the racquet as though it were something that might at any minute bite him, Mr. Ridd went slowly homeward, to work at his Weekly Football Forecast Competition (entrance fee sixpence). Cheroots and racquet were carefully put in a corner cupboard, as both Mr. and Mrs. Ridd agreed that by rights they belonged to Mr. Pidler in the circumstances of the non-payment of rent.

## 3

Suddenly the village was disturbed and animated by the news that the police sergeant had arrived in a taxicab, after a telephone call in Arty Brooking the grocer's shop from Mrs. Bullcornworthy, who informed the sergeant that her husband had arrested a burglar, who had made a confession and signed it. There the police sergeant was, outside the cottage of COUNTY POLICE, the taxicab with engine running, with Mr. Bullcornworthy in blue uniform and helmet, and gripping his staff under his cape, and scared children and alarmed mothers looking from a safe and silent distance at the figure of the young chap in the boots from Uncle Joe's old cottage.

A villager named Mrs. Tigg was among the spectators, trying to make herself bold enough to tell the sergeant that she had seen a motor car with blazing lights stop outside the cottage at nine o'clock only two nights before.

While the sergeant and the constable were talking there, two boys called by their schoolmates Mustard and Tikey rushed up, hair wild and caps in hands, and gasped out that a murdered man with his head battered and bleeding was lying on the rocks of Vention Sands. As Mr. Bullcornworthy adjusted his cape and drew a deeper breath Mrs. Tigg ran forward and threw her arms around her nephew Tikey.

"What be ut? What be ut?" she screamed faintly, and when the yellow-faced Tikey gasped out his news, she moaned and staggered back into the hedge.

More telephoning; and while Mustard and Tikey, now green-faced, mute, apart, and forbidden to speak by the sergeant, waited through an unreality of drying throats and beating hearts, another taxicab was churning up the steep no-man's-hill leading to the village from Crosstree, two police constables behind the driver.

A mechanical and pedestrian expedition then proceeded to the cottage.

"What times us be living in," said Mrs. Revvy to Mrs. Tigg.

"My dear soul, whatever next I wonder," replied Mrs. Tigg, who looked dishevelled with the tremendous events. "There, I knew that Mustard would be leading Tikey into mischief afore long." Later, Mrs. Revvy reported this to Mustard's grandmother, Mrs. Taylor, who said she would flatten Mrs. Tigg if she didn't look out. As for Mustard, he learned bad ways from Tikey. She forbade Mustard to go about with Tikey; and Tikey's mother said she would kill him if he were seen again with Mustard; so the boys became closer friends than before.

While the sergeant and another constable were questioning

62

the Captain, whose eyes in a thin grey anxious face looked as sharp as his moustache-points, the villagers were hastening up from all directions. The two local taxicabs, with engines running—for once they stopped running there was no knowing when they could be restarted—waited in the road. Inside the mystery cottage, whatever could be happening? A search for blood-stained hatchets, hammers, knives? Mrs. Revvy dared to walk past the open door, and saw the old man twisting his moustaches and heard him saying, several times in a high throaty voice, "I tell you, sir, I know nothing about it. I am completely ignorant of what he has been doing. I am a cripple, sir, as you can perceive for yourself. On my word of honour, I know nothing about it."

Her face alight with excitement, Mrs. Revvy said to her neighbours "What about that motor car with the blazing headlights? I know someone visited 'n, for I saw 'n enter with my own eyes."

By this time it was known that the young man had been seen the night before, walking with a sack over his shoulder, by Mr. Bullcornworthy on duty on the Santon road. Next morning, report had been made at the police station that several huts on the sandhills had been broken open, and the contents stolen. Putting two and two together, Mr. Bullcornworthy had gone down to the cottage to make enquiries. He had come out again ten minutes later, with the young man under arrest. Mr. Bullcornworthy was the hero of the village: alone, in the execution of his duty, he had entered the cottage, which rumour said was the headquarters of a desperate gang.

"My!" said Mrs. Thunderbolt Willy, to me, one of the spectators. "But what times we're living in! So close to our doors! Fancy that! We might all have been murdered in our beds! Oh dear, I feel quite funny when I think of it." Mrs. Willy had come out into the crowd; but her pale sister-in-law Bessie was upstairs, peeping through the curtains.

At length one of the cars, containing the sergeant, a constable, and the two boys, went off with a roar of engine and grating of gears, at a very slow pace, towards the distant Vention Sands.

"It will be in all the papers," said Mr. Willy to me. "Can't you write something quickly, and get in before the others? You'll get the fame you're always talking about quickly then, won't you?"

On my Norton motorcycle I dashed after the car going to Vention Sands.

I returned before the others, reporting that the car was stuck in Vention Lane, and the policemen were walking back. Tikey and Mustard had disappeared somewhere.

"Oh my dear soul," moaned Mrs. Tigg. "Where be'm to, for goodness sake?"

"Vanished, Mrs. Tigg. They're hiding, I expect."

Tikey's aunt gave a faint scream. Mustard's grandmother, muttering to herself, looked round like a cat ready to dash at anything in defence of her kittens. I thought my joke of adding to the confusion had gone far enough; and explained that the murdered corpse on the rock had turned out to be a cliff-fallen sheep, dead many days.

After the departure of the police with the young man, I learned from Mrs. Revvy what had been found in Dark Cottage. On the old chap's bed was a pillow filled with the hair of Mr. Jaggers' Angora rabbits. The old chap said the young chap said he had bought them. A tin of sardines was found, empty; one had been stolen from the Santon huts. Cigars, too, were found hidden behind the pictures. Up the chimney was a box of used tennis balls, a bathing dress, a shrimp net, an old pair of canvas shoes; and an empty biscuit tin was on the larder shelf. All these had been stolen from Santon. Goodness knows what else, for there was the car with the blazing headlights which had waited outside the cottage two nights before.

"I know about that car," I said. "For the man came into my cottage."

"Goodness, how horrible!" cried Mrs. Thunderbolt Carter, who had just come into Revvy's kitchen. "Have you told the police?"

64

I shook my head.

"Don't you think you ought to? Everyone's talking about the car with blazing headlights. Can you shed any light on the mystery, Mr. Williamson?"

"I thought there might be too much light already," I ventured to declare.

"But how, I don't follow, what do you mean?"

"Those blazing headlights," I said, after which Mrs. Thunderbolt Willy disappeared.

That afternoon Mr. Bullcornworthy, a big man with a face like a large round cheese, walked on rubber-soled boots slowly past my cottage. To me he said, with a significant glance, "You won't be troubled any more for a while, I reckon, sir."

To Mrs. Revvy he said, further on, "Got him away smartly, don't you think? Evidence all complete."

To Mrs. Thunderbolt Willy he said, "You can sleep easier now, I reckon. You won't be worried any more."

Mr. Bullcornworthy went down the lane, as though realizing that he was the admiration of all.

Uncle Joe's old cottage remained as before. At night the smallest light glowed behind one of the blinds, but that was put out at 8 p.m., just as Mr. Ridd, concealing raquet under his coat and cheroots in his pocket, knocked on the door. Mr. Ridd waited in the cold for five minutes and knocked again. When the door was opened, he said, "I've brought these back. Thank you, but I do not wish to retain them."

"I know nothing about them," said the Captain's voice through three inches of door-space, "I don't know what you mean. Good night."

He attempted to close the door, but Mr. Ridd put the racquet between door and post.

"I shall leave them on the doorstep if you don't take them in," he said.

"I tell you I know nothing about what my man may have been doing."

At this moment Revvy arrived with the phonograph and

records. They also were refused; and the door being shut against them, cheroots, racquet and phonograph were left beside the boot-scraper. They were gone in the morning.

## 4

Two days later I knocked at the door of the mystery cottage. I was invited into the kitchen. It was a cold day, with N.W. clouds passing black over the village.

The grate was grey with a dead fire. Unwashed plates were on the table, with bread-crumbs. Stale air, tobacco smoke, ancient paintwork, darkened wallpaper, homeless furniture, oppressed me with a sense of desolation. Thin as a heron, the old man, one foot in a mass of sordid rags, stood there, leaning on a stick. His moustaches drooped mournfully.

"I'm afraid I haven't a cigarette to offer you, sir, or a drink. . ." he began.

"Forgive me asking, but I know what it is to be friendless, and—please don't think I'm merely curious, but have you had anything to eat lately?"

The old man sat, or rather collapsed into a chair, and putting his thin hands over his face, began to sob.

"I'll be back in five minutes," I said. "No, sooner." I returned with some sticks, and lit the fire.

"I left some milk warming. Just a minute."

When the Captain had drunk the milk with an egg beaten into it, he looked less haggard. His voice reassumed its former attempts at precision. He produced an envelope, and taking out the contents, handed them to me.

"The fact is, sir, I am not entitled to the rank of Captain, and I am worried about possible discrepancies between what I have said to the villagers here and what is written on my discharge papers. I am a time-expired infantry soldier, sir, with a disability pension of twenty-four shillings a week only. I was for seven years an officer's servant to the late Captain Reginald Lowndes, whose testimony you will find there. The young man with me

# THE MYSTERY OF A DAMP COTTAGE

I gave a home to, he being recently an inmate of the Borstal Institution. The rent of this place is beyond my means, and for the past month we have existed on practically nothing. He brought home various things, with a story of having been given them. How was I to know otherwise, sir? The gramophone is legally his, I know, for it was given him by the Borstallian Old Boys Aid Society, together with the clothes he wore, on his leaving at the expiration of his attendance there. I agreed to find a home for him, and paid him all I could afford, two shillings a week, which latterly I was forced, by the general high cost of living, to reduce to a nominal wage of sixpence per week. He did nothing; he refused to work; he was sullen, and would not speak. Now, sir, I have from the first recognized you as every other inch a gentleman, and I give you my word of honour as an old soldier that I am completely innocent of any confederacy with the youth whom the police have arrested in the course of their duty. My pension is still three days away; I am practically destitute until then; but I am too proud to beg. All I have, sir, is a tennis racquet and a gramophone, which were given me by my late servant. It is true I sold the gramophone to a man in the village, but he will be refunded in three days' time. Meanwhile, I am in dire distress; thanks to your generosity, the inner man is momentarily satisfied. What I desire, sir, is to leave this cottage, with its soul-destroying atmosphere, at the earliest possible moment. I see a bus leaves the village at 4 o'clock; and if only I can acquire my fare to my sister's place in Union Street, Plymouth, where her husband keeps a nice little off-licence, I would leave to-day. The gramophone, sir, is, as I think you know, a good one, made before these days of standardization and crash-stuff. Do you smoke, sir? These cheroots are not bad, and are in good condition. For a pound, sir, all are yours; and I give you my word of honour, as an old off—an old soldier, that ten of the shillings I hope to receive from you shall be refunded to the labourer before I depart, as I trust I may be enabled to, on the 4 o'clock bus from this horrible village."

"Very well," I said, after a pause. I gave him a pound note.

# THE MYSTERY OF A DAMP COTTAGE

"Thank you, sir. The action of a perfect gentleman, if I may say so. The only one in the village who has treated a stranger kindly. Thank you, sir, I can never repay your kindness."

"Revvy the labourer was kind, surely?" I said, as I was leaving.

The Captain shrugged his shoulders. "The woman certainly mended a couple of socks for me, but she only offered in order to find out about someone else's affairs. Sir, may I give you some advice? Leave this haunt of meanness and parsimony; don't demean yourself by treating them as though they were gentlemen. Why, what do they say behind your back? I assure you, if I repeated to you the tales I've heard about you, your ears would burn to a cinder. No, sir, take it from me, this is no place to live in."

The Captain, one foot in a bundle of rags, one hand carrying a pressed-paper suitcase, left for the 4 o'clock bus, ignoring the stares of all who watched him go. One villager, John Kifft, said, "Bliddy rogues, both of them; if I had my way, I'd hang the two of 'em!"

Did Revvy get his money back? Yes, but not from the Captain.

And the phonograph? It went out of existence with flying colours, or *accelerando fortissimo*, or whatever the correct technical expression is. Screaming, in a shrill *falsetto*, *Sailors Don't Care*, and standing on a pile of worn-out records on my table, the phonograph suddenly collapsed with a screeching and a whirring, smitten by No. 5 shot from a left-and-right of my 12-bore gun.

And the car with the blazing headlights, was that mystery ever solved? Yes, for I had had the honour, on that never-to-be-forgotten night, of a visit from the district inspector of the Astronomical Life Assurance Company, Limited, whose organisation is as a tooth-comb.

And the racquet? The mystery of its origin is as yet insoluble: even Mr. Bullcornworthy doesn't know. Ernie played with it until all but three strings were broken, then Madge had it, then

Baby Megan, and after Megan, well, dry-rot or the death-watch beetle or the stream or the flames had it.

As for the youth, he went back for further attendance. Sam Pidler never got his rent, Mr. Ridd never won his football competition, and the Captain was not heard of again. But for weeks and months Mr. Bullcornworthy, as he passed the cottages below the churchyard, gripping his staff under his cape, was wont to remark modestly to one or another of the neighbours down there, with a significant glance at the closed windows and drawn blinds of the cottage, "Bit quieter down here nowadays, I reckon?"

# Chapter Five

## AN OLD-WORLD COURTING

### I

One evening when I went into the gravedigger's cottage where (having given up cooking for myself) I used to have my meals, I interrupted a dance by an old woman of eighty years of age, the mother of my landlady, named Mrs. Hector. The name suited her. The dance, a mixture of skirt and jig and clog, being over, her smiling and middle-aged daughter suggested that I should hear the story of mother's courting. After a hearty burst of laughter, and a slap with her huge hand on her knee, so vigorous that it would almost have broken the neck of a cat had one been sitting there, Mrs. Hector began eagerly,

"I were crippling along, and 'er wanted vor to cut me carns."

This puzzled me; and the daughter, proud and smiling, hastened to explain,

"Mother was sixteen, do 'ee zee, and a chap wanted vor to court her, and Mother pushed'n in the stream. He wasn't put off by that, and followed her about still, do 'ee zee, and one day he offered to cut her corns, when he saw that her feet was bad. What did 'ee answer back, mother?"

" 'I can cut they myself,' I told'n.

" 'Yurr,' he said, 'When be I and thee going to get married?'

" 'What's that,' I told'n. 'Marry 'ee? Noomye, I damned well work hard now, and if I had thee, thou miserable old mommet, I'd have to work a damned sight harder. Get out of my way, I've got vor to milk ten or twelve cows.' "

The neighbours sitting in the kitchen roared with laughter. Old Mrs. Hector bellowed with them. She had light blue eyes, and massive forearms bared to the elbow. What was a mommet? I enquired. A scarecrow.

"Aiy, a miserable old mommet he was, a mumbling boy if ever there was one," went on Mrs. Hector. "Wan day 'a came in the furnace-house as I was taking a ham out of the furnace, and started messing and pulling me about, until I told'n I'd put'n i' th' boiler, and I would'v, too, if 'a hadn't cleared out! 'A were full of words as a dog be vull of vleas, a nimpsypiminy chap, 'a were. No cop."

"Mother worked on a farm, you see," explained the daughter, while Mrs. Hector listened with keen delight and approval. "She started at eleven years of age to work, beginning at six o'clock in the morning and going on to the night."

"One day 'a met me carrying a yoke, and 'a wanted to carry it for me, and when I told'n to shog off, 'a pulled my bonnet off, so I catched'n holt, and shoved'n right in the ditch, and chucked a pail of milk over'n. That stopped'n. Oh! a miserable old mommet 'a was, a proper mumbling boy."

I gathered that was the end of that romance; the young milk-maid later married a bullock tender named Harry Hector.

One of the listeners in the kitchen was Uncle Joe, the old fellow who lived in a cottage near mine. He was a lonely figure, living without cat or dog; going at the same hour every night to the Higher or Lower House to drink his pint of fivepenny ale, and listen to the talk of the men there. Sometimes he spoke, but his words were not much heeded. He was ponderously interested in his garden, his weekly pension, the weekly newspaper he received from a daughter far away in service—coal strikes, murders, these yurr Red chaps from Roosha, flying the Atlantic. He believed everything he read, although he often prefaced a description of week-old news with the statement "'Tes perhaps a lot of lies in the paper, but, did you see that—" His cottage was dark and rarely ventilated, and smelled of stale tobacco smoke, musty wallpaper, and mouldering clothes. Like most of the villagers, he disliked an open window, believing that colds and diseases came in with fresh air. Uncle Joe clipped his beard three times a year, usually on a Sunday, and for a day everyone he met was informed of it. He had an old photograph of his six sons, with himself in the middle, taken eight years before, at the outbreak of the Great War. He was very proud of the photograph, and showed it to me several times each year, with the same remark each time. "Now just you give me your opinion of these fine boys of mine."

I had noticed during the dancing of the eighty-year-old Mrs. Hector that the eyes of Uncle Joe had lost their usual faded vacancy. There he sat in the corner, bowler hat on head, laughing and wheezing, "Did ye iver in all your life zee anything like it? My dear soul!" and the pipe dropped out of his gums with excitation. The next morning, coming into the cottage for my mid-day meal, I overheard from the sitting-room this conversation between Mrs. Hector and her latest admirer. It took place after dinner, when the daughter and her husband were out of the kitchen.

*Uncle Joe*, puffing at pipe, hat on head, hands in trousers pockets. "Did 'ee ever think of taking another husband?"

*Mrs. Hector*, promptly. "Noomye!"

*Uncle Joe*, after several puffs, reflectively, "I've been thinking I'd like to see a woman about my place."

*Mrs. Hector.* "I wouldn't have another man, not if 'a were decked in diamonds!"

*Uncle Joe.* "What then, did your other man serve 'ee bad?"

*Mrs. Hector.* "Noomye! 'A were as proper a man as ever walked ground! 'A were as good a man as ever broke bread! I never heard'n swear, noomye, he never even zaid dang to a dog!"

*Uncle Joe.* "Wull, I've been thinking I'd like to have someone to do the cooking down in my place. 'Tes a nice comfortable house, and not damp, like some be."

*Mrs. Hector.* "I don't trouble."

*Uncle Joe.* "I thought 'ee might suit me, that's all."

*Mrs. Hector.* "Not if 'ee were decked in diamonds!"

*Uncle Joe*, scraping to his feet, puffing pipe, and preparing to return to his cottage, "Oo well, tidden no odds."

## Chapter Six

## A VILLAGE DAVID AND GOLIATH

Farmer Hancock, having no sons, could work his farm only with the help of two labourers; and so two labourers were employed by him, reluctantly, for much of his thought ran along a single line—that one labourer could do all the work if only he would work reasonably hard. He was a strong and successful farmer, although he never admitted, even to himself, that any season had been really successful. Broad-bodied and ruddy-faced, always wearing a bowler hat and breeches with leggings and a coat of horsey style, "Champion" Hancock looked "a proper farmer" as he passed you in the lanes on his cob. There was a ring-and-hook in the walls outside the Lower House, wherein before the coming of the motor car the reins of many a cob or pony would be slipped; but nowadays it was used by one farmer only. Champion's horse waiting there was a good sight.

When Champion rented the glebe field from the Rectory, his cob was occasionally seen outside the Lower House any time between the hours of 11 a.m. and 2 p.m., and 5 p.m. and 10 p.m., the legal hours of inn-opening. He was popular in the

Lower House, where he never drank more than he needed as drink. If someone asked him to have a pint, and he accepted, he always returned it, after the custom of those who go to inns for company and entertainment. His nickname "Champion" had been given when he was the owner of a ram which during the best part of its life had been responsible for more lambs per acre than any other ram in the parish. He had the reputation for being a good man of business: for example, during the last three years of his tenancy of the glebe field he had not dressed it with dung, but for three seasons had taken the hay at the cost only of mowing and carrying and thatching the rick. The incoming tenant, knowing this, had acquired the glebe field at a reduced rent from a sympathetic Rector, who, to save the legal costs of collecting his stipend, collected the tithes, and the rents of the glebe, himself. Thus, by thinking he knew better than his agent, the rector did not know that "Champion" had depleted the fertility of the field by removing all the hay from it: and thereby lessened its value.

A tithe is an ecclesiastical tax on fields, by which immemorially the parson had been able to exist. All farmers hated the tithe, but most of them paid it, sooner or later with a good grace. The Rector was understanding about the hayfield that had "gone back" after the hay had been taken repeatedly without "putting it back" in "dressing", or manure. So the Rectory lost by managing its own affairs, but the Rectory was sympathetic to Arty Brooking the new tenant, who, meeting Champion in the pub, said:

"I reckon the parson is a good old fellow. He was very reasonable about that field."

"Well, he's supposed to be a Christian, ban't he?" replied Champion.

"There be no flies on you, farmer," said Arty Brooking. "You pay the tithe on your own land by the hay you took second and third year off the glebe, I reckon. Now, be 'ee going to have one along o' me?"

"I don't mind if I do," replied Champion.

73

"I'll play you a game of skittles?" asked Arty, who was very good at skittles.

"Aw, I ban't no good."

"Yes you be, come on!"

The loser of a game of skittles paid for drinks: thus a pint from Champion was assured, in addition to that owed by the standing of the pint. Get it back somehow.

After Champion had left, a small nondescript man who voluntarily had been pegging during the game of skittles—marking the score by pegging the burnt matches into the holes of the score-board, thus earning, according to custom, a pint from the loser—this little man slid along the form to where I was sitting, and putting his hand over his mouth, although we were alone in the room, asked me in a whisper if I had heard the story of how he had bested Champion.

This story he told me, while darting his eyes about the room in the traditional manner of a conspirator, and talking behind his hand. Yes, thank 'ee kindly zur, he would have a pint of beer.

The name of the sly and furtive conspirator—or respirator, for most of his breath went directly into my ear, sometimes with a spray of beer—was, he told me, "Andy" Lovering. Andy Lovering was the hero of his story, Champion Hancock was the villain; which was another way of saying that Champion was once the little man's employer.

Very astute the little man had been, according to himself. If what happened had taken place in the way he described, something like this must have occurred:—

Andy went to work for Farmer Hancock as a labourer. Thirty shillings a week, and a dark little old place to live in, hardly fit vor put a pig in. The walls were spotty as a leper, and his missus had to walk three hundred paces vor get water from the well. After awhile Andy said to Champion,

"Tidden sanit-airy, maister, vor keep food to ait in a dark place like a coal-house. Plaise to make a window in the wall, and stop up they rats' holeses. Tidden sanit-airy, like it be now."

# A VILLAGE DAVID AND GOLIATH

Champion wouldn't do this, and Andy had two courses open to him; one, to write an anonymous letter to the sanit-airy inspector; two, to ask the village carpenter to run him up a box outside made of a bit of match-boarding, as cheap as he could do it. He would fix it himself. As Champion would have knowed who writ the letter, Andy got a sanitairy box outside the north backdoor, fixed to the wall.

"Iteming job number one—putting up and fixing sanit-airy larder."

I shook the beer out of my ear-hole, and prepared for further spraying, after Andy's long nose had emerged from the pint pot.

The coos got through the li'l old thin hedge into his garden, and ate up his lettuces and cabbages. Andy told Champion about it, asking for a ditched wall or a wire fence. Champion said there it was, and if Andy liked to quarry Champion's stone and load it and build the ditched wall, he would lend a horse and butt and he could do it in his own time. He could have the stone and horse-butt for naught.

"You see?" hissed Andy. "He would'v liked me vor be a fule to improve his own property at my expense, see?"

I wondered what sort of landlord Andy would have made. However, I couldn't escape now. I had to have it all. Andy stopped the hedge gaps with old buckets and sticks and rummage, but the pigs got through next, and ate up his beans and carrots. Andy complained again, but maister said naught that he hadn't said before. Then the bullocks got in again and ate up all the currant bushes. So Andy, out of his own pocket, paid for wire and posties—he wouldn't cut them from Champion's hedges, noomye, he paid for them out of his own pocket.

"Iteming job number two—putting in of posties and fixing same with three strands of barbed wire."

Some said he was a proper fule, improving another man's property, planting currant bushes in place of they ones ate up by bullocks, and the bushes all having big-bud, too. Andy said naught. He was biding his time.

75

"Iteming job number three—planting of currant bushes, and gooseberry bushes in addition to same."

After awhile Andy couldn't work no longer for such a maister, and getting other work, and a cottage, he gived maister notice. Came day before Lady Day, and all his things loaded on a long-tailed cart. Champion was there, for a purpose. Ah, Andy knew he was there for a purpose. Iteming jobs numbers 1, 2 and 3.

Iteming job number 1. "Be you going to take that sanit-airy larder away?" asks Champion.

"I be, and you can't stop me taking away that sanit-airy larder."

"Can't I tho? That be a landlord's fixture, let me tell 'ee."

"Wull, farmer, would 'ee like vor offer me a price for this same sanit-airy larder?"

"It be mine already," says Champion.

"Not if I know it. I be offering it to you for what it cost me, material and labour."

"If you take away thaccy sanit-airy larder, which is fixed to my property, I shall go to Town," saith Champion.

"I ban't afraid of your sort," I replies, "Bella, hand me that screwdriver. For I must inform 'ee that it ban't fixed to the wall by nails druv into wooden plugs, but be screwed in, and thereby constitoots no landlord's fixture."

Champion looks fit vor kill, but he saith:

"Wull, what do 'ee want vor the same sanit-airy larder?"

"I ban't selling now, Farmer." And I unscrews'n and loads'n on the long-tailed cart. Iteming job number 1.

"Now, Farmer," I says, "you knows all about the law, so will 'ee make me an offer for the wire and posties?"

"They be landlord's fixtures," saith Champion. "And if 'ee takes them up, I'll have 'ee to Town on a summons for theft."

"I be still open vor offers for thaccy fence," I tells'n.

"If you attempts vor take 'n up, I be going to fetch the police-man," saith Champion.

"That would suit me very well. Plaise to fetch the police-man."

# A VILLAGE DAVID AND GOLIATH

Champion gallops off on his roan, and returns with Mr. Bullcornworthy on his bicycle.

"It is my purpose and duty to warn you, Andy Lovering," saith Mr. Bullcornworthy, "that according to the law which I represent and uphold in this yurr parish, you have no right vor take away another man's property."

"Such an act of larceny or robbery is not my intention," I replies, "and I asks you to note particularly my words."

"I warn 'ee that anything you say will be taken down and used in evidence against you if things so take their course before the Justices into Town, you being the defendant and Mr. Hancock here the plaintiff."

"That suits my purpose, Mr. Bullcornworthy, meaning no disrespect to you as an upholder of the law, Mr. Bullcornworthy," I says. "Mr. Hancock, will you plaise vor make me an offer for thiccy fence of wire and posties before I removes same, being claimed as my property?"

"I claim same as landlord's fixtures," saith Champion, turning to Mr. Bullcornworthy.

"Bella, bring me my saw!" I saith.

So I cut one of the posties level with the ground, leaving the stump therein, in accordance with the requirements of the law, same being landlord's fixture.

"Stop," saith Champion, "What be asking for the wire and posties?"

"I ban't selling now," I tell 'n. Iteming job number 2.

Then we goes to the currant bushes. They was different from Champion's bushes, which his bullocks ate, but the moots (dead roots) of 'n were still in the ground.

"They be my bushes," saith Champion.

"Not likely," I replies.

"They be," saith Champion, looking to Mr. Bullcornworthy.

"You claim they bushes, Mr. Hancock?" said Mr. Bullcornworthy.

"I do," saith Champion.

# A VILLAGE DAVID AND GOLIATH

"I am of the opinion that the law upholds you in your claim, Mr. Hancock," saith Mr. Bullcornworthy.

"Meaning no disrespect to you or to the law you uphold, Mr. Bullcornworthy," I saith. "But I be of a different opinion. You be a witness to the fact that I am willing to sell these yurr currant bushes, which are free of big-bud and better bearing than those old worn-out miserable parcel of old moots and mores yonder."

"You be exposing for sale another man's property," saith Champion. "For the reason that if you dig them up and take same away, you will be taking some of my soil with the mores."

"Will you buy them?" I asks.

"I will not," he saith.

"Bella," I saith, "fetch me that fork and that bucket and scrubbing brush."

"What be going to do?" asks Champion.

"I be goin' vor take away my currant bushes," I replies, "first making sure, with Mr. Bullcornworthy yurr as a witness, that I take none of your property away, same being the soil in the mores (living roots), Mr. Hancock," I saith.

"Aw, us don't want to fall out about a dizzen currant and goosegog bushes," laughs Champion. "What will you take for 'n? I'll give 'ee two shillin' for the lot."

"I bain't selling now," I tells 'n. "Champion you be called and no doubt Champion you be, I'm not disputing that, but let me tell you this, I'd sooner work for a German Jew from Scotland than work for you again, Jos Hancock."

And to Mr. Bullcornworthy I says, as I walks off with me currant and goosegog bushes, "Meaning no disrespect to you or to the law you legally represent, Mr. Bullcornworthy, but let me tell you this, to be used in evidence against me at any time or place, 'There be no flies on Andy Lovering.'"

"So saying, I bids them a civil good morning and drives off, and now I be working for Mr. Furze, who is as proper a maister is ever I've worked for."

So the nods, winks and sibilances ended; and the little hero finished up his beer and went home to his supper in the modern cottage-bungalow down the road, recently built for him by Jonathan Furze on the site of the proposed New Cemetery, complete with every sanit-airy convenience.

## Chapter Seven

## THE OLD COB COTTAGE

For those who were born there, or who are of the working life, the village has two parts of a name—Higher Ham and Lower Ham—often pronounced Am. Higher Ham is north of the church, and most of the cottages stand in a row beside Rock Hill, which is an exact and sufficient description of the place. The hill lies east and west, and a horse drawing a butt has to pull its hardest, on the toes of its iron shoes, for fifteen or sixteen yards before easing up opposite the Higher House, where the rugged grey shale surface is smoothed under the threshold by the feet of hundreds of years. Thereafter the pull eases off on a slight incline for fifty yards, where the cottages end, and the red lane leads on level between high hedges away from the village.

Seen from the glebe field opposite Rock Hill, the cottages were roofed unevenly, but all of them were lime-washed. Near the top of the row, smallest and probably oldest, stood a little thatched cot hardly wider than the length of a horse. Its brown roof of reed—unthreshed wheat straw—rested against the rough-cast wall of its large and modern neighbour. This neighbour had been built a year after the Great War by the hard work of Charlie Tucker, the mason builder, working himself and employing his brother, John Tucker, the carpenter; the work on the new building had been almost entirely inspired by a Government subsidy of £260.

Most cottages have a look of a human face about them, the

79

upper windows being like eyes, with the door below in the place of a nose; and when I used to stroll over the glebe field, looking for the nests of larks and pipits (while the village boys were in school) the little cob cottage beside the new subsidy building seemed to me to be part of the ancient man who lived within it. The resemblance was not obvious, for the small flat white mask facing south, with its heavy thatch overhanging the single upper casement that was seldom opened, and door and lower casement, did not look like his face. Rather, it was the effect of the taller and newer cottages rising on both sides of the tiny old-fashioned cot, grey lichens on its thatch, the doorway with its rude-hewn oak lintel and its string latch, the threshold slab worn hollow, the hart's-tongue ferns which grew from the loose outer stones of the chimney, its lonely survival of thatch in the row of more modern slate roofs. Under its frontal mask of mortar, which had scaled in patches, the thick walls were mud and stones, bound by cow-dung, and held by straw. "Cob be good lasting stuff, until the wet gets in," said Charlie Tucker, when the oldest inhabitant had died and been buried; and at last the windows were opened to the sun. "But us won't see any more of they old-fashioned places built. Be 'ee coming to the auction this afternoon? 'Tis a dark li'l old place. I shouldn't care vor to live in it." He had bought the cot ten years before for forty pounds; and had been waiting for possession.

An ancient man had lived in the cot for more than seventy years. Old men and children called him "Sparker", or "Zsparker". His name was Jacob Ley. In an oak box, about a foot square, and eight inches deep, he kept his money, five silver spoons, his marriage certificate, his dead wife's golden wedding ring, worn thin as the edge of a man's thumbnail, a thirty-year-old pencil, and a penny note-book almost filled with nigh on three hundred similar items, dated and signed, of quarterly rent received—fifteen shillings a quarter. The bottom of the box was neatly lined with a square of newspaper, a calendar of the days and months of 1882, cut from *The North Devon Herald—published bi-weekly, every Thursday morning and Monday afternoon.* I saw these things when the contents of the cot were auctioned, and the box became mine for three shillings and sixpence.

Sparker Ley, for many years the oldest man in the village, spoke a slow and beautiful dialect, the broadest I ever heard. I used to see him about Rock Hill, always with the same thick ash-staff in his mittened hand, and his trousers hitched up below the knees with string. He was short and sturdy, with a long nose and strong, regular features, and carried nearly a hundred years with stowed strength. In the days when some of the Old Age Pensioners of the parish were children, sitting still and strained in church, overawed by the clerk and his stick kept for talking or fidgeting or otherwise being natural, Sparker was a figure of admiration in the village. Every Sunday before the annual Ham Revel he would get out of his pew, after the sermon, put his beaver firmly on his head and walk slowly up the aisle to the pulpit, and back again. This was the yearly challenge, with the silver spoons won at previous Revels stuck in the band of his hat. When he had sat down again in his pew the parson would give out from the pulpit that the men of the parish might consider themselves, after the custom of Ham village, challenged by the champion's parade to beat him at wrestling on the morrow. "Quiet! Hold your tongues, men!" his reverence would boom; and the murmur would be silent immediately.

On the morning of the Revel, the parson, who was also squire, would observe his yearly custom. Booted and spurred, and wearing a buff-coloured double-breasted waistcoat with his cutaway riding coat, his weasel-coloured beaver, with its rough nap, pushed firm over his right temple, he would walk slowly up the drive from the rectory. He carried a long coaching whip, with which he flicked at leaves and sticks and stones. More than a hundred men and women and children would be waiting for his reverence in the road outside the gate, silently watching his big red face, with its grey whiskers cropped short like arrish, and his hard blue eyes. A broad-shouldered shape of a man, well over six feet tall; a three-bottle man, with a fist-battered nose, relict of a lusty youth. Jacob Ley minded how his reverence was a masterpiece with a whip, for once with a single flip of his whip he had killed a dishwasher—a pied wagtail—as it was running on the grassy border of the drive.

He was greeted by a respectful chorus of "Y'r Reverence!" as they opened a way for him to walk across the road to the stable yard, and so into the glebe field. As though clearing a way among ghostly revellers with the wide airy figures he cut with the whip, his reverence strode on, followed by the wrestlers, and greeted by the yapping of terriers tied along the hedge. There was a badger shut up in a tub under the stable wall, but that sport was for later in the day. Near the badger was a pig in a three-cornered pen of hurdles. Skittling for a live pig was one of the other big events of the Revel, with guessing the weight of a sheep, and climbing the greasy pole for a saddle of mutton. But the biggest item was the wrestling bouts.

"Off with your hats, men!" shouted his reverence, and those going in for the wrestling, who had been awaiting the command, flung their hats at the feet of the parson. The bare-footed boys mingling in and out of the crowd began to wag their wabs in wonder and admiration, but they ceased, like the starlings which had flown up from the grass a minute since, when the clerk bawled, "Shut that rattle, you!" and his reverence stung them with precise flips of the far-reaching lash. "It was right and proper to trim they boys," explained Sparker to me, for the ceremony of the ale was about to be held.

Three thirty-six gallon casks, already tapped and hissing at their spigots, lay on frames against the wall, near the ewe and the brock. Each wrestler—close-sheared for the lesser chance of a grip on his hair—took his beer-pot from his wife or maid whom he was courting, or friend, and waited for his pint. Sparker said that the ale, brewed in the rectory outhouse, in the furnace wherein parson's shirts were washed, "put them all in proper temper."

"Pass'n's man did boil thiccy malt, that was the tithe barley of Varmer Brown, of Crowcombe, who growed th' best malting barley i' th' parish. Pass'n's man was as proper a man for brewing ale as ever broke a bit of bread. 'Twas zaid one time when a' opened the zack o' malt that a master girt rat zat there scrupeting and chittering, and pass'n's man tippeth rat and malt into vurnace together. 'Twas master ale from his reverenz' barrels, aiy! master stuff. 'Twould spring in flame out of the vire when you drowed a spoonful to the hearth."

It was the custom of the wrestling champion to spill on his hearth, for luck, a spoonful of the winner's ale brought home in his gallon firkin, or wooden keg.

After the temper of a pint had been put into his reverence and each of the "wrestlers", the long whip would bend and swish and crack again, clearing a way back to the hats on the grass. The polished toe of his reverence's boot would be inserted under a hat, which with a kick was sent flying, a second hat after it. Thus the two wrestlers for the first bout were selected.

Aaron Kift, the blacksmith, remembers that his father used to tell how the wrestlers came, a week or two before Ham Revel, to the smithy in order to have iron hacking caps with edges like plough-coulters hammered to the fronts of their boots. For practice they used to go, after work, to the top of Norman's Hill two miles away, where the road led down to the largest village in England, to meet the men who had walked up to meet them. On Norman's Land, a narrow incult strip at the fork of two ways, they practised on each other, and the blood ran down into their boots, and the earth was scored and trampled, and the brambles broken from the roots going down through the dust of suicides anciently buried there, each with an oaken stake through its middle, in the light of lanthorns at midnight. A local hate and distrust existed between the villages of Ham and Crosstree, and so the practice wrestling was as hard as the championship bouts.

Long legs were not the best legs for wrestling. The shorter, sturdier man could kick quicker. He who remained off his back was the winner. Sparker was famous for his quickness in shifting and catching his opponent's hacks against the insteps and heels of his own boots; and for his terrible double kick when, in grunting fatigue, his opponent's feet came together. The first hack glanced from the shin of one leg to the ankle of the other, to be followed by a cross kick with the other boot that once cracked the ankle of the Morte champion. Sparker used to practise the cross kick on a rope stretched between posts in his garden, until he could cut it through with one kick. Nobody in the district could stand up to him from his twenty-fifth to his thirty-first year. "It were a grand sight to watch him making his feet zspark," the blacksmith's father had told the blacksmith. That was over sixty years ago.

On his ninety-fourth birthday I met the old champion in the lane outside his cot, and invited him to come with me to the Higher House, and drink a pint of beer. Too late I realised that a half-quartern or a quartern of whiskey would have been a better drink to put the old man in temper. I wanted him to tell me of the parson's hounds, which Sparker used to tend and feed; a mixed and savage pack which was kennelled in a small stone shed with a hayling roof in the meadow now called Kennel Field. The hounds were fed on whole dead sheep, on rats, on each other. One night a man who hated the parson (who had flogged him for getting a girl, employed in the rectory, in the family way) went down to the Kennel shed, and knocked a hole in the slates to drop down the poisoned carcase of one of his reverence's goats. The man slipped and fell in through the hole. Next morning Sparker found the body of the goat under the outer wall, its eyes picked out and its tongue torn, with two dead rats and a magpie near it. Some buttons were also found inside the shed.

"Aiy, zur," said old Sparker, sitting still in the corner of the Higher House, by the little round table, and sipping at a pint of sixpenny. He looked at me uneasily, having lost the habit of going to pub.

"'Twas in th' days of his rev-rr-rence th'ould zsquire what you'm telling, zur."

He finished the beer in slow and uneasy silence, and I asked him to have another; but he got up, took his stick, thanked me and said something about tilling his tetties while the ground was "plumm".

"Isn't it rather early for tilling potatoes?" I asked, when he had gone.

"'Tis nigh on half-past seven, do 'ee see, zur," explained Stroyle George, of Hole Farm, standing by. "And ould Sparker doth love to hear his clocks striking. He doth set one half-an-hour before the other, to hear them periodically."

A grand word, *periodically*, culled out of the *News of the World*. Tiger Kift, waiting to play whist, enquired the meaning of the word. Stroyle George replied, "It be simple, if you unnerstand. Many gennulmen, like the Admiral up to Pidickswell, leave England periodically."

"In the winter, like," observed the landlord of the Higher House, who was sitting in his shirt-sleeves, on a form, staring meditatively before him and picking his teeth with one of the burnt matches used as pegs in the whist scoring-block.

Tiger gave one of his intense quick frowns, and then a bellow of "Corbooger, if my glock ban't be a better wan than thaccy! My glock strikes periodically and in summer, the weather don't make a bliddy bit of difference!"

They were puzzled and silent, thinking that Sparker's clocks also struck in summer and winter. Stroyle George laughed. "If that bain't the best thing I've heard for many a day!" he shouted.

"Well, 'tis like this, don't 'ee see," explained the landlord to the puzzled Tiger. "There be two meanings to the word. They long eddicated words often mean many things to once, if you follow my meaning."

Tiger was silent, fearing that he was showing his ignorance. He could neither read nor write; but there was not a man in the parish who knew the lobster holes on the north side of the headland so well as he, or the way about the rocks in a stormy night.

But Tiger remembered; for when Jacob Ley died a week

afterwards, he was heard to say that, "Clocks or no bliddy clocks, Sparker died periodically."

Grannie Carter helped to wash and lay out the corpse in the new all-wool nightgown that Lady Maude Bullace, the village benefactor, had given Sparker some years before, but which he had never used, keeping it for his coffin. Grannie Carter told me that Sparker's ankles were "all plood (ploughed) up with blue scars."

The auctioning of his few effects took place on Saturday afternoon, when most of the men were home from work.

The dark kitchen, or living room, was filled with village people, come for the same reasons as myself; curious to see inside the old chap's place, and hoping to get something good and cheap. Those two grandfather clocks; the oak dresser; the willow-pattern plates and dishes; the woollen blankets ("I mind her Ladyship givn'n to the old chap dree Christmases agone"); the table; chairs; mattress; pillows. The dealers had not bothered to come out to such a small sale. The auctioneer stood by the blackened hearth. At first we were rather shy of our own voices. That reluctance to reveal oneself before others, which ingrowing with a sense of property so often isolates and hardens the individual! The auctioneer made jokes to draw out our natural sense of fun.

"Nice little village, Ham. Proper little old village" (laughter). "That's better! Someone knows I'm yurr!" (a cackle). "Yes, sir! How's the old horse gettin' on, Varmer?" ("Aw takes I 'bout still, y'knaw, midear!" — and laughter). "Now we're getting along proper, ladies and gentlemen. Now then, let's hear the rattle of your wabs! (Sudden shouts of laughter at hearing a stranger use the intimate village expression). The first item on my list, ladies and gennulmen, is a pair of vases. Now then, who'll start the bidding at five shillings? Five shillings, five shill'gs, five shill'gs—"

"Sixpence," says a voice.

"Sixpence, sixpence, sixpence, sixp'ns, sixp'ns, sixp'ns, sixp'ns, six'—he took up a nod—"shilling, shilling, shill'ng, shill'ng, who'll make it one and six, going for a shill'ng, shill'ng, shill'ng, shilln'g, last chance, going for a shill'ng, come on, make it one and six, don't be shy, going for a shilling, shill'ng, shill'ng"—his hammer rapped on the table—"Gone. Name, please? Mrs. Butt. How old's the baby, Mrs. Butt? Proper baby. Two nice blue eyes and all—(laughter)—boy or girl?" ("Get out," says young Mrs. Butt, reddening: it is her third girl.) "Now then, a pair of bellows, a nice pair of bellows, chance for some of you to pick up a genuine old antique. Who'll start?"

The auctioneer's success was partly due to his memory, for once having heard the name of a purchaser, he did not forget it; but used it again to inform his clerk after a further sale. The successful bidders felt more important, and their manner encouraged the more timid. I bought Sparker's old pint pot for sixpence—a beautifully light cylinder of Marland white clay, coloured brown, with white and black rings. The upper black ring had been smeared in three places by the potter, for the colour to run down the wet slip and to spread into the shape of beech trees. That pot had held the famous rectory ale, a spoonful of which had made the flames spring out of the fire! The rim of its base was worn down, the bottom cracked with fine hair lines like a fine net.

While I was admiring my pint pot, I missed the next item, which was a china figure of Napoleon Bonaparte as a young slim ensign, with a cocked hat and incredible waxed moustaches. It went to Tiger Kift for sixpence. Determined not to miss anything more that was good and olden, I bid seven shillings and sixpence for a pair of brass candlesticks. Later, I had two hollow feelings of doubt in respect of those candlesticks: the first feeling, that my recurrent nervous glances at the eyes of the chanting auctioneer were raising my own bids each time: the second, that the candlesticks had been brought to the sale for the special benefit of one such as I, for thousands of similar antique brass (Birmingham) candlesticks are sold each summer to English and American visitors to Clovelly.

Mine was not the only irresponsible buying. Mrs. Clibbit

# THE OLD COB COTTAGE

Kifft was bidding for most things in her quiet, pure voice, that was like the lone sorrowing notes of a blackbird calling her young in a leafy copse. Her brown childlike eyes smiled at me from the corner where she was resting her big body. She wanted the things to furnish the bare farmhouse on the road to Morte, where she was living with her younger children, peacefully at last. But when it came to the turn of the grandfather clock, I hardened my heart. The clock did not go, but that did not matter. On the night that Sparker died, missing the hands on its winding chains, it had groaned, and struck nearly a hundred times, and ceased work. I liked to think that it had told the age of its owner. The hands were of wrought iron. Its face was painted with flowers never found along hedgerow or landsherd, but they were beautiful and of olden time. Its door inside was inscribed with the initials of the clockmakers who had cleaned it during the past hundred and forty years.

At twenty-five shillings, Mrs. Butt dropped out of the bidding. At thirty, Mrs. Revvy Carter, the mother of Ernie standing so quietly in the corner, with his sweet face watching mine high above him. At thirty-five shillings, Charlie Tucker, who muttered that a modern alarm clock was as good as that old-fashioned thing. At forty, with a mild oath and a spittle-squirt between his boots, Stroyle George. At forty-two and six, the wife of the carpenter, whose thin and gentle face went pink as she shook her head, released from an uneasy prominence. At forty-five, with a regretful gasp out of her red round cheeks, Mrs. Clibbit Kifft. At fifty, the village schoolmaster, with a smiling shake of his head. At fifty-two and six the clock belonged to—speak up sir, don't be shy, what's the name?—Mr. Henry Williamson. I could hardly refrain from giving a shout, and carrying the tall brown brittle case out of the place forthwith. I was going to be married in a week or two.

Afterwards, the table was sold; and the Windsor chair worn by the fireside clasp of Sparker's hands and the back of his head —mine for fifteen shillings. What things of the English country I would write sitting in that chair, listening to the slow tick-tock of the clock, with its strange remote murmurs and bee-like dronings in the candlelight, and drinking out of the pot of Marland clay? While I mused, the oaken dresser was sold for thirty shillings; it was a warren of worm-holes and frass, and falling abroad. I saw Mrs. Clibbit Kifft giving her new possession a pleased and mournful look-over; and then the auctioneer led us all up the stair-boards.

There were two rooms upstairs, one more than I had expected. The back room was very small; a barn owl could hardly have made a flying turn in it, without breaking the broad downy tips of its pinion feathers. The room was half filled with innumerable pale green stalks, rising off the floor towards the little window. Their heads, set with small leaves like green ears, were turned towards the window. Some had reached the panes of the fixed frame, and were peering among cobwebs and the dusty wings of moths. They seemed to be watching for the old man; their thin stalks were pathetic. They longed for the earth, but were doomed to the air; and the old man had longed for the air, and the earth was dark around him evermore.

After resting myself in the little room among the starving and hopeful stalks, I went into the bedroom, where stood the second grandfather clock, a painted ship moving in its face. It was not for sale; Sparker's great-grandson and heir had decided to keep it "for the sake of the old man".

Sparker's bed was put up first. This weighty and rusted arrangement of knobs and bosses and coupled iron webs—each about nine inches square—was bought by Mrs. Clibbit Kifft for half-a-crown. "It will defy Clibbit, missis," said the gaunt tenant of Hole Farm, and there was a united shout of laughter. Clibbit Kifft's violent smashing rages were notorious far beyond the parish. "Ah, yes," said the middle-aged woman, with a slow movement of her head. She had the eyes of a cow standing in shaded water, filled with deep patience, that suffereth old wrongs of men, and knows not hope or despair, but submits, and is innocent. She smiled in the corner, standing under the sooted spider lines that looped and quivered with the warm air arising

89

in the musty room. The auctioneer looked at her, hesitated, but made no comment; and sitting on the pillows, started to sell the bedding.

When the sale was over, and only those who had goods to claim and pay for were remaining, I looked around the kitchen. It was a lime-ash floor, of the kind never laid nowadays, when cement is everywhere available. Those old floors were made of gravel, carted from Cryde Bay at the low spring tides, and after being washed to get out the salt, mixed with the ashes of slaked lime, and a quart or two of cider. For days, and nights too, it had been trodden underfoot, until all the air bubbles were broken out of the hardening mass. Under the slide and press of boot-nails through the years the floor had taken on a hard and polished surface. Around the hearth the floor was chipped and cracked and troughed with blows of axes which had missed the chopping block.

The pitcher, filled from the pump under the rectory wall a hundred yards away—through the cottage garden, and down the sunken lane parallel to Rock Hill, and all the way up again— had made its last dull-ringing sound as it was dumped on the whitened border of the floor. On Saturday nights, when he had shaved and changed his shirt, Sparker had always lime-washed the border round his kitchen floor, making one or another of his three patterns—plain, engrailed, or embattled—for he was a man of originality. Had he not invented that double kick which none could copy? There his pitcher was, its sunken water floating the still dust of empty months, on the yellowing border.

While I was making notes my friend Revvy came up to me and begging my pardon (O ever-courteous Revvy) asked me if I would like to write down the words of two songs he had heard Sparker sing sometimes.

"Many's the time ah've heard Zsparker zay that when'r were a boy he often didden have only a slice o' bread and lard all day. They wasn't so well off in they days as they be now, noomye!"

# THE OLD COB COTTAGE

### Shrove Tuesday Chant

*Lencrock a pancake*
*Fedder for my labour*
*I see by the string*
*There's a good old dame in*
*I see by the latch*
*There's something to catch*
*Nimmy nammy no*
*Trippy trappy toe*
*Please to give me something*
*And I'll be go.*

He told me another, which ragged crowstarvers, twirling clappers and holloing across the fields, may have been shouting to one another when Shakespeare was alive.

### Ploughboy's Chant

*Over to Pickwell*
*Mongst the trees*
*Barley bread*
*And vinned cheese*
*Reasty bacon*
*Tough as thong*
*Darned if I stop*
*There very long.*

In another version, *thang* and *lang* were used. *Vinned* or *vinny* is green. A variation was the line *Sour cider much as you please.*

Just as I had written down these songs I heard a low voice say, "'Tes jonnick, that clock," and I saw Mrs. Clibbit Kifft looking at my granfer clock. "It went too high for me, but 'tis a gude thing all the same, for I've spent all me money twice over, I was so overtaken."

I was glad to buy from her an elmwood box, about three feet

long and two feet tall, with old wrought iron hinges and lock, for eighteen pence, the bidden price; and the smaller oak box in which Sparker kept his spoons, his marriage certificate, his rent book, and his money. The great-grandson and heir, who had ordered the sale, wanted to keep the key of the box "for the sake of the old man", but I persuaded him to let me have it.

"They say you'm gettin' married soon," said Mrs. Kifft. "Be 'ee, surenuff? You wouldn't like to buy that bed I bought, would 'ee?" She laughed, divining my thoughts.

"Aiy, tis' a monstrous great bed, surenuff," the heir informed me in a whisper. "Very heavy," he said, staring down at his new black shoes, which probably he had bought on the strength of the auction. "That was the trouble, between me and you," he added confidentially. "Else I should have kep' that bed for the sake of the old man."

Those who did not know the cottage in the time I have written of would not, perhaps, find it easily in Rock Hill nowadays. It is still there, but it has, like its former occupant, moved with the times, which solves all things. The upper part of the wall, the cob, is gone, scattered as top-dressing over the glebe field. Rains have broken up the light brown lumps, unlocking, after centuries in darkness, the yellow blooms out of the charlock seeds.

The subsidy house has a new small stone wing added to it, covered with a modern rough-cast of cement, and roofed with blue slates. Charlie Tucker is pleased with his work; he gets forty-five pounds a year rent for his new house.

Larks and pipits still make their nests in the glebe field, and the summer wind shines in the grass.

## Chapter Eight

## THE ACKYMALS

One full-summer afternoon, following a stormy night, when the shadows of the walls and thatch lay sharply on the drying road, a shot rang out in the hollow of the village, and a little boy walking in the shade past the nettles growing out of the wall of Hole Farm, stopped, and said to himself, "Coo! I bet that one knacked'n vlying!"

"Hullo, Ernie," I called from my window, glad of any excuse to leave my desk. "What's been knocked flying?"

"'Tis Janny Kift shooting th'ackymals on his pays!"

I ran out of the room, and down the steps to the road, crying, "So that is what has been startling my baby, day after day! Why does that fool want to shoot tomtits? They don't eat peas. They eat insects on the peas. Poor little tomtits. Would you shoot an ackymal, Ernie?"

"I ain't got no gun," murmured Ernie.

"That's why the eleven nestlings in the hole in my garden wall died this spring! He shot the old birds."

"When Janny Kift finds an ackymal's nestie, he blocks'n up if he can't tear'n out. Father see'd'n doing it. Be 'ee gwin to the funeral?"

"What funeral, Ernie?"

"They be gwin to bury a babby up to churchyard this afternoon. I be gwin. Be you gwin?"

When he is quiet, Ernie's face has an expression that rests in beauty; his brown eyes brim with a sweet and gentle luminousness, as though a spirit were looking forth from the eyes of a child.

"Us be gwin," said Ernie.

I remembered hearing about the baby. Four days before, a treble toll of the bell in the church tower had brought the cottage wives to their doors. After an interval, a single toll; and the women had waited, to learn the age of the dead child. The bell was silent. One year old! Then Mrs. Ridd's babby were dead, poor li'l mite.

The swallows were twittering over the village street, and the martins were busy with their late brood in the nest over the door of Hole Farm. The black and white droppings, remains of thousands of flies, splashed the wall, and the sett-stones under, every year, for the farmer "liked seeing the birds about". No, I was not going to the funeral.

Ernie knew all about death, although probably he had forgotten what he had told me three years before, when he was four. Graves he called pits. Before burial, dead men "had a good tea first, and then they take their boots off and put them in pits. They can't see nobody any more when they be in the pits, because the earth be in their eyes." I remembered asking him, trying to probe the child-mind, how he would like to be buried; but he had shaken his head, saying he "won't never go into a pit, because he can't never die." Asked how he knew that, Ernie said, "Jesus said so," and told me that it was in Sunday School. Later, his mother had told me that Ernie had been shown a biblical picture of the disciples walking through a cornfield, shod with sandals, and eating corn; and this had made the above impression on his mind.

The Lower House stood at the top of Church Street, where it joined the road to Windwhistle Cross and beyond. Passing the carpenter's cottage and shed, with its large enamelled iron Navy Recruiting advertisement, lime-washed after the War with the rest of the wall, I reached the sunken thatched cottage where John Kift lived. "Plaise to come right in, midear," invited Mrs. John Kift, an elderly plump woman, dressed in black clothes smelling of moth-ball. "Mind 'ee don't brish against they walls; they'm spotty as a leper. 'Tis the damp, zur. No matter what be done, they walls remain spotty as a leper!" I stepped down into a damp, dark passage, and into a darker living room, lit by a small square window. A percussion-cap

single-barrel gun was laid on two rusty nails driven into the
great oaken beam crossing the smoky ceiling; the beam, as in
all the cottages, had been lime-washed. I noticed photographs
on the high chimney piece, and bunches of herbs drying along
the beam; and then I heard the craking voice of John Kift calling me from the end of the passage.

At the passage-end were sheds, cluttered with old gins, and
pails, and shovels, and boxes; bedsteads, bicycle frames and
wheels, pea-sticks, and barrels. Rust had worn away the iron
lying there, the death-watch beetle—the "worm" of the countryman—had bored the wooden supports and rafters. Cobwebs,
loaded with the frass of the boring insects, and with mummied
moths and flies and wasps, filled the upper spaces of the sheds.
John Kift stood beside a box with a wire-net front, behind the
webs of which a ferret was moving, trying to get out.

"You shoot tomtits, what you call ackymals, don't you?" I
asked.

"Aiy aiy!" he cried. "Every wan I zee near my pays! I load
me gun with a half-charge, and blow ivry wan of the li'l beggars
abroad! Seventy-eight I've shute this year, and in the spring
my son blocked up half-a-dizen nesties in holes in walls round-
about." His voice grew louder and louder. "Yes, zur! And if
us didden do that, us wouldn't have a pay left, noomye!"

"But tomtits eat insects," I protested.

"And pays as well! Yes, zur! They be master birds for pays,
the rogues! But this one won't ate no more pays." And with
the toe of his boot he kicked a tiny bundle of feathers lying on
the ground. I picked it up. Half its feathers were blown off its
breast, its legs broken, its eyes filmy in its loose and backward-
rolling head. Its neck and head were a deep black—a marsh tit,
weighing, perhaps, half an ounce.

John Kift took me to the rows of peas and showed me pods
three inches long, with ragged tears along the length of shucks,
as though rats had gnawn them. "Knack, knack, knack, the li'l
hellers go on them, and I'll shute ivry wan I zee!"

Four kinds of titmice were lying on the ground under the

95

peas—great, blue, coal, and marsh. I knew that great-tits and blue-tits could chip and hack expertly with their strong beaks—the name ackymal or hackmal, and its numerous variations, is derived from the blows they deal—but I was certain of the innocence of the marsh-tits.

"I'll shute ivry beggar I zee on my pays!"

"That's so, zur. John Kift be quite honest, zur," said the rough and pleasant voice of Mrs. Kift behind me.

He agreed to allow the next tit time to feed before shooting, and then to bring the slain bird to me for dissection.

"You'll zee I be right, midear," he called after me, as I went into the gloomy passage, wondering what sort of a fool he thought me. I had seen sparrows and finches pecking the fresh green leaves of sprouting peas in early spring, for I had seen them walking down my own rows, and had thrown stones near them. What business was it of mine if birds slew peas, and a man slew the birds? Slugs and snails ate my seedling cabbages, and I burned them with quick-lime; but John Kift did not interfere with me for it. Was this feeling of pity for little happy birds shot in the sunshine an unnatural feeling, arising from discarded instincts; a useless feeling, as unproductive as a rainbow? Thought made me miserable.

The village street was bright and quiet. I noticed a hand drawing a curtain across a window. A girl ran past the gate, saying in a loud whisper, "They'm coming," and hustling a young sister into a cottage. The old terrier called the Mullah lying at the bend in the road by the shop got up, scratched, stared at something invisible to me, and sauntered away. I heard a shuffling of feet. Then round the corner came four youths, clad all in black, except for white bow-ties and white collars and white gloves. They moved very slowly, carrying a small white coffin on two cloth slings, one at each end. I saw blackness behind them, and hurried away.

Women were standing by the low churchyard wall, looking over the green mounds, and I stood among them, next to Mrs. Butt, who immediately told her three little girls—heavy Saxon type—to shut their rattle; and then smiled at me, showing her ruinous teeth. Mrs. Butt's five-month baby, without a stitch on its grubby body or a tooth in its gums, lying in a perambulator near, also smiled. I felt its chubby legs, and remarked how well it looked, but how cold it was in the shadow of the elm trees. "Ah, I likes 'em to be 'ardy," said Mrs. Butt, smiling again, and asking after my baby, who was born on the same night as her own. "Fine li'l boy you've got!" I agree, and smile at the recollection of what Mrs. Butt is reported to have said to the parish nurse when told that her baby was not a boy. "Cor darn, what beats me is where all these girls come from."

"Tikey, get down!" scolds Mrs. Willy Gammon, mother of innumerable children and grandmother of several, to the seven-year-old merry boy who robbed one of my apple trees last year. Tikey laughs, and won't get down; he is the unconquerable sort, nervously and physically strong. Even when I whacked him hard, over that apple business, he didn't whine; but, with angry tears in his eyes, picked up apples and earth and flung them at me, crying, "Ha, 'it 'im agen, wull 'ee? 'It 'im agen, wull 'ee, ye ould booger?" We respected each other afterwards, and I gave him the hazel stick for a souvenir; and now we meet as proper friends.

Daisy is Tikey's younger sister, then comes Boykins, whose round brownish face—all the Gammons have ruddy-brown faces—is still rather scared of me; it was Boykins, aged nearly four, who from the road below tearfully urged Tikey to kick me during the mock whacking. Daisy, red lips and soft brown eyes, regards me from the wall, as she cuddles the Gammon baby, a petulant and spiteful child, aged three, "the last Mrs. Gammon will have, surely, at her age," says the village. Daisy's face is full of love; the little maid will make a good mother when she weds later on.

So I muse by the wall, whereon many children sit, eager for the sight of a baby's funeral. The bell tolls. Scientists tell us that the bony structure of the bat is nearer to the human frame than any other mammal: and lo! here are great human bats following the coffin with slow and shuffling steps, old women with strange and ugly faces, clothed in black. Their eyes peer under shapeless bonnets; their clothes, like wings of black shrivelled skin, seem to suffocate the personality. Tears drip out of their old eyes. They walk into the graveyard, and follow the parson into church. Only then does Grannie Carter dare to call out, in a loud threatening whisper,

"You come away from that grave, my boy! Young reskle, you! A-a-ah! You wait till I catch 'ee!"

"Ya-ar, ould booger!" cries a minute urchin playing alone by the small shallow grave. He does not care for his grannie, whose voice, harsh and broken, has just threatened him over the wall. The young rascal has blue eyes, and a split lip; his toe caps are kicked broken. His widowed grandmother looks after him; her daughter is in service in another part of the country, and rarely comes home. He is Ernie's cousin, and was christened Vivian Somerville Carter; but Ernie and his friends call him Babe. What a temper Babe had when he was really small, two years or so; when granfer was alive, and used to shut him up in a shed! Dreadful screams of rage! "A very backward baby" his grannie said to me once. "Two and a half year old and 'a can't talk yet. All 'a can do is to swear." But now he goes to school, and plays and fights with other boys, and is happy.

The mourners were in the church; the curious were looking over the wall; the bad boy was sitting by the shallow grave. He was scratching at the earth with his nails, and trying to push something into a hole.

" A-a-ah, you young limb!" scolded old Grannie Carter over the wall.

"Ya-aa-ar, ould booger! 'Ee can't catch I now!" taunted Vivian Somerville. He was planting a kidney bean in the earth by the grave.

The grave was twelve feet from the wall. Like all the other graves, it lay west and east—the tiny feet would lie towards the east, awaiting the coming of Christ beyond the sunrise. By one of the trunks of the great elms many wreaths of flowers were laid, piled one on another, each with a card and lines of sympathetic writing; for the baby's death had touched many hearts. A red-haired man stood by them, copying the inscriptions into a penny notebook: he was the village correspondent of the local newspaper, which would describe the flowers as "a wealth of floral tributes", and for every name included in his list he would probably sell a copy on the following Thursday. He used to keep a motor-car, plying for hire in summer when the visitors came; but the red omnibuses took the visitors, his car grew shabby and out of date; he became a labourer again, and his little boy took round papers, for times were bad.

The children on the wall were merry and noisy as the starlings on the church tower. Grannie Carter stole into the churchyard, grey and lumbering as a badger; but Babe saw her, and with a shrill laugh ran away among the tombs. "Ya-aa-ha! Ye can't catch I naow! Ye can't catch I naow!" he taunted her, waiting for the intense delight of being chased, and plucking at his middle. "Ould Granmer Carter, ye can't catch I!"

Granmer Carter retreated, for something white had appeared out of the church porch, between the stone heads of the gargoyles, one chipped and frowning, the other whole and serene. The Rector, in his vestments, walked slowly, with composed face, his hands clasped before him. Behind, the youths bearing the coffin, and the black straggling files of mourners. Vivian Somerville gave a startled look and ran out of the churchyard. Children on the wall were pulled down by their mothers, or hushed into silence.

Slowly the mourners settled round the grave. The father was a tall man, with a face yellow as tallow, and a black moustache; a thatcher by trade. He swayed, and looked in the grave, with dull, dry eyes. The face of his remaining child, a youth of eighteen, was also sallow, but puffy with weeping. The old grandfather stood beside the grandmother; sometimes he gulped, like the grandson, and stared wildly as the priest recited, in a low and placid voice, the words of the Church of England Burial Service.

"Man that is born of a woman hath but a short time to live

. . ." the mother, shrunken in black mourning, gave a whimper-
ing cry— '. . . and is full of misery. He cometh up, and is cut
down, like a flower; he fleeth as it were a shadow, and never
continueth in one stay."

The parson spoke without feeling. No beauty bloomed in his
words, to raise an image in the minds around him. He was sixty
years old, and looked forty; perhaps if he had been deeply
moved by all the services for burial he had conducted he would
have looked eighty. A heavy trundling sound, and the far-away
singing of many voices, caused some of the women by the wall
to look northwards; children's faces followed their gaze. Round
the corner of the Rectory wall came a big yellow motor coach,
filling the roadway, and the singing grew suddenly loud. The
service went on. A hatless man stood with his back to the
driver, conducting the choir with his hands. Dust swirled behind the coach, which quickly slowed, and as it rolled past the
burial place the voices sank, but did not die away. The Welsh
miners on holiday were singing one of their grand and inspiring
national choruses; eyes were brightened when they had passed,
except the sad ones by the grave.

As the coffin was being lowered, the mother uttered stifled
whimpers, while she stared as though penetrating the white
composition of the lid, to the small pale face within. She clutched
her husband, longing to fling herself down to break the shut
lid and to take the little one, whose every laugh and wail and
cry in life were still part of her living heart. She heard words,
well-worn words, that since childhood had never entered her
consciousness: words, "O Lord God, holy and most merciful
Saviour, Lord most holy, O God most mighty, O holy and
merciful Saviour." She tried secretly to smile to herself, and
whimpered, "I believe, I believe;" while her husband held her
tightly, his face a duskier yellow.

*Zip-chee-chee. See-see, see-see!* A family of marshtits flittered in
the shadowed leaves over us, restless and happy as they peered
and lit on the twigs, hanging head-down to peer with bright
eyes for green-fly and caterpillar.

"Earth to earth, ashes to ashes, dust to dust; in sure and certain hope of the Resurrection to eternal life, through our Lord
Jesus Christ; Who shall change our vile body, that it may be like
unto His glorious body, according to the mighty working,
whereby He is able to subdue all things to Himself."

*Sit-ee sit-ee sit-ee!* A coal-tit was wandering with them. I could
see the streak of white on his black head. *Zip-chee zip-chee*, as they
passed, some high in the tree, others just above my head. They
swung and fluttered, always calling to one another, sometimes
peering for hawk or owl on the branches. For days and weeks
they had been wandering in the spinneys and orchards and gardens, sleeping in holes in trees, in the eaves of thatch, ivy on
walls, warm and together. I saw the parent birds fly over the
Lower House to the hollow of gardens beyond; and then I was
listening to words that seemed false and unnatural, and harsh to
the miserable beings standing black, as though charred, in the
summer sunshine.

"We give Thee hearty thanks, for that it hath pleased Thee
to deliver this our sister out of the miseries of this sinful
world . . ."

After the service, the priest turned to the mother and said,
in a voice more like his own, "Do not grieve, Mrs. Ridd. She is
now safe in the arms of Jesus, and one day you will see her
there." "Aiy, aiy!" said the old fisherman, the baby's grandfather. "She'm safe i'th' arms of Jesus," and looked at the sky.
He walked away, to get a glass of beer, and looked into the sun's
face, which dried his tears, and gave strength of life after grief.
I heard the report of a gun.

Children scrambled down from the wall, forgetting what
they had seen. Observing Vivian Somerville Carter back on the
grass by the flowers, I went to him. He was banging ants with a
stone, watched by a small quiet boy who wore an enormous
cap. This boy was a visitor to the village, and whenever I had
seen him, on the sands, in the street, or on his own doorstep, he
was wearing the same large cap. He did not play with the boys
of the village, but stood about near them; and once, when I had

playfully thrown a minute apple at him, he had gone away with injured dignity, and told his father, who had complained to me.

"Don't you feel sorry, Babe, that this poor little baby is dead?" I asked.

"No."

"Would you be sorry to see Ernie laid in a grave?"

"No."

"Wouldn't you cry, Babe?"

"No."

"What, didn't you cry when Granfer died?"

"No. Uncle Bill did. I zeed un going home down the road crying."

Uncle Bill was Ernie's father, called Revvy because, years before, he had worked in the Rectory garden.

"Would you care if I died, Babe?"

"Booger, no!" he replied, furiously digging with his nails.

"Well, then, will you come and live with me, as you are not happy with Granmer?"

"No, I tull 'ee, you bloomin' vule you, no!"

Yes, I was a blooming fool to continue the inquisition; and I continued:

"But, think, Babe. You will have a nice time, go to bed late, have all the apples you want, and go down to the sand-water every day. Won't you?"

Babe called the sea, sand-water.

"Ya-aa-ah-ee! Ould Daddy Wisson!"

I was Ould Daddy Wisson.

"And think, Babe. You will have a nice bed, all to yourself."

Then the large-capped boy joined the conversation.

"I've got a bed of me own where I live, in a big house up to Exeter."

"Ya-aa!" jeered Babe, "It's a poop bed!'

"Vivian Carter," the other solemnly warned him, "remember you are in the churchyard." Five years old, and already matured, thought I; poor little man. Then I saw John Kift look over the

102

wall, and lean his elbows along it. He was the brother of the fisherman, and great-uncle of the dead baby.

"Well, well!" he said to me, in his loud voice, as I stopped by him. "Did ye ever see anything like it? Look at that, now! Look at them all. Well, well! I call that a turrible waste of money, all they flowers." He stared round again, as though unable to realise what he saw. "Well I never. Did 'ee hever zee anything like it now? Pounds and pounds, I reckon, they flowers must have cost. No flowers will bring it back, noomye. Aiy, pounds and pounds. Well, well! Much better to have given the money to the parents. Pounds and pounds, they flowers must have cost. More than all the doctors' bills, I should say."

He put his hand in his pocket, and drew out two dead marsh-tits, which he put on the wall.

"I don't reckon they doctors be much cop," he mused. "Five doctors Liza took the baby to, and all described bottles and bottles of medicine, but with all of them twarnt no gude. No, zur! I reckon she would have done better, and saved money, if she had kep to one doctor, instead of trittin' around from wan to anither, from Crosstree to Town, from Town to Combe. Tidden no sense in it. What do 'ee think, Mrs. Carter?"

Granmer Carter was looking at the flowers again.

"Poor li'l mite," she croaked, slowly and sadly. "'Tis most butiful flowers I ever did see. 'Tis a loss for the mother, 'tis a loss, and after eighteen year."

"'Twas going on fine the night before, too!" said the cheerful voice of Mrs. Butt, returning with her perambulator and three yellow-haired girls. "Why, only the night before the poor li'l mite died, it ate nearly a plateful of tinned salmon, so Mrs. Smaldon told me."

So small were the bodies of the ackymals, and so strong the fingers of John Kift, that it was a difficult matter to find, among the feathery pieces, the crops of the birds. Vivian and Ernie stood on the iron toe-tips of their boots, to see the interesting *post-mortem*. The gullets were far too small for the passage of a pea; and no green fragments were found in the crops. Nevertheless, John Kift, pointing to minute black specks, cried, "What did I tell 'ee? I knowed I was right! What more could ye want? They ackymals be master rogues for stealin' pays, and I'll shute ivry wan I zee!"

*Chapter Nine*

## BILLY GOLDSWORTHY'S BARN

When first I came to live in the village I used to go to the sea at least once every day, and immediately after walking out of the drang or passage-way from my cottage to the roadway I passed a barn. It was built against the eastern wall of another cottage; the angular ridge of the sloping tiled roof lay out from, and below, a tottery brick chimney. After awhile I noticed a shrub growing out of the ridge, a small-leaved shrub, which later I learnt was a laurustinus. It grew in the middle of the ridge, and at first was not specially remarkable.

The first time I saw it, the shrub was no taller than a perching sparrow. It bore about a dozen leaves. A bird, perhaps, had carried up the seed, and lost it there; rain had sprouted the roots in a crevice of crumbling mortar between the ridge binders. In the dust of spiders' webs, swallows' droppings, and the rich frass of colonising wood-lice, the roots had found their food. How long would it last in that strange place, I wondered.

That summer was the driest within living memory. No rain fell for months, and yet the shrub growing among the sun-baked tiles did not wilt. Day after day of unclouded heat of the high and brilliant sun; week after week of blinding sun-dust furiously and incessantly beating on all life, as though heaven would breathe flame into the very rock again. On the chimney tuns and walls of farmhouses and cottages the wall-rue and hart's-tongue ferns, and the pennywort and stonecrop—camels

among plants—shrivelled brown as the brittle thatch. Only
lichens held their forms and colours in the over-pressing sunlight—the lichens that were like mummies: and the green mysterious plant growing in solitude out of the red tiling.

The drought broke, and from the grazing fields, which for
months had been hard and rough like cocoanut matting, there
sprang the green loveliness of young grass. Beautifully the ferns
uncurled in the mortar'd chimney tuns. The swallows on the
ridge of the barn twittered as though it were spring again, and
no autumnal farewell looming through the serene days of Little
Summer. Soon, too soon, they were gone, and the damp, yellow
leaves were falling from the churchyard elms; and the ferns
were rusting, the fields lying grey and sodden in sea mists,
the lanes but empty places along which to hasten in the afternoon walks—but haste was vain, for no immortal country,
changeless in solitude dream of sunlight, was ever found over
the next hill.

In that autumn and winter, when youth had not learned the
source of its illusions, and human love and friendship seemed to
hold only pain and bitterness, the little shrub growing so high
and solitary in its evergreen sturdiness became more than a
symbol of aspiration and endurance. Sometimes I saw it against
the star-great winter sky, when Orion was lying bright over the
elms. Once it was snow-clogged, and a hungry rook, watching
the bare yard of Hole Farm opposite, huddled beside it. Year
after year it remained there, a marvellous small tree serene in
the burnt-clay desert of the barn roof.

One day in passing I stopped, thinking that I had never seen
the doors of the barn open. They were drab and weather-worn,
and secured by a rusty padlock of old pattern. Breaks in the
ragged skirt were rudely patched with sheet-iron, or stopped
with pieces of rock. Sometimes a small black and white cat was
to be seen walking with slow, as if reluctant, steps in the long
grass before the doors, squatting on the threshold to wash its
face, and then, after harkening and flicking the tip of its tail,
creeping under and disappearing. If one listened, one might

hear a remote mewing, and the rustle of straw, and a blend of purring noises.

The wood of the upper part of the doors was almost hidden by bills stuck one on top of the other. Of all colours and types, the bills announced auctions, grass keep for sale, whist drives and socials and fêtes organised by political committees, or for funds for the Church School, circuses, sales of boots and shirts and breeches and other cheap clothing. Occasionally, a religious text with Love as the theme was found there, stuck upon the others. Youths on motor-cycles slung with canvas bags and iron paste-pots used to stop before the barn, give surreptitious glances over their shoulders, hastily paste up their business notices, and quickly ride away; but the religious texts must have been affixed at night, for no one in the village seemed to know who stuck them there.

Wasps flew to the doors in summer, to rasp the paper with their jaws, and carry it away to their nests. Children sometimes pulled off thick many-layered wads of the bills, which were cast away to litter the streets for days and sometimes weeks.

Passing late at night down the quiet village street, on my way to a haystack roost in the fields, I frequently heard the noises of knocking and thumping in the barn. Streaks of light shone through the chinks of the closed doors. Sometimes, instead of knocking, there would be the sound of low voices, but rarely after eleven o'clock.

I came to recognise the low and continuous flow of one voice; but the voice accompanying it, and usually vainly trying to override it with laboured words, which were unable to pass easily off a tongue recently immersed in ale or cider, seemed to be different on each occasion. After I had passed the half-closed door about a score of times, three voices, vain accompaniments to the continuous and dispassionate flow, became recognisable. One of them was the farmer of Hole Farm, who, I fancy, had come to complain, but had remained to argue.

The low-voiced man, I decided, was the owner of the barn, and, like all men, he did not like the expression of his ideas being thwarted; for one night, when the vain accompanying voice had raised itself almost to a shout in order to be heard, or perhaps to restore an ego's inner harmony, the knocking began vigorously, and shut down all words. The door was pulled open; a figure stumbled out and fell on the grass; picked itself up swearing; and shuffled away up the road, making uneven progress. Twenty yards farther on it halted, shuffled, spat, and yelled hoarsely, "You'm a bliddy old vule, Billy Goldsworthy!" and shuffled on again.

A couple of nights later there was another discussion behind the closed and multi-papered doors; and this, too, ended abruptly, when a woman's voice cried with angry reproach from the lane, "How much longer be 'ee going to bide there rattlin' away? I've got to be up to work early in the morning, and I want to be to bed some time to-night, even if you don't. 'Tes nothing but a parcel of ole flim-flam you both be telling, anyhow!"

I recognised the voice as belonging to a small middle-aged woman who passed by the barn several times every day, always carrying a rush-bag. She would stop on her way to speak to puppies and children in low and friendly tones. Every year she walked more than a thousand times between her cottage at the west end of the village and the inn called the Lower House, always carrying a rush-bag with a bit of newspaper hiding the contents on the return journeys. Sympathy, tenderness, and understanding welled out of the plump little ageing body; and if she and her husband had rough words sometimes in their cottage, it was so inevitably, since the main trait of her nature was perpetually being stimulated and magnified at the expense of the rest of her being.

My curiosity about the owner of the barn was now active, and the next morning I asked my neighbour Revvy who it was.

"'Tis Billy Goldsworthy," said Revvy.

"Where does he live?"

"Down by Zeales. Funny chap, he be: proper old oyl (owl), he be, always working at night, when most volks be up auver."

Up over was a regular village expression for being in bed.

Time went on; I got married and moved into the cottage adjoining the little barn. One day, from the writing-room above, I saw the left section of the double door wide open, and going downstairs, I went to the door and called out, "Good morning!" There was no answer, and I peered in. The sun laid a bright parallelogram on the uneven floor littered with old straw and broken, worn, slates. Beyond, in shadow, I saw barrels, planks, posts, a ladder with rungs fallen like teeth in old age, and many other wooden things, broken and hoarded.

The barn was a museum of things of old-time village life. On rusty nails driven into the dry cob wall hung a reed-shearing hook, and a reaping hook beside it. The shearing hook was more circular than the reaping hook, and of iron beaten flatter. Both blades were brittle and dark with rust. The wooden handles were riddled with worm-holes.

Near them were other thatchers' tools: the flat wooden mallet used for banging level ends of the reed-motts; a standing bittle, or small thatching step, with iron prongs curved like an otter's eye-teeth, for sticking into the thatch; leather knee guards; a shearing board. All were riddled, dusty, and draped with old slack cobwebs.

As I was looking round, the barn, lit by the doorway light, grew suddenly dimmer. A small man, whom I had often seen before, but never spoken to, stood there.

"Good morning," he said guardedly, standing still.

"I was just looking at these relics of old times," I explained, and added. "I've no right to be here, and must apologise for—"

"You'm quite welcome," he replied immediately.

"The thick cob walls keep it cool, don't they?"

"Ah, they can't build to-day like they built in the old times."

"It's a fair size, too."

" Ay. 'Twas a dancing barn when I was a boy. Many's the time I've a-zin young men and maids a-dancing in this yurr barn by lantern light. And it was proper dancing in they days, too."

Before I could say anything he went on,

"Twadden like these days, you know, when they'm all up to the Institute night after night, all dressed up like young leddies, with jazz bands and all. There ba'nt no sense in volks to-day, that's my way of thinking."

"But don't you think times are better now?"

"You'm quite right, zur," he replied, unexpectedly. "'Tis an old barn, surenuff." He added meditatively. "Aiy, it be. Tidden like times be now, when things be different. A man had to work for his living in they days. Aiy, he did." He began to gather some straw.

The floor was of lime-ash, and a broken hollow like a pig's trough lay across it. He noticed that I was looking at the break, and paused in the act of picking up the armful of straw.

"Now that was done by my father and his father avore'n, beating out corn with a dreshel. I've a-zin my father knacking all night, when I was a boy. Twadden like to-day, you know, they was hard times, and no mistake." He put down the straw. "Aiy, they was."

He took down the dreshel and showed it to me. It consisted of two thick wooden sticks linked together loosely. The longer length was the handle, four feet long. To one end a horn joint was lashed with raw hide strings fitting into grooves, to allow the leather thong attached to the horn joint to turn with the flail, or wooden striker. Thong and horn made together a universal joint: the dreshel was swung from left wrist and right elbow, so that the flail turned just above the floor and banged on the corn along its whole length at once. The flail was two feet long, and made of holly two inches thick.

"In they days volks was poor, and couldn't afford a floor of oak planks for the dreshing barns, so they had to have lime-ash. An oak floor was best, you see, to give a jump to the flail after every knock."

He showed me a thing like a low wooden stretcher, which he said was a pig form.

"'Tis many a pig I've seen killed on that one," he said. "'Tis

the proper way to kill a pig, too, none of this yurr modern stab
and spill the blood all over the place. Why, my dear soul, men
couldn't turn the pig up to-day! They ban't got the strength
the old volks had. Noomye!"

I looked at Billy Goldsworthy. He was about sixty-five years
old, small, lean, and long-armed. His nose was long on his thin
face; his adam's apple large in his thin neck. He wore always
the same kind of semi-starched, semi-grey linen collar and shirt-
front, never quite clean and never quite dirty. "A proper old
oyl," Revvy had said; and as he stood before me he looked like
an owl, but an unfledged owl, a nestling barn owl that blinks in
some dim day-chinked tallat as it sways like a decrepit, moth-
eaten, very ancient featherless bird. His long nose and blinking
eyes, his slightly bowed legs, the quiet grey night-look about
him, all these things were owl-like.

"No, it ban't like the old days to-day," said Billy Goldsworthy.

He pointed to an unfamiliar wooden machine like a great bee-
hive, and said it was a wimbling machine. It had seven square
sieves of iron wire graduated in size, each size being numbered
with tallies, or cuts, on the wooden frame. After the threshing
by the flail, the corn and the doust were shovelled into the winnowing machine; and when the handle was turned berries and
doust, or seed covers, were scattered in the confined whirlwind,
until the whole grains found their way through the first sieve;
the broken grains through the second; the "charlick" (charlock)
and dock and scabious seeds (if the binding of the sheaves had
been careless) through the third sieve, and afterwards, to the
crops of the chickens waiting outside the door.

By the winnowing machine lay a hand rake for combing the
wads, or sheaves, set aside for thatching after they had been
threshed and pitched. The best motts, or unbruised wheaten
straws, only were used. He demonstrated how a wad was first
bound with a straw rope, and then tightened with a driff, or
wedge of extra reed-mots: then it was pitched, or tapped on the
floor, in order to get the cut ends of the motts tight and level.

The pitched sheaf was then combed with the hand rake, whose wooden teeth pulled out the bent or loose motts. The reed was then ready for wetting under the fall of the stream, before being laid as thatch.

"There won't be any more reed laid to new houses again, unless it be for these yurr gentry's fancy houses, 'tis my way of thinking," said Billy Goldsworthy. "Apart from other things, you see, a man can't get his money back on reed. Why, 'tis nigh on a hundred pounds to thatch a farmhouse 'vore and back nowadays, and 'tis all gone again in twenty years. That's five per cent. depreciation for your money, and where's your money coming back by? That's how it is to-day. Modern, that's it."

He blinked, and fell into a reverie.

"What's that?" I asked, pointing to a frame of iron, about a foot square, with cross bars like a drain, fixed on an ash pole with a double handle.

He came out of his reverie, and explained that it was an old-time stamper for threshing barley. The iron bars broke the brittle beards of the barley, which was then shovelled into the "wimbling" machine, to be thrown about from sieve to sieve as the cumbrous engine revolved inside its wooden frame.

"Aiy, they was bad times in they old days," said the quiet little man, stooping to pick up his armful of straw, and laying it down as some thought itched within his mind.

He stared around his pile of old wood which he had been hoarding for nearly half a century. "It don't seem right, nowadays, young men picking up three pound and more a week so easy, when you think what the old folk earned. To-day folk don't have no children, but in they days a man might have seven or eight childer, and bring home seven shillings and sixpence vor to feed them all on. My dear soul, I've a-zin men in the harvest field working fifteen or sixteen hours straight off, and the vrost showing through their leather belts the whole time, as they stooped behind the reaper to bind the sheaves! And get one shilling and threepence for it!"

"The frost through their belts?"

"Well, that's what us calls it hereabouts. 'Twas so hot, you see, that a man would sweat all the time. Yes, there was beer, for those that wanted it, but twadden all who might want beer. 'Twas small ale, and likely to give a man the guts-ache. Some used to like it, no doubt. My dear soul, men used to sweat when they worked in they days: tidden so to-day. Why, they do say that a man to Morte once drank two pecks of ale and two pecks of cider between sunrise and sunset, and could walk straight after it! That's only what I've heard my father tell, you know, but 'tis right enough, no doubt. And 'a could'v drunk more if he'd a mind to—'twas more in the house, you know. Tidden like these days, when the farmers won't give naught away!"

A peck was two gallons, carried to the harvest field in a hand keg, or firkin. Four pecks would be sixty-four pints.

"Yes, sir, a penny an hour was all they old people was paid. And if a man saved up enough to slap up a cottage, what ground could 'a get? Vor to put'n up on? My dear soul, the landlords wouldn't let a man buy a bit of land! Look at my place down to Zeales, by the stream! There's a nice muddy place, under water in the winter. That's what poor people had to put up with in they days! A poky li'l old place for volks to live in. Tidden right, zur?"

He bent down once more to collect the straw.

I wondered what was right in these days or they days; but I said, "Surely labourers to-day don't earn three pounds a week?"

He stood up again promptly.

"No sir, but these young masons pick up that, and more. For a labouring man, you have to pay one pound, twelve shilling, and sixpence to-day," he said. "And what do 'ee get for it? Why, if it rains, they'm oomwards! 'Tis the same all over the country to-day. Look at these Trade Unions! Why, there ban't no sense in it! People don't know when they'm well off."

I attempted a question about the difference between the wetness of muddy cottages and the wetness of working in muddy fields, but I was caught up in a flow of words like the stream in flood. The monologue consisted of a sort of cold mincemeat of talk, that had been cooked many times already; a mince of what he had read in newspapers, heard at political addresses, and reluctantly absorbed from more persistent orators in his barn. Sometimes I put in a word or a sentence into the flow, when he would most unexpectedly pause, stare at the ground, say, "Yes, zur," as though in profound meditation (but really in politeness), and then he would start again, gradually working up to a rapid rant.

For more than an hour, while the swallows sped over the barn and the furze-grown wall of Hole Farm opposite, the monotonous flow ran on, washing and rattling around the stones and rusty tins and sherds and rags of Unequal Ownership of Land, Rates and Taxes, Money, Artificial Silk Stockings for Village Maids who thought only of Dancing, Parish Roads, the Scandal of the Sewer, the Scandal of the New Cemetery. No more mental nourishment in his words or ideas than there was use in the things thrown away in the stream by the village people.

At last the tax-collector, Charlie Tucker, passed by, and stopped to give us each a demand note for the rates of the last half-year. Bill Goldsworthy stooped down to gather up his straw, but—

"Now just look at this," he exclaimed, laying down his armful of straw again. "Five shilling and eightpence in the pound! And for what exactly be you and me paying it? Do us get any benefit for our money? Five shilling and eightpence in the pound!"

Laboriously he read out the items in the demand note.

*General Expenses of the Rural District Council (including Highways)*, 1s. 9d.

"And did you ever see the roads in such a dirty state? Now just look at all that grass and weeds by the roadside. They'm supposed to have all that cleaned up, and look at it! That's what us be paying for, my dear soul! Modern! that's what it is."

*County Police and Education Rates County Contribution*, 2s. 4d.

"What be the good of all the education children be getting to-day? The old volks could neither read nor write, and were better off like that, too. And to-day the young volks be above themselves, and won't do this, and won't do that, and are all for this yurr jazz dancing and pleasure. Aiy, they be."

*Expenses of Overseers, including voids and balance, 6d.*

"That's what us have to pay for to have our money taken from us!"

"What's this next item?" I asked him.

*Expenses (other than under Adoptive Acts) of Parish Council or (where no Parish Council) of Parish Meeting, 2d.*

"Ah," said Billy Goldsworthy, like one who had waited long for that moment.

Deliberately he stuck a pitchfork, its handle scarred and brittle with age, into the bundle of straw-bedding for his cows that he had come to fetch about an hour and a half previously. He lifted it waist-high, then put it down again.

I realised that his silent action was meant to express his full feelings about that twopence.

I waited. Billy Goldsworthy stared at me with a knowing expression on his face. No, he was not like an owl; his face was like that of a slow-worm, greyish, with little eyes.

I waited. He blinked.

"So you want to know the truth about that item, you say?"

I waited. This man did not know what words meant.

"Well, shall I tell 'ee?"

He put the pick carefully by the wall.

I waited.

No, not a slow-worm: he was a toad-stool in a wide cloth cap. A blinking toad-stool.

He gathered the straw on the pick, and hoisted it on his shoulder. "Ha, Ha! *Modern,* that's what it is to-day, everywhere!"

I waited, and I waited.

He laid down the straw again.

"Us calls that Clitter Clatter Rate," he said at last. "That's

what us has to pay for the talk in the Parish Council. At the
moment 'tis this yurr New Cemetery; and if tidden wan thing,
'tis another. And it be your and my money that has to pay for
it. Aiy, it be."

Once again he hoisted the straw, and moved towards his
rotten, paper-tattered doors.

"A good expression, *Clitter Clatter*," I said. "It just expresses
all the unknowledgeable rant and rubbish and superficial spate
of words that wimbles and wambles on and on for ever in this
village, particularly at night. Nothing but parcels and parcels of
old flim-flam."

"You'm right," said Billy Goldsworthy, smiling: and yes,
he put down the straw again!

"You'm just about right! That's how it is everywhere to-day!
Tidden like the old times, noomye!"

Then he picked up the straw. Then he moved into the sunshine, blinking towards the roof. Then he put down the straw
again.

"Ah, I'd almost forgot that there shrub. I've been meaning
to do it for some time now, only I've always been so busy."

He opened the door again, and the imperturbable life of the
little roof tree was a mystery no longer. For I saw, against the
cob wall, the crooked and wandering greyish stem of a shrub
that had pushed under the eaves by the farther wall, and, climbing to the rafters, had found a way to the light through the
ridge. The shrub had its roots in the garden of Thunderbolt
Carter whose cottage was hidden behind the barn.

"The dark green leaves looked rather pretty up there: can't
you leave it to grow?"

"Ah, but 'tis growing out of another man's garden, you see,"
he replied. "And has no right to be on my property. By rights
he should have cut it himself; but us'll say naught 'bout that.
You can't do what you like with another man's property, you
know! Noomye, tidden right. What if it breaks my tiles abroad?
What will I have to pay for a new roof? And how long will it
last? Why, some masons break the tiles they'm laying, just to

make work for themselves! 'Tis true what I be saying, mind! Tidden no lie! You've got to look out for yourself to-day, for no one else will if you don't, will they?"

He took a rusty billhook from a nail in the wall.

"I think it looks nice up there," I mumbled. "And it's hardly grown all these years. It won't break your tiles."

"Ah, but tidden right that another man's tree should grow otherwise than on his own property, do you see?"

So saying, he hacked the straying trunk of the shrub.

"Aiy," he said, moving away. "And it's the Same Thing Everywhere throughout the Country to-day, you'll find. There's not the sense in volks now as there used to be, that's my way of thinking. Now just take these yurr Trade Unions—"

From the window of my writing room I watched him walking away up the road in his quiet, inoffensive shamble, veering slightly out of his line towards the docks and grasses growing by the wayside, to pluck with his free hand at the seed-heads, but reluctantly, for another man had been paid to remove them.

## Chapter Ten

## P.C. BULLCORNWORTHY

London policemen have had much publicity in the news-papers of the world; indeed, the first thing any American visitor was reputed to want to see on arriving in the town, during the 'twenties of the twentieth century, was the figure of the tall and immaculate London bobby, with his calm and benevolent attitude amidst the swirl and roar of traffic and hurrying pedestrians. No longer can the London policeman be called a "cop"; certainly never a "slop".

Now you may take trout from various rivers, each differing by the spots and marks of its home river, and put them together into a stream, and in time these trout will grow to the shape of the local trout, assuming local spottings and colour. There is a spirit in every river which controls and orders the life which it bears in its flow. Food: acidity or alkilinity of water: oxygen content: rate of flow—all these mould and form its fish and other life. So it is among men in cities, which are no more unnatural in the light of the sun than men in a village. The New York policemen, or patrolmen, recruited from other states or from Europe's nations, after a lapse of time in the streets and avenues of the city, are worked upon, and changed, by the spirit of the place. They resemble one another in manner and physical appearance. Slowly the red roll of flesh begins to push itself from the back of the neck, between neckband and cap. The blue-uniformed cop learns to walk on his heels, to ambulate with his knee-joints, to twirl his stick, to stare about him, to lean up against a wall, to get irritable with the ceaseless metallic streams of traffic. He looks like a man who has seen so many interesting things that he cares for none of them. He becomes, in the triturating streets of New York, a slop.

Among the police of the entire English-speaking areas of the world, it is doubtful if another like Police Constable Bullcornworthy, of our North Devon village of Ham, exists. Transfer him to New York where the slops flip the traffic back irritably, to Paris where occasional gendarmes seem to be aloof spectators of life, to Berlin where the Politzei were like pike among carp, to Madrid, to Oslo, to Timbuctoo, and he would remain himself, P.C. Bullcornworthy. Beyond saying that he weighed eleven score, liveweight, and was six feet tall, it is impossible to describe him; his words and actions must do that.

Lest it be thought that a mere book comic character is being created at the expense of this dutiful officer, it should be understood that what follows is an exact transcription from reality. The man who told me the story did not tell it merely to put me in the right frame of mind, and my jaws in the best position, for the extraction of my last wisdom tooth. He was conscious of no technique in the matter; something of great interest had happened to him the night before, and he recounted it to me. He is well-known and respected in the city of Barum, and at any time will no doubt be willing to verify the following account.

I had made an appointment with Mr. S—, a dental surgeon in the old town by the river Taw, and at the duly appointed time I found myself waiting before a fire in a room panelled in sixteenth century oak. During the few minutes of waiting, my thoughts were for some reason occupied by a mental picture of P.C. Bullcornworthy. It may have been because Mr. Bullcornworthy, after his recent successful apprehension of the burglars of Ham, had lately been transferred to the Town Police, where no doubt his services among the more cunning thieves of the neighbourhood would be of great value in the keeping of law and order. It was known that one inn served drinks sometimes five minutes after closing time; Mr. Bullcornworthy would be quite capable of dealing promptly with such crime. Just then a soft and charming voice informed me round the ancient oak door that Mr. S— would now see me.

Soon afterwards, I was seated in a chair which, if it were in my writing-room, would give much comfort and a variety of elegant postures. It is a fact that I always looked forward to visits to Mr. S—'s place, because he was so gentle an artist as he was an interesting personality.

"By Jove! I must tell you what happened to me last night. You know P.C. Bullcornworthy, of course?"

I nodded gravely, while eyeing an affair of nickel, glass tubing, and needle, with which he was toying.

"You're looking at my shaking hand," he observed.

"It looks a very steady hand to me," I murmured, while I could.

" I was out very late last night," he said.

I raised an eyebrow, for my mouth was wide open.

"Very late," he repeated, looking at me over his spectacles.

"Glarg?"

"You needn't maintain that uncomfortable position," he said softly. "You may close your mouth. Or shall I inject first, and tell you afterwards?"

"Tell me now," I replied hastily. He put the syringe down.

"I was burglar hunting," he said, picking up the instrument again, and toying with it.

"Did you kill?" I enquired, eyeing the sharp needle, while he dipped it into a bottle labelled POISON.

I felt happier as I saw him put down the bottle and the hypodermic syringe, and remove his spectacles in preparation of telling me the story. The wild hope came into my mind that if I could keep him at this story for the next half-hour, then my appointment would have elapsed, and chivalrously I could refuse to keep the next patient waiting, and slip out, promising to return another day; or I might even never come back. After all, my wisdom tooth was not hurting me. I didn't even know of its existence. "You had better have it out," he had said, "a wisdom tooth is no good to anyone."

"Is wisdom?" I asked; but he was not to be drawn. "It won't take me long to tell you this story," he continued. "First of all, I will inject your gum with novocaine and by the time I have finished telling you about Bullcornworthy, everything will be ready—"

"I am in your hands," I murmured. "But why don't they call them something else?"

"Forceps? Oh, they're nice little things," he said, reprovingly. "I once had a mechanic who set up a practice elsewhere. His only experience of using forceps was the trueing-up of bicycle wheel spokes with a pair of pincers, but I hear he is very successful. The forceps do nearly all the work, you see."

"You have a bicycle too," I remarked, as I opened my mouth and shut my eyes.

At last the thing, clattering against my teeth, was withdrawn, and put on a glass table. A football seemed to have been pumped up inside my jaw.

"Now for the story," he said: "Last night, just as I was thinking of bolting the door and going to bed, an urgent rat-tat-tat made me wonder who was there. Opening the door, I saw P.C. Bullcornworthy's round face and blue helmet.

" 'Aw, Mr. S—, have 'ee got a telephone, 'av 'ee, surenuff?' I said 'Yes, Bullcornworthy, what has happened?'

" 'Aw, Mr. S—, there be a burglar trying to get into Mr. Cramp's house round to Heavitree Lane. I must telephone to the Station.'

"He took off the receiver, and in a voice shaking with excitement he got through to the Station.

" 'Be you there, Sergeant? This be Bullcornworthy. There be a burglar trying vor get into Mr. Cramp's house round to Heavitree Lane. Can 'ee come up along quick with a couple of men, as soon as possible, Sergeant? I will go back along now to take up my position to watch in case 'a comes out.'

"He hung up the receiver with a trembling hand.

" 'Was there only one?' I asked.

" 'I only zeed one,' he replied. 'Thank 'ee, Mr. S—, thank 'ee. Do you think I had better be going back along now?'

" 'Perhaps you had better,' I said. 'Would you like me to come along with you?'

" 'Aw, thank 'ee, Mr. S—, sir, thank 'ee,' he said. 'I was going along to watch if 'a comes out. It's very kind of 'ee, I'm sure.'

" 'What have you got in case he attacks you?' I asked.

" 'Aw, I've got my staff,' he said, pulling out his truncheon.

"On the way, hastening round to Heavitree Lane in the darkness, I asked him if he had ever used his staff.

" 'Aw, yes, aw yes, Mr. S—, I have used 'n, surenuff, scores of times. Why, I used 'n only last week.'

" 'How was that?' I asked.

" 'Well, it was about two in the morning, Mr. S— and I were down by High Street, when I saw a man come hurrying up. "What be you doing about this time of night?" I says to myself, and I grips my staff and slips into an alleyway. He was carrying a little black bag, Mr. S—. Just as 'a comes level with me, I steps out and I says "Stop! Where be you going with that little black bag?" "What do you want to know for?" 'a says. "I require you to tell me," I replies. "What be you carrying in that little black bag?" "You mind your own business," 'a says to me, only 'a sweared, Mr. S—, aiy, 'a used indecent language.'

" 'Then what did you do?' I asked.

"Well, Mr. S—, I grips my staff, and before 'a could swear again I daps 'n one on the head, and 'a droppeth down into the gutter. While I waits for 'n to get up, I opens up the little black bag.'

"By this time we were coming near to Mr. Cramp's house, which was in darkness. Cautiously opening the gate, Bullcornworthy and I crept on our toes up the path. We listened, but heard nothing. We went forward again and waited in the porch.

" 'I be gripping my staff,' said Bullcornworthy. 'Do you think 'a will come out this way, Mr. S—?'

" 'Well, if he does,' I replied, 'You will be just in the right position to stop him, won't you?'

" 'Aiy,' said Bullcornworthy. 'Proper suggestion, sir. I got a grip on my staff, Mr. S—.'

"We waited for some minutes in silence. By this time I was enjoying myself very much. Bullcornworthy was trembling with excitement and suspense. After a while it seemed safe to enquire what had happened to the man lying in the gutter. 'You were telling me about the little black bag,' I said.

" 'Aw yes, Mr. S—. I opened 'n!'

" 'And what did you find in it?' I asked.

" 'There was a small packet of sandwiches, Mr. S—."

" 'What did you do with them?' I asked.

" 'Aw, I put 'n back, and shut up the little black bag.'

" 'And what happened to the man lying in the gutter?' I enquired.

" 'Aw, Mr. S—, after a while 'a got up and I told 'n to be off, and not to be loitering around.'

" 'Oh,' I said.

"Time went on and we stood quite still in the porch. At last we heard the noise of a motor car approaching. Bullcornworthy seemed very happy to hear the sound of that car. It stopped outside the gate and its lights were turned off. Up the path came the Sergeant with a man from the garage and young B—, who works in the bank. One of them carried a big spanner, and the other a leather gauntlet filled with sparking plugs, which he intended to use, I suppose, as a sort of swinging knuckle-duster. Bullcornworthy gave it an approving glance.

"Mr. Cramp, the owner of the house, was also there. He opened the door and switched on the electric light, and we began a search of the premises. While the others went upstairs, I kept close to Bullcornworthy, who was making a room-to-room search downstairs.

" 'Hadn't you better look under that table?' I would say to Bullcornworthy. And Bullcornworthy would go down on his knees and look under the table.

" 'What about down the back of that sofa?' I said. And gripping his staff, Bullcornworthy would approach the sofa and peer over. He seemed to wait for me to tell him what to do at every turn. Every little cupboard, in the umbrella stand, behind the coat rack, in the coal boxes, behind a crate of empty beer bottles, up the chimneys—everywhere.

"The whole thing was a big joke to me, but Bullcornworthy was entirely serious.

"At last we had searched everywhere downstairs except in one place, and that was a small ventilation door built into the wall. The door was about eighteen inches square, up at the top of the wall by the ceiling, and nobody could possibly have got in there; but I said to Bullcornworthy. 'You haven't looked up there. He might be in there.'

" 'Yes, Mr. S—, I must look there.'

"And holding his truncheon ready, he pulled the table against the wall and climbing on to it, opened the ventilation door. He then gave a screech, for something jumped out. You will probably not believe me when I tell you that it was a small mouse. And to see Bullcornworthy pursuing it over the floor with his staff, was the funniest thing I had ever seen. The mouse, I am glad to say, escaped."

"Was there a burglar?" I asked, gingerly exploring the football with my tongue.

"There was nobody in the house," he answered.

"Well, who was the man?"

"It may have been the little man going home with some more sandwiches. Now just open your mouth. All things come to an end."

After the interval I was able to tell Mr. S— what was not exactly a sequel to the story he had told me, but another incident in the life of our late constable.

Recently he had bought a baby motor car and was to be seen when off duty, day after day, sitting at the wheel, gripping it firmly and staring straight ahead with pale face and fixed eyes, while an amiable instructor sat beside him. After a while Mrs. Bullcornworthy took the place of the instructor, and whenever I saw them, he was either in low or second gear, moving very cautiously and hooting frequently. He told me once, when I was admiring his car, that the times were very dangerous, so much fast traffic on the road.

For several days he drove his car, until one afternoon it stopped, and he had to leave it by the roadside. Remembering instructions to keep the radiator full, he had done so; and for caution's sake, he had also filled the petrol tank—with water. Mr. Bullcornworthy sold the car.

But that is not all. You have not heard the last of P.C. Bullcornworthy.

One day, glancing at a copy of *The World's Evening News*, my eye was arrested by the photograph of a face which surely I knew. It was set at the top of a whole column, with the caption A WONDERFUL EXPERIENCE, and the face looking out at me, round and big and with teeth like a buck-rabbit's, was that of P.C. Bullcornworthy! I must transcribe what I read in full: for it is, indirectly, also indicative of the historical trend of the period—the aimless 'twenties.

# P.C. BULLCORNWORTHY

## A WONDERFUL EXPERIENCE!

The remarkable recovery of Mr. Bullcornworthy has been the topic of the West Country for weeks past, but our special representative is privileged to-day to give for the first time his own personal story of how he was restored to health. "I have only one thing to thank for my remarkable recovery," he said, "I took *Dr Shapland's Nervkicke Pillules*."

"I understand you were very ill, Mr. Bullcornworthy," our special representative remarked.

"Yes," was his reply. "My health seemed to be completely broken down and I thought that the happiest days of my life were past."

"You suffered a great deal?"

"I did. Everything seemed to go wrong with me. Since I retired from the Police Force, at the expiration of my term of service, I found that I was missing something very big from my life. Whenever I looked at my truncheon hanging in the hall on its nail, I felt that my life was as good as over. What with pains all over my Body, Poor Digestion, Weakness, Feeble Eyesight, Twitching Muscles, General Weakness, Desire to avoid my Fellow-men, Rheumatism, Gout, Bad Breath, Biliousness, Headaches, and Lack of Appetite, I was a proper 'Sick Man'. And whatever I tried seemed to do me no good. All day I used to feel tired and at night I could not sleep."

"How were you persuaded to take *Dr. Shapland's Nervkicke Pillules*?"

"I read about them in the newspaper," explained Mr. Bullcornworthy. " I learned that they contained 24 special stimulating, tonic, nerve-building, and health-giving properties. So I thought *Dr. Shapland's Nervkicke Pillules* MUST do me good."

"And they did?"

"They sure did. It was a wonderful experience to feel Strength and Health returning—to be able once again to wake up cheery and bright after a good night's rest, to enjoy my meals again, and to be free from those Terrible Pains in my Head. I never thought it was possible to feel so FIT again. In a word, I was the man again I was when in the Force."

"How glad I am that I took *Dr. Shapland's Nervkicke Pillules*! There is no remedy in the world so Wonderful! They, and they alone, restored my Health, and never again shall I be without them in the house."

There it was, staring out of the paper; and as everyone knows, advertisement is stranger than fiction.

## *Chapter Eleven*

## CEMETERY OR BURIAL GROUND?
### *A DEMOCRATIC STORY*

### FIRST YEAR

### I

Here lean the tombstones, casting their shadows under the morning sun, above the shades which vanish with the human memory maintaining them. Nevertheless, human emotion has caused to be graven in stone words which express a joyful certainty of a deathless state beyond death. The olden mounds of grass, and the new stone rectangles containing live and dead and artificial flowers, lie east and west, in the heavenly track of the sun. Every coffin of elm or oak, lowered amidst sobs into the graves of centuries, has rested in the deep earth with its wider end to the west, so that the corse within may "ope its eyes to Christ's Sunrise".

"It be so, zur, it be so, surenuff, it be so," said Clib the sexton as, clad in his postman's trousers and Admiral Bamfylde's old tweed waistcoat, and holding in knobbly fingers a long-handled Devon shovel, he rested on the edge of a pit.

"But how do you know, my old earth-heaving friend?"

"It be so, zur, it be so. You know it be so, zur. His reverence saith so, zur, his reverence. His reverence saith so. It be on the Book, the Book. It be on the Book, zur."

"Well, I hope I see you, Clib, when that happens."

"Thankee zur, thankee. I'm sure I'll always be plaized vor zee 'ee, midear, always be plaized. My wife will too, my wife. My wife her'll be plaized vor zee 'ee anytime. Mary will too. Us often talks of they days when you come to our place to have your food—food—your food, like. Sh-sh, here cometh his reverence. His reverence cometh, surenuff. His reverence." Clib bent himself to his work again.

The Rector was coming slowly, as though pensive about the lack of vision of the Church Council over the question of the impossibility of extending the Burial Ground. He came slowly down the path leading from the Rectory, past the western door of the grey stone church. He was dressed in a cassock which hid in its sweeping black skirts all but the welts of his Driped boots. On his head was an academic hat familiarly known as a mortar-board. One of the questions which puzzled the village was, Did the Rector wear a wig, or was it his own dark brown hair? Another thing frequently said was, When the Rector goes, then the village will find out how much he had done for them, and for the children.

"Good afternoon," said the Rector, cheerfully, to the two villagers. Just then the clock struck eleven. He passed on, his lips pursed again, his brow knit, his finger-tips pressed together before his girdle. He was going, confided Clib a little fearfully, to see Charlie Tucker, the Clerk of the Parish Council, to tell him what had been decided the previous evening at the meeting of the Church Council.

Clib seldom looked anyone in the eyes; he was thin, shambling, tender-hearted, the most innocent man in the parish. The Rector said he was sly. Clib never said the Rector was anything; he never even said yea or nay to the question of the wig. Very occasionally Clib was to be seen in semi-darkness at the hatch-window in the passage of the Lower House, nervously sipping a glass of milk-stout, the earth of a new grave on his elbows and red-striped trousers. Sometimes in the privacy of his own cottage Clib dared to smoke a cigarette, holding it carefully between two fingers, and sucking at it like a maid who has reddened her lips for the first grown-up Institute dance.

"Only don't 'ee say I told 'ee," whispered Clib, "I don't know naught about it, I knoweth naught, naught, naught like."

"Pooh, you're too windy, my dear Clib. Heaps too windy. Why should I?"

"They do say graves be too expensive, but the burial ground be full up, that's what they be saying," said Clib, levering himself, all elbows and knees and mud-clumped boots, into the pit again. "There'll be a new cem-e-tary, so parson told Admiral Bamfylde, that's what they be telling. I know naught about 'n, so please don't go saying I told 'ee, wull 'ee?"

"I've heard it already, not that I care a damn—"

"Sh-sh! Naughty man! You be! Sh-sh! In the churchyard. Lookee, lookee, do 'ee ze thiccy bone?" Clib's hand, like the root of a rose-bush, held out a long brown bone. "Us 'v all got to come to it, haven't us, zur? Poor old John Hancock, this be his grave, zur. His grave, poor old John Hancock. Many a time I talked to poor old John Hancock, in this very place. It makes you think, don't it, zur? Us 'v all got to go sometime, haven't us, zur? All got to go sometime. Sometime, all of us."

How old was the acre of ground in which the grey church stood? It was "made" ground, that is, levelled ground, its western end held in by a ditched wall, covered by nettles in summer. Sometimes when he passed under the wall, Revvy the labourer saw a brownish matter which had run over the stones in patches; this, he declared, was from the corpses. It was, I thought, more likely to be sap from the elm-roots. What did

# CEMETERY OR BURIAL GROUND?

Revvy think of immortality? "I reckon a man be like a horse; when you'm dead, you'm gone."

## 2

The oldest known grave had been set with its stone two hundred years before. The earlier nameless mounds were levelled, and over them flowers and rose bushes grew in tended beds: the work of one who had succeeded, after years of almost solitary work, in making the graveyard a place more tranquil than a garden. More tranquil because of contrast with the yews, dark and inscrutable as the death that is ever behind the gayest flowers.

Some of the stones, which for centuries had leaned sombre and sunken in the grass, now stood against the church wall, with their Angels crudely carved, with their names and dates, their child-heads with fore-shortened wings like large ears, and little parish pedigrees. Crudely carved? They held the eye almost with a start, and raised thought as one stood in meditation before them; the handcraft was in them, they were different from the cold modern white marble stones, with their overlaid gilt letters. Yes, they were beautiful, for something living existed on the worn stone, the rude carving was the work of a man truly expressing himself.

Those villagers who since the War had bought their own cottages, and the farmers' wives and daughters, thought that the new marble stones, with their immaculate letterings, and the artificial flower wreaths made of marble-chip waste from the stone-mason's yards, "very nice" and "lovely". Perhaps the appearance of the wire-caged "everlasting" marble flowers on the graves of their dead made them feel superior in the eyes of the other church-goers walking in their best clothes through the lych-gate on Sunday morning. It is doubtful if the human mind would connect the glass domes and wire-cages with the dead; and yet, when the Rector wrote in his parochial letter in the *Monthly Bulletin* that the "lobster pots and bird cages" on the graves were unsightly, there was much indignation because he had spoken thus about the sacredness of the dead. One man named Matthew Hammett was very upset by the comment; his mother had recently died, and he had ordered an extra large marble bouquet at twenty-five shillings.

It was not long, however, before the churchyard was void of marble flowers. Tulips, wallflowers, pansies, bell-flowers, aubretia, and other flowering plants grew in their places. Where once nettles and docks grew under the western elms, over the unmarked mounds of the suicides and nameless drowned sailors, daffodils and primroses flowered in spring, appraised by the village.

The Church Council approved the scale of charges laid down by the Rector for burials. Mr. Clib the sexton got 5s. for digging a grave; the Rector, who after all had to live, got 200s. for the use of his words and gestures, the modern varnished, rubber-tyred, ball-bearing coffin-carrier, and the soil.

Now the time was come when in spring and summer the visitor might roam among the tombstones and peer at the ancient names and inscriptions without need to glance over his shoulder and see, to his embarrassment, that a slow black procession, led by white-surpliced priest with a most grave, or graveyard expression, and finger-tips pressed together, was moving in his direction. There was room for but three more graves; already above the paths the grass was too high, covering the risen brown soil which was the dust of anger and laughter, misery and kindness and agony, of the village of olden time.

HERE LIETH IN HOPE OF A JOYFUL RETURNING
THE BODY OF GRACE BADCOCK OF THIS PARISH
WHO DEPARTED THIS LIFE THE 1st DAY OF MAY,
1811, AGED 70 YEARS.

> Farewell vain world I now must bid a Dieu
> And all my friends I take my leave of you
> For here on Earth I lived in Grief and Pain
> But yet I hope to see you all again
> To sit in Glory with the Lord on High
> And Sing his Praise to all Eternity

# CEMETERY OR BURIAL GROUND?

SACRED TO THE MEMORY OF
THOMAS MORDE OF THIS
PARISH WHO DIED THE
20th DAY OF OCT. 1830
AGED ONE YEAR AND NINE
MONTHS.

Grive not for me my parents dear
Nor be for ever sad
The shorter time I lived here
The lesser sin I had.

SACRED TO THE MEMORY OF HENRY THE SON OF
JOHN AND MARY TUCKER OF DARRACOTT IN THE
PARISH WHO DIED THE 28th DAY OF AUG. 1833
AGED 5 YEARS

ALSO ALEXANDER SON OF THE ABOVE 18 YEARS

Afflictions sore long time we bore
Physicians were in vain
Till God did please to give us ease
And release us from our pain.

IN MEMORY OF
WILLIAM SON OF NICHOLAS AND MARY REDMORE
OF THIS PARISH WHO DIED MARCH 25 1825

All in the blooming of my days
To send for me the Lord did please
My morning sun went down at noon
Happy for me it set so soon.

5 YEARS

# A DEMOCRATIC STORY

IN MEMORY OF
SERGT. JOHN HILL
OF THE 40th REG. OF INFANTRY
A WATERLOO MAN AND THROUGH THE
PENINSULAR WAR WITH THE
DUKE OF WELLINGTON
DIED THE 28th FEBRUARY 1861 AGED 77

> Nor cannon's roar nor rifle shot
> Can wake him in this peaceful spot
> With faith in Christ and trust in God
> The sergeant sleeps beneath this clod

ALSO OF
ELIZABETH
BELOVED WIFE OF THE ABOVE
DIED DEC. 31 1884
AGED 91 YEARS

> For me my friends lament no more
> I am not lost but gone before
> My glass is run my days are past
> And yours is running out so fast.

## 3

The Church Council meeting of the previous night had ended thus:—

"Our alternative," said the Rector, speaking slowly, pronouncing his words meticulously, as though he were conscious of the need to be explicit to an audience whose mentality or understanding was inferior to his own: he had been a Council School teacher in London in his youth,—"Our alternative, then, is to ask the Parish Council to procure for us, that is, to procure for the parish, for the needs of our beautiful village, and its more immediate neighbours, a public cemetery." He smiled suddenly and went on in a less slow, more conversational voice,

"Where they will get it from, I don't know. But that is their business, not ours. Now any questions? I must hurry, for I have to start the motor to charge the batteries for your electric light in church on Sunday, as the horrid thing has an earth-leak which no one seems able to trace."

He glanced round the faces in the vestry, some of them guarded. What a pity they .could not be more friendly, he thought.

"We have room to lay but three more souls to rest in our churchyard, which is looking so beautiful now owing to the unsparing efforts of our Lady Bountiful, to whom we all owe so great a debt of gratitude. Yes, to return to the problem before us at this meeting. The Ecclesiastical Commissioners agreed with me that it was inadvisable, nay impracticable, to extend our present Burial Ground. We have gone most carefully into the whole question. To set against the loss of burial fees, which will occur if a parish cemetery is made, there is the loss by depreciation of the glebe land if an extension of God's Acre is made thereon. Besides, it would not add to the appearance of our beautiful village, and those of you who help to make others happy in the summer by letting them your rooms for their holidays will agree with me, that if tombstones were visible against the skyline, for the glebe land lies above our main street, as you know, it would spoil the appearance of the village. Besides—" and here the Rector's voice resumed its tone of careful slowness—"Besides, the consecrated ground of the Chapel is also full, and we must consider the needs of others as well as ourselves, in a Christian spirit. Now who will move that we make demand on the Parish Council for a New Cemetery, on the grounds that we are unable to extend our Burial Ground, and who will second the motion? Don't all speak at once," he added humorously, looking round the mass of faces. In the silence of blank faces he went on:

"Then when the motion is proposed, seconded, and carried, I, as Chairman of the Church Council, will go to the Parish Council, and deliver our decision, and tell the Clerk that, as, we are unable to extend our Burial Ground, they must see about acquiring a Cemetery for the parish."

"May I suggest, Rector," said a quiet voice, belonging to the lady who had made the churchyard into a beauty spot with its shrubs and beds of flowers. "May I suggest that the province of the Church Council does not extend to instructions to the Parish Council? I make this suggestion only in the interests of precision and harmony."

"It is good of you to correct your Rector," smiled the Rector. "But surely the Parish Council would not be so stupid as to quibble about a few words. As you wish, however. We will not impinge on the Parish Council's dignity."

"It is merely a question of the minute book," said the voice of Colonel Ponde, "of a correct minute entry. Precision in such matters is surely advisable."

"Well, the motion is not yet even proposed," retorted the Rector. He felt the need to be tactful and urbane with both Lady Maude Bullace and Colonel Ponde, two difficult members of the Church Council, who wanted their own way too much, he considered.

# 4

The oil engine driving the dynamo that charged the batteries that lit both rectory and church was hard to start. When started, it would not run slowly. It boiled the water in the tank. The Rector had paid £160 for the beastly worn-out thing five years before. It was a horrid nuisance, always giving him blisters to start it and liable to break his wrist if it backfired. Coneybeare, his gardener-butler-chauffeur, was missing again, on one of his irresponsible meanderings from village to village, calling at every inn and making a fool of himself by greeting every man he met as a long-lost brother, poor silly fellow. That morning the Rector had discovered Coneybeare, haggard and woeful, in the engine-house, where he had slept in a pool of oil; and Coneybeare had wept, and begged forgiveness, but the Rector was tired of the anxiety and uncertainty and the bouts of drunkenness of Coneybeare. Coneybeare had gone away, a pitiful figure; but he had got money from somewhere, for here he was back again, in a different suit, wearing a bowler hat and carrying a Malacca cane, and puffing at a cigar.

"How are you? All reet? Everything all reet?" the silly creature said, holding out his hand, and refusing to be put off in his drunken benevolence, "Everything all reet? All reet? I'm happy, sir. You're frowning, Rector? Why so? Everything's all reet. I'm grand. Aren't you grand?"

He lunged towards the Rector and inadvertently puffed smoke from the cigar into his face. The Rector, who neither smoked nor drank—if one excepted the sips of communion wine taken in the course of duty—pushed Coneybeare away.

"Go away from me, and never come back," he said sternly. "The farther you go away from here, the better for all concerned."

"All reet," replied Coneybeare between puffs of the cigar. "I will—go—*puff*—to my father—*puff*—who is—*puff*—in Heaven."

No, thought the Rector, as he jerked the starting handle of the worn-out engine, Coneybeare has had his last chance. I have forgiven him on sixteen previous occasions. Coneybeare has had his last chance. Definitely his last chance.

Two days later a very sober Coneybeare was digging the rectorial potatoes. On the third day he was singing at his work. For the next four months he drank only tea and water. And for the next four years—the period of the controversy over the burial ground, or new cemetery—Coneybeare lived at the Rectory, witness of the humanity and tolerance of his master.

# 5

"The official from the Ministry of Health," said Charlie Tucker, in a low voice, "is in the Lower House. He's a great big fat chap—or gennulman, p'raps I should say."

Charlie Tucker, the Clerk of the Parish Council, wore his best suit of grey cloth, and his best bowler hat, his best boots, a clean

shirt, and his best tie, a black one. It was five minutes to two
o'clock. Six other members of the Parish Council, also in their
best clothes, were standing by the lych-gate of the churchyard.
Two other members, Jonathan Furze and Rear-Admiral Bamfylde, D.S.O., R.N.(retd.), had yet to arrive. The nine members
of the Parish Council were to meet the official from the Ministry
of Health at two o'clock, for the purpose of viewing the eleven
fields which the Parish Council, after much argument and
friction, had selected as possible alternative sites for the New
Cemetery.

At intervals during the past two months various members
of the Council might have been observed in the act of regarding
one or another of these eleven fields; and the owners of the fields,
knowing of what was about, looked grim at intervals—except
Jonathan Furze, who appeared unaffected as he went about his
business and his pleasure (which were identical) the buying and
selling of bullocks, and generally increasing his substance by
persistent work and good judgment in buying.

Shortly after two o'clock the great big fat chap or gennulman
from the Ministry of Health in London, came out of the Lower
House, after his meal of pigs'-trotters, potato, cabbage, prunes
and custard, and bread and cheese with beer. Mr. Taylor, pro-
prietor of the Lower House, had ordered his favourite trotters
for himself, and by good luck they were also a favourite dish of
the gennulman. Mr. Taylor had to be content with a couple,
instead of the half-dozen he had been anticipating. "Eels and
pigs'-trotters, I could eat 'em all day and all night for a pastime,"
Mr. Taylor had declared on many occasions.

The Ministry of Health official was greeted with a chorus of
"G'afternoon, zur," and Mr. Furze having arrived a moment
later, the nine men went to see the first prospective site. They
were about to enter this field when the squeal of brakes pro-
claimed the arrival of the Admiral in his grey Morris-Cowley
motor van. He wore his oldest clothes, and greeted them with
a cheery apology for being late.

It was a three-acre field of grazing land, called Isaak's Splatt, owned by Billy Goldsworthy. Its advantages were lanes along three of its sides; it was level; it was far enough from any buildings; and it was rock three feet under its topsoil—an advantage in the eyes of three Parish Councillors, for then the departed relatives would rest fairly dry and not "sleep away" quickly into dissolution. Many parishioners, including the owner, considered that some of the springs which fed their wells ran under this field, and if it were selected, they were prepared to raise objections. It was valued, by the owner, at £100 per acre—although he had bought it for £40 per acre—as the field was now, "in view of the opening up of the village," available for building sites. The official made notes, and they moved on to the next field.

This was the larger glebe field. The Church Commissioners, advised by their agent, a solicitor in Barum, after consultation with the Rector, had valued it at £240 an acre. It was claimed that springs ran also under this field.

The third site was in the other of the glebe fields belonging to the Church, called Kennel Field. It sloped north-east. Years before, a former parson's hounds had been kennelled in a small shed built at its bottom, where a streamlet ran. Charlie Tucker's mouth became firmer when the official looked at this field. He owned the field opposite whereon he contemplated the building of a cottage as soon as possible. If this field were chosen, no one would want to be the tenant of that contemplated cottage; funerals and gravestones were not cheerful sights. The official asked where the stream ran. Through Crowcombe Farm below, owned by John Brown. Was the water used for domestic purposes?

"Certainly," replied Charlie Tucker. "The hill be dripping wet in winter." The official was about to make a tick on his list when Mr. Furze said:

"Pardon me, sir, but I fancy the field at the top, No. 4 on the list, be well-drained, sunny, and level. This be only a little parcel of it down here. Up top be out of view of any dwelling house, too."

# A DEMOCRATIC STORY

Charlie Tucker muttered something to another councillor as the procession went to the top of the field.

Proposed Site 4 was a field rustling with yellowing wheat on the other side of the lane, up the hill again. It was owned by Farmer John Brown of Crowcombe. It sloped gently up from the lane, and from its higher or southern end the official, mopping his brow with a handkerchief taken from his cuff, heard the sound of the Atlantic waves beating on the distant and unseen sands of Cryde Bay.

John Brown, aged about forty-seven, had inherited Crowcombe Farm when his elder brother had died in the war. I remember the two khaki figures, Labour Corps, working there in the summer of 1916, when I was on sick leave and they were on long farming-leave, having been released for awhile under an Army Order issued at the request of the Ministry of Food. They gave me and my friend ready permission to shoot rabbits in the fields, which we did, having been lent guns by the kind Farmer Furze. We shot several rabbits, bottles, rats, and I shot my hat several times to make it look in keeping with my imagined reputation for wildness, a reputation gained by drinking a dozen quarter-noggins of brandy in succession one night in the Higher House, after saying good-bye to my friend, aged seventeen, who was going back to the nihilism of the Somme. It so happened that a week or two later Farmer John and I drove in the same pony jingle to the station, and travelled to London, and shook hands, both of us thinking, but not speaking, of the quiet fields and lanes of the far-away village. Now, more than ten years afterwards, Crowcombe Farm bore first and second mortgages, and John Brown's contemplative grey eyes regarded the official's face with an interest that was nearly impersonal. He seemed to me tired. Rows of marble tombstones black clothes, solemn depressed people, wilting flowers . . . Time took the colour from everything, from the record of a dozen quarter-noggins of brandy, from the hat I had shot, from my friend who was gone for evermore, and now, perhaps, from this cornfield.

## CEMETERY OR BURIAL GROUND?

It was a fine field, brown soil that crumbled richly between the fingers; free of poppy, couch-grass or stroyle, and charlock, and sheltered from the south-west winds. The wheat loved it. Any known springs near? None. It was near the village, yet was overlooked by no cottage windows, and it fronted on the lane. It was certainly a building site; and Farmer Brown, after consulting the mortgagor's solicitors, had fixed its value at £180 per acre. His quarry was near, and he could supply stone at 1s. a butt-load, excluding digging and haulage costs. This was neither known to nor to be reckoned by the Ministry's official, who considered the suitability of a site for hygienic and not economic reasons.

"Good field, this—Fourteen Acre, I see it's called," remarked the official. "Curious how many cornfields are named only by their acreage."

Charlie Tucker and Jonathan Furze looked easier. John Brown said, "Well, sir, I'm pleased to hear you say it's a good field, for I've known it for nigh on fifty year."

Mr. Alford, after clearing his throat, said, "Well, sir, in my o-fficial capacity as Chairman of the Parish Council I believe I am in order to ask if you wish to see the other prospective sites we have selected?"

"Certainly, Mr. Chairman. Which way?"

"Backalong to the lane, sir."

The next three sites were quickly rejected; one because of its shallow soil and subsoil, which meant that graves would have to be blasted; the second because the entrance was through Frog Street, an old sunken sled-track leading from the lane, which was a water-course in winter; the third because the dark splayed overflow from the runnel leading out of the village cesspit was visible from it.

"We can rule that out right away, I think, gentlemen," said the official. "Any more for me to see?"

There was a pause, for the next site was in a field owned by Jonathan Furze, the largest property owner in the parish. The feeling among the councillors was this: the cemetery would

lower the value of any land around it, for the village was opening up, and the days of the old agricultural standards were gone.
Any land nowadays was a possible building site. Therefore he
who could most afford to have the cemetery on his land should
be the one to have it: and that one was the man they all envied,
Jonathan Furze.

"The next prospective site, sir," said Mr. Alford, "is at the
southern end of Netherhams, the field yonder. As you can see,
it lies against the parish road leading to the sea. The acre we
selected is in the south-west corner, one hundred and fifty yards
from the nearest building, which is the Church School. There
are no wells in the vicinity."

They went down to look at Netherhams.

"Very good building sites, as you can see," said Mr. Furze,
to the official. In a mutter he continued, "In my opinion, the
best and healthiest in the parish for new cottages and bungalows.
That doesn't affect your judgment of course, sir."

"We have to examine thousands of sites every· month as a
matter of routine," replied the other, pleasantly. "And every
aspect is taken into consideration. The Ministry does not select,
in the precise meaning of the word; rather, it approves and dis-
approves, and final choice, as you know, lies with the Parish
Council."

"Yes, yes," muttered Mr. Furze.

"Ideal spot," remarked Charlie Tucker. "Well drained, sunny,
practically level." The next field on the list belonged to him.

Mr. Furze heard, but said nothing.


# 6


At the following Parish Council Meeting, Charlie Tucker, the
Clerk, read a letter from the Ministry of Health, "appertaining
to the recent visit of the o-fficial regarding the prospective New
Cemetery". Of the eleven available sites, said the letter, eight
were deemed unsuitable, but the Ministry approved of the

remaining three. They were the fields called Kennel, Fourteen Acres, and Netherhams.

The upshot of the discussion that ensued was that Mr. Furze proposed Kennel Field as the most suitable, since it was most convenient for funerals from both Church and Chapel, and nearest to Cryde village and the hamlets of Buckland and Cott. His proposal was seconded by Harry Zeale the carpenter, another of the Chapel brethren.

The Chairman asked for any amendments, and Charlie Tucker immediately objected that Kennel Field was uphill from both Church and Chapel, and too far from the village, and people from Cryde had to come some distance already. He proposed an amendment that the site of Netherhams was much more suitable as it was downhill, and distressed mourners would not be so put out to get there. His amendment was seconded by his brother Jack, the mason.

"Gentlemen, I question the procedure of proposing an amendment to a motion that in effect is another motion," said the Chairman, Mr. Alford.

Arguments went on for nearly an hour, and at the end four councillors voted for Mr. Furze's motion, and four councillors for Mr. Tucker's amendment. The Chairman, of course, did not vote. Accordingly, a minute was entered into the Minute Book, and the matter of the site for the Proposed New Cemetery was "referred back for further consideration" at the next meeting.

The argument was continued by Mr. Alford in the Lower and Higher Houses, with whomsoever would listen to him.


SECOND YEAR

7

It is not possible to narrate in correct order the events in the controversy which ended in the grand uproar in the schoolroom four and a half years after the Church Council wrote to the Parish Council for a new cemetery; nor is it possible to find the order in the Minute Book of the Parish Council, for the book had vanished before the conclusion of the affair. "Lost, Stolen, or Strayed", as Tom Gammon remarked at one meeting.

The Parish Council, under the chairmanship of the venerable Mr. Alford, had still to choose one of the three prospective sites selected by the Ministry of Health—Kennel Field, owned by the Ecclesiastical Commissioners, and valued by their solicitor at £240 an acre; Fourteen Acre Field, owned by Mr. Brown of Crowcombe, valued by him at £180 an acre; Netherhams Field, owned by Mr. Furze of Inclefell, valued by him at £160 an acre.

At the next meeting, after discussion, it was decided to refer back the matter of the choice of the site until the Council knew the real value of the land in prospect. Mr. Brown proposed, seconded by Mr. Furze, that an outside valuer should be appointed. So Charlie Tucker, the Clerk, wrote to the County Council, who sent down a valuer, charging his fees and expenses to the Parish Council.

This visitor looked at each of the three fields, picked grass blades and clover stalks, and crumbled earth betwen finger and thumb. He walked alone through Kennel Field and Fourteen Acres, but when he got to Netherhams Mr. Furze was there, looking at his bullocks.

"Good morning, sir," said Mr. Furze.

"Good morning to you," replied the visitor, with extreme affability.

After talking about the fine grazing for bullocks, Mr. Furze said:

"Many people would like this position for a bungalow, you know. Did think of living here myself when I be too old to farm."

"You'll never be too old for farming, Mr. Furze," declared the land valuer, who knew of his reputation.

Mr. Furze accompanied him as he went round the field.

"I was thinking of cutting the dashels next week," said Mr. Furze. "They'm very thick on this land. Dashels won't grow thick on poor land," he muttered.

"Yes, they need cutting," observed the visitor, looking at the mass of thistles. "Hullo, a mushroom. That's early."

"Some years there be a lot of mushrooms in this field and the next. People come then, and take them away. Scores of 'em, trampling the grass, can't ever get a basket for myself. Could stop 'em I dare say, by putting up a notice that mushrooms be cultivated hereabouts. Howsoever, I've no objection to 'em taking a few now and again, don't fancy 'em a lot myself somehow."

"Let me see, there's a right of way across this field, isn't there, Mr. Furze?"

"Yes, sir. But not a lot use it. Mostly Pidickswell folks coming and going."

"Let me see, it was in corn years ago, wasn't it? When Major Gate farmed the manor, eh?"

"Oh, it's good land, surenuff," declared Mr. Furze promptly. "It don't pay to grow wheat nowadays," he added. "All this foreign wheat being dumped."

"Just so," said the valuer. "Well, I think I've seen all I want to see."

At the next Parish Council Meeting, held in the schoolroom, Charlie Tucker, the Clerk, read, in a voice as impersonal as he could make it, the report of the land valuer.

"Agricultural Glebe land called Kennel Field, property of Ecclesiastical Commissioners, valued at £120 per acre."

He paused a moment.

"Agricultural land called Fourteen Acres, property of John Brown, farmer, valued at £100 per acre."

He took another deep breath, and after another interval,

"Agricultural land called Netherhams, property of Jonathan Furze, farmer, valued at £80 per acre."

Mr. Furze half rose in his seat, then sat down, muttering, "It ban't right, you know. Mine's the best land in the parish, by a long chalk."

"It seems reasonable to suppose," said Mr. Alford, the Chairman, "that to save the ratepayers' money, we should select the cheapest site. If any councillors wish to propose and second that, and the motion be carried, we can enter it in the Minute Book—"

"I rise to a point of order," interrupted the voice of Charlie Tucker, "I think that Councillor Furze should step outside as he is an interested party."

"But no motion has been carried yet," said the Chairman.

"Quite right," replied Tucker, sitting down. "My point was that an interested party should not sit in council."

"Then you ought to get out of it," Mr. Furze was heard to mutter.

"Well, who will propose the motion?" asked the Chairman.

"I will," said Charlie Tucker, half rising in the small dark desk, which trapped his knees, and half holding up his hand. "Aw, darn the desk," he muttered.

"I beg to s'cond that motion," mumbled John Tucker, also half rising.

Jonathan Furze laughed to himself.

"The motion is before the meeting, is before the meeting, that the site for the Proposed New Cemetery be that which is least expensive, I said least expensive, having due regard for the burden to be put on the ratepayers," announced the Chairman. "All for the motion show assent in the usual way. One, two, three, four. Four. All against, one two, three, four. Four."

"I rise to a point of order," said Charlie Tucker, cracking his knees again in his agitation. "Councillor Furze should not vote in this motion. The Council should adjourn. These proceedings ban't in order while Councillor Furze be here. If it were my field, I should be outside long ago."

"Perhaps," remarked Councillor Furze.

"No perhaps about it," retorted the other, angrily. "I move that the Council adjourns for the purpose of the business of the site in Netherhams field."

"I s'cond that motion," mumbled John Tucker.

"It seems to me, gentlemen, I said it seems to me that no useful purpose will be served by getting heated, I said getting heated, gentlemen. We as the Parish Council have been requested to acquire a site for a Public Cemetery, and we have to do our duty. Nothing personal should enter into the business, gennulman, I said nothing personal. Nothing at all."

The argument went on about the procedure of an interested party sitting in council with power to use a vote.

"Perhaps you'd like me to leave the village while you're making up your minds?" enquired Jonathan Furze, at length.

"Not at all, Mr. Furze, not at all," said the Chairman. "It is a question for you to decide. We have our duty to do by the parish, and intend nothing personal. If you so wish, you can step over there, or we can move over there, same thing, for the purpose of adjournment."

"The public be allowed in, so long as'm don't speak," remarked another Councillor.

Mr. Furze ignored this remark.

"Order, gennulmen, please," said Mr. Alford.

Mr. Furze said he had no intention of leaving the council, because in his opinion the whole procedure was out of order. The matter was therefore referred back; and the remaining business, connected with the open sewer and the monthly rubbish cart, was done. About the sewer, it was decided to write to the District Council again.

# 8

Mr. Alford was reputed to be indisposed with a cold when the next meeting took place in the schoolroom, and as senior councillor, Mr. Furze took the chair.

The minutes of the last meeting were read, and then Councillor Charlie Tucker proposed that the Council should adopt the necessary measures to select and secure for the Parish the cheapest of the three prospective sites approved by the Ministry of Health, to wit, an acre of the field called Netherhams.

"I beg to s'cond that motion," said Councillor John Tucker.

The Chairman hesitated for a moment, then a faint smile passed over his rugged face.

"Those in favour of the motion, please signify in the usual way," he said. "One, two, three, four. Am I correct, I wonder. Four, yes. But remembering the objections of last meeting, about an interested party, I fancy someone else should be in the chair."

He got up.

"Mr. Brown, I believe I'm right in saying that you're next in seniority, and therefore I vacate the Chair for the purpose of becoming one of the public." He glanced at the Tucker brothers as he left the room.

Three votes were recorded for the motion, three against it. The matter was referred back in the Minute Book; and other business was done in connexion with the open sewer, which, in dry weather and southerly winds, was distinctly a public nuisance. It was unanimously decided to write to the District Council yet once again.

# 9

As has been explained elsewhere, the Church School stood at the western end of the village, in the south-eastern corner of the field called Netherhams. The field for several centuries had been part of the estate of a noble family. At the end of the nine-teenth century the Pidickswell estate was sold to a gentleman farmer who was also a brewer. Soon after the Great War, which had hastened the coming of high wages and motor cars to the villages, the manor house—transformed by the gentleman farmer at a cost, so it was said, of twenty thousand pounds—was sold to Rear Admiral Bamfylde, D.S.O., R.N. (retired) for about a third of what it had cost; and the fields were sold, in lots and separately, by auction to the various highest bidders. Mr. Furze bought the four fields called the Netherhams.

For many years the Managers of the Church School had been allowed to rent a small parcel of ground next to the school, for a garden. The children, under the care of the schoolmaster, dug with their miniature forks and spades, raked and hoed with the small tools provided by the benevolent Manager, a rich woman who also tended the Churchyard; the children sowed their penny packets of seeds, and worked for prizes in the summer. This parcel of land, or splatt as it would be called locally, was one-quarter acre in size, or one-one hundred and sixtieth part of the field.

It was bright with flowers, and green with lettuces and cabbages, and the apple trees were in bloom one May morning when Mr. Furze, walking down Netherhams with a stranger, climbed over the tarred wooden fence and said:

"A proper picture. Faces south. Good soil, as you can see. There's the lane, all handy. Church or Chapel quite near. Nice dry corner, well drained. Handy to the village, if you understand my meaning, and yet away from the noise, you'll get a bit of quiet here all right, sir."

"Quite. But the playground—"

"Children only there just before school, and during the break at 11 o'clock. The school is eastwards, you know, and shields the east winds of course. For building a bungalow, it's an ideal spot, in my opinion. Near the sewer, too."

"Er, where is that, Mr. Furze?"

"Down there, sir, down the valley, way down. They're talking about a new scheme, but I don't know much about it."

"Quite. Is it—"

"Progress, you know, sir. Cryde be growing, and Ham too, and no doubt the future will see many changes."

"A pity, in a way. Such a beautiful, old-world village—"

When the other had ceased speaking, Mr. Furze said, after a pause, "Well, what do you think, sir?"

"I think it's quite attractive, Mr. Furze. I must, of course, bring my wife to see it. She loves flowers."

"Ah, pretty things, ban't'm?"

"Quite. I see you've got a very good show of polyanthus over there."

"Yes. Afraid flowers are a bit out of my line, tho'."

Suddenly the stranger, who had been examining the flowers intently, said to Mr. Furze, "I suppose £40 is your lowest."

"Yes sir. I can make that anytime. Several people already—"
He waved his hand.

"Quite."

As they went away, the stranger said he would like a week's
option on the site. Mr. Furze readily agreed.

Shortly afterwards Mr. Furze returned. From the western
fence—that nearest the corner chosen as a proposed site—he
began to pace, counting his paces. He walked hastily, not wanting to be seen there by the children who any moment would be
running out of school. At the one hundred and sixtieth pace
he was by the hedge. He laughed to himself. The official from
the Ministry of Health had said that a new cemetery must be one
hundred yards from any dwelling; and the east side of the cemetery, if it were made there, would be ninety yards from the
bungalow site. Ought he to have taken the £35 offered by the
visitor, and sold it there and then? No, he knew his man; he
would buy the site, and then Charlie Tucker and Alford and
their gang could go to Halifax.

Mr. Furze was as careful about his language as he was about
his property; and he had not sworn or used indecent words
since he was a young man. He had cursed only then because
his father, an elder of the Chapel, had been brought home one
Sunday afternoon, just as folks were going to chapel, in a horse-
butt, snoring, sewn up in a raw sheep's-skin. This was the work
of a neighbouring farmer, famous for his practical jokes, to
whom Luke Furze had been trying, all the previous Saturday,
to sell some fat stock. They had not been able to agree about
the difference of a shilling, and so the bargaining had gone on
all night, while the cider barrel became more and more hollow.


10

The school garden was sold. Arriving in the autumn to sign
the agreement with Charlie Tucker for the building of a bungalow before Christmas, when he was retiring from the Post
Office, the owner saw that the trees and plants and flowers were

gone. Even the stones making the path borders were removed. However, the contract was signed.

Already, secretly at night, Charlie Tucker had measured the distance from what would be the western foundations of the new bungalow to what would be the eastern wall of the New Cemetery. One hundred and ten yards. He laughed to himself: the bungalow would be outside the 100-yard limit.

Mr. Furze, expert judge of cattle, careful business man, had never in his life thought to check his pace as thirty-six inches.

A week before Christmas the bungalow had been finished by the two brothers. It was square, with a roof of grey asbestos tiles, resembling any of half a million others being built or already built in England at that period. Ancient local characteristics were all going.

## II

The following appeared in *The North Devon Herald*, following several meetings of the Parish Council in the New Year.

### HAM CEMETERY

#### END OF LONG CONTROVERSY:

##### COMPULSORY PURCHASE OF LAND

Official confirmation is to hand from Ministry of Health *re* the compulsory purchase of land for a burial ground at Ham. The Ministry's confirmation was only forthcoming, however, after a local enquiry into all the circumstances. The Parish Council of Ham, having adopted the Burial Acts 1852 to 1906, sought to acquire on reasonable terms land for the purpose of a burial ground, but failing to do so appealed to the County Council. The outcome has been the order known as The Parish of Ham (Burial Ground) Order, 1926, and land, owned and occupied by Mr. Jonathan Furze, has been compulsorily acquired, the price to be decided by arbitration.

## THIRD YEAR

### 12

"Now then, you boys," said Mr. Taylor importantly, from the raised threshold of the Lower House. "You be off. Be about your business. Out of it!" In his black cap and black suit he looked like an old prize-fighter. The Mad Mullah, his decrepit and scarred badger-fighting terrier, stood shivering beside him. The boys who had been playing among themselves in one of their favourite spots, the joining of the main road and Church Street, shuffled away silently. At any other time Tikey or Boykins would have cheeked Mr. Taylor, or at least would have answered him back; but to-day they understood the importance of the big shining motor car standing outside Grannie Carter's house. The school bell rang, half-past one, and they ran down Church Street with shouts and cries.

Quietly Mr. Taylor went back into the bar, where Mr. Alford was sitting. Two pint glasses of beer were on the mahogany counter, one of them level with Mr. Alford's ears.

"They'm gone into school now, they Gammons is the noisiest bliddy boys I ever knowed," remarked Mr. Taylor, picking up his glass and draining the ale almost violently.

"Aiy. Boys will be boys," said Mr. Alford, turning round to take a careful drink.

The reason for Mr. Taylor's concern was that two of the arbitrators who were that very afternoon to decide the question of the new cemetery once and for all, were having lunch in his front parlour. One of the gentlemen, Mr. Taylor fancied, was from the County Council at Exeter; the other was one representing the Parish Council. Mr. Taylor was waiting for Mr. Alford to open the subject; he, Charlie Taylor, wasn't going to poke his nose into business that didn't concern him, like all the other boogers did in the village, not likely!

Every day, from 12.30 to 2 o'clock, excepting Sunday, Mr.

# CEMETERY OR BURIAL GROUND?

Alford sat in the same place in the Lower House, ordering, paying for, and drinking two pints of beer in that time. Mr. Taylor considered him a dogmatic person, listening to no one else's views except his own; but he looked forward to the daily meeting, and would have missed the older man if he had fallen ill or died.

The long gilt hand of the clock in the south wall of the grey church tower, which Mr. Taylor could see as he lounged behind the bar, made another circuit of its ancient Roman numerals. Mr. Alford drank the last of his second pint, put down his glass, rose to his feet, shook and buttoned his tweed jacket, took his stick and mackintosh which had hung from the hook behind the door for many years, picked up the daily paper which he would not open until the evening, then turning to Mr. Taylor as he was about to go out, said in a low voice:

"Well, it be a good thing it's all over, eh? It's been a proper nuisance. But there! we have only done what was asked of us. No man can do more. I said no man can do more. But asking £240 for an acre of Netherhams! Disgraceful! But that's finished now! That furze bush will be cut, eh? by arbitration. That's it!" He laughed at his own joke, "Furze by name, and furze by nature! Well, good day, Mr. Taylor."

"Good day, Mr. Alford," replied the landlord, promptly locking the door of the bar behind the slow figure of the old man. "You bliddy long-winded, kelt-gutted old bull-trout!" he muttered to himself. In his younger days, Charlie Taylor had been a fish-poacher.

Then he went into the kitchen, calling out peremptorily, "Missis! Ready for that sheep's head!" followed by the Mad Mullah, who had been waiting for this moment for the past three hours. The ancient dog had watched the skull's arrival from Arty the butcher's, observed its transference to a plate and a shelf, thence to a pot on the stove; and thereafter his nose had informed him of its imminence.

While her husband was eating sheep's brains, Mrs. Taylor, looking younger and stepping lightly in excitement, kept him informed of what was going on outside. First Charlie Tucker, in his best clothes, arrived, and was waiting by Grannie Carter's wall. Then Mr. Furze himself, wearing bowler hat and best chapel-going clothes, came yawing down past the churchyard. Then another motor car stopped outside, and Mr. Furze's lawyer got out, and shook his client's hand.

"They'm gone in!" whispered Mrs. Taylor excitedly. "They'm all in now!"

Mrs. Taylor's excitement might well have been due to the fact that five big men had succeeded in wedging themselves into her parlour without crushing the furniture or causing the strangulation of one another. Like every other parlour in the village, it was an assembly place of its owner's treasures collected over a number of years. Mrs. Taylor had often meditated the removal of some of the furniture, but every time the articles under consideration had seemed to give out a feeling so intimate that they had remained. The visitor could hardly move without entangling his legs with the legs of tables, chairs and sofas, or knocking pictures off the walls.

The five men having fitted themselves into the room, the walls of which were papered red, the representative of the County Council read over rapidly the agreement that had been drawn up. By this, the Parish Council of Ham and Mr. Jonathan Furze, farmer, agreed to abide by the decision of the arbitrators. Copies of this agreement had already been read many times by Jonathan Furze and by Charlie Tucker, Clerk of the Parish Council. Everything was in order for the signatures.

Taking the pen, Charlie Tucker wrote his signature plainer than usual, with a hand that was shaking. Jonathan Furze watched every stroke of the pen until it was transferred to his hand. He wrote his name beneath the other. His signature was more scrawled than usual, and his hand was also shaking.

Having extricated themselves from the room, the five men lingered for a moment outside the Lower House.

"Well," said Mr. Furze's solicitor, "we leave the field to you, gentlemen."

# CEMETERY OR BURIAL GROUND?

"Yes, I must be going, too," muttered Charlie Tucker. Touching his hat, he murmured shyly, "Good day, gennulmen;" and feeling that everyone was staring at him, he hurried down the road to get out of his best clothes into his easy boots and comfortable carpenter's overalls. Standing on her scrubbed and polished door-stone, Charlie Tucker's wife was eagerly waiting for him to hear what had happened. Other neighbours came up too. However, seeing the three gentlemen walking down the road, Charlie disappeared muttering into his workshop, the neighbours vanished, and his wife shut the door and hastened upstairs to peer at them through the curtains.

"He'm a tough customer," said Charlie later, to his wife. "The idea of it, asking two hundred and forty pound an acre for Netherhams, and his expenses, all to go on the ratepayers! With all his money, he could afford to give the land to the parish. What good be all that land to'm when he dies? Who can he leave it to? Two hundred and forty pound an acre, and he bought it not six years agone for thirty! But 'tis the same everywhere to-day, whether you'm acting for yourself or for a representative body, if you don't look out for yourself, you'm gone!"

"Aiy," said Mrs. Tucker, "the parish knows'n well enough by now, I reckon. Furze by name, and furze by nature, they say, don't'm? He won't get elected back again on the Council in a hurry."

The elections for the new parish council had recently taken place; and Jonathan Furze, seeking re-election, had received the lowest number of votes, due to his demanding £240 for the acre of Netherhams.

"Furze by name, and furze by nature they say, don't'm?" repeated Charlie Tucker. "But I reckon this customer won't prack (prick) the Council no more over this question, noomye! Us'v got'n by the short hairs now all right!"

## 13

But at the next meeting of the Parish Council a very subdued and serious clerk read from a letter the amount of compensation fixed by the Arbitrators—a sum that caused Mr. Alford, the Chairman, to stare aghast and mutter, "Well, well, did you ever"; and John Brown, struggling against the mortgages on Crowcombe farm, to wish that after all his land had been selected for the Cemetery; and Harry Zeale the carpenter to make up his mind to be the first to tell Mr. Furze that it only served those other councillors right; and Colonel Ponde, elected in Furze's place, and nowadays entirely water-minded, to think instantly that his trout lake would be safe against any possible pollution for some time to come, as the parish now could not possibly afford to undertake another sewerage scheme for some years; and the other councillors to feel various emotions either of envy or indignation, according to whether their interests inclined them for or against Jonathan Furze and the proposed new cemetery in Netherhams.

That evening little business was done by the Parish Council. Almost automatically the question of the improvement of the existing sewer and cesspit was referred back for further consideration; and the lowest tender for keeping the borders of the parish roads clear of grass was accepted without comment. Two hundred guineas compensation for Jonathan Furze, plus eighty pounds for the acre, plus his expenses and the Council's expenses of valuation and arbitration—near on three hundred and twenty pounds.

It was decided unanimously to refer the matter back to the next meeting. Three hundred and twenty pounds an acre for Netherhams!

## 14

As the third year drew to a close many letters were written to and received by the Parish Council from the County Council and the Ministry of Health. The other sites were reviewed, but non-committally, for both the Ecclesiastical Commissioners and the Mortgagors of Crowcombe Farm were aware of the possibilities of compensation.

While the matter remained unsettled several old parishioners passed away, and were laid to rest at £10. 5s. a time in the churchyard, space being found for the new graves among the unknown and unmarked dead of the sixteenth and seventeenth centuries. The months went by without any decision being taken. Meanwhile Jonathan Furze sold a quarter-acre of his field adjoining Netherhams; and the new owner, a carpenter by profession, immediately began to dig the foundations for a bungalow as square as the one erected by the Tucker brothers in the old school-garden.

This site lay against the hedge which was to have been the western boundary of the Proposed New Cemetery. Immediately the Parish Council wrote to the new landlord, protesting against "the proposed new building". No answers were received to their several letters; and the brick walls of *Mon Repos* arose thin with rapid growth.

"You'm making a mistake, midear," said Bale the trapper and would-be wit to the owner-builder, as he passed by in his wind-ragged coat and stone-chafed leggings one morning, "*Mon Repos* should be next door." He indicated the grassy field of Netherhams beyond the hedge.

"A man must live somewhere," replied the builder, tapping a brick into position.

"Aiy, and be buried somewhere, midear."

The Parish Council considered this new move. "Disgraceful, unlawful, the man has signed before witnesses, agreeing to arbitration, then he goes and sells a building-site within a hundred yards, almost a hundred inches of the site—disgraceful, no public spirit," muttered Mr. Alford in daily conversation with Mr. Taylor in the Lower House.

"Well, why don't you boogers in the Parish Council go and do something about the bliddy site, then?" cried Mr. Taylor, at last. He had heard Mr. Alford talking on the subject during, literally, more than a thousand middays. Mr. Taylor removed his pipe and squirted violently but accurately into a sawdusty spittoon. Then rapidly swallowing half a pint, "What do you boogers do, tho'? You'm all talk, talk, talk, meanwhile us be gettin' older and older and soon us'll all be as stiff as gurnets, and nowhere to be put when us be gone. Talkin' never got a man nowhere, you'm all alike, clitter clatter and flim-flam, dravin' away like a proper ole local praicher, like the wind you be, and saying 'disgraceful', 'Should be stopped', 'Where be the Country comin' to', 'Tidden like it was in my young days'— Bah! if I'd my way I'd drown the lot of you like a litter of kittens!"

There was no real ill-feeling between the two men, but that was Alford's way, and the other way was Taylor's; and Alford, when he spoke in a roomful of men, always raised his voice until it became strident, but there was no heat or personal feeling in his words, just the habit of an unimaginative old man who for most of his life had been secretary to a body of excitable miners in South Wales.

Ill-feeling, however, caused many words and petty actions about the village.

One night an argument went on outside my cottage for more than half an hour between Charlie Tucker and Harry Zeale. Their voices, one deep and insistent, the other high and mewling, were going together most of the time. Neither apparently had any new effect upon the other, for at the end of the half-hour they concluded with the following dialogue,

"You said you were going vor do it, tho'!"

"No I didn't!"

"Yes you did!"

"No I didn't!"

"Yes you did!"

"You'm telling lies, that's what you be doing!"

"So be you telling lies!"

"You'm just a bliddy fule!"

"You'm a bliddy fule yourself!"

"Oh, I be a bliddy fule, be I?"

"Yes, you be a bliddy fule!"

"Aw, I ban't going to waste my time on your sort!"

"Nor be I on yours!"

Then the climax: Charlie Tucker leaning forward, and declaring as he snapped his fingers in the other's face, "I don't give a flip for 'ee!"

"I don't give a flip for 'ee, neither!" retorted the other, snapping his fingers; and both turning round at the same moment, they walked away in opposite directions.

That the climax of what had been almost a violent quarrel was a derisive snapping of fingers may appear restrained conduct to some; but during the decade I lived in the parish there was never a fight or a blow struck in a quarrel. Only once did I hear of blows being struck, when a gang of youths and men encountered, as he returned from the inn at Cryde one dark night, a sporting, elderly, and very friendly visitor who owed money in the village. They tripped him up, kicked him as he struggled on the ground, cracking several teeth and nearly breaking an eyeball, among other abrasive injuries, then running away into the darkness. They came of folk who a generation before had been wreckers on the coast; and Porky, as the old fellow called himself, owed their families money. Usually the villagers were too peaceful or what may be the same thing, too fearful, to carry their dislikes or hates into action.

## FOURTH YEAR

## 15

The last of the pink asbestos tiles were being nailed to the battens of *Mon Repos* by an industrious and cheerful owner-builder, when the news sped round the village that Jonathan Furze was actually about to build a cottage on the very site chosen for the new cemetery! There was the lorry, which had brought the builders from West Moor, a village seven miles off!

West Moor, a collection of damp valley cottages, had recently arisen from its century-old obscurity because the villagers, disagreeing with the behaviour of their parson, had broken a pig's bladder of blood over his gate-post in preparation for the immemorial Devon custom of hunting him with "rough music".

Charlie and John Tucker the masons, Harry Zeale the carpenter, Tom and Willy Gammon, and others who got their livelihood by building, came to look at the digging of the foundations. So did Admiral Bamfylde and Colonel Ponde, two of the Parish Councillors. The well-sinkers were at work when they arrived.

At the next Parish Council meeting it was decided to call a Parish Meeting, to be held in the school-room, when the main facts would be put before the ratepayers. Both Mr. Alford and Charlie Tucker were resolute in grimness against the action of Jonathan Furze. "Whatever next?" cried Mr. Alford. "Disgraceful, disgraceful, no public spirit, I said, no public spirit! Never have I heard the like of it in all my sixty years' close connexion with the parish, sixty years, I said, never once heard the like of it! Furze by name, and furze by nature, I said, 'furze by name, and furze by nature!' I say we have adopted—." He went on like that to Charlie Taylor, in the inn.

In due course the meeting was held. Jonathan Furze attended. The Clerk, Charlie Tucker, read in a rapid and monotonous voice—he was nervous—the minutes of the last meeting. Then he read the twenty-seventh letter from the Ministry of Health, and letters from the County Council, from the Arbitrators, and from Messrs. Buydon, Buydon, and Lamprey, solicitors for Mr. Furze.

"Our client," wrote the lawyers, "has over an extended period of time suffered considerable annoyance owing to the apparent inability of the Ham Parish Council to come to a decision about the exact boundaries or confinements of the acre of Netherhams field which your Council agreed to purchase at a price to be fixed by arbitration, the said agreement by arbitration having been signed by our client and yourselves in November of last year. We should, therefore, be glad to have from you at your very earliest convenience your decision of what is considered by your Council to be the most suitable site for the Proposed New Cemetery, having due regard to all the points to be considered in its selection.

We beg to remain, Sir,

Your most Obedient Servants,

BUYDON, BUYDON, AND LAMPREY,

*Solicitors.*"

"Disgraceful!" cried Mr. Alford, getting on his feet, "I said disgraceful! The lawyers know very well that the site specified by this council lies on the south-west corner of Netherhams, the very place where the builders are now erecting a new cottage for Mr. Furze, and sinking a well for that same purpose. Disgraceful! It's all a monstrous bluff! It's a conspiracy! What is Parliament doing to allow this sort of thing, hall over the country, I said, all hover the country! The ratepayers' rights are being played fast and loose with, and we are going to see that it is stopped!"

Shouts of approval greeted his oration as he sat down.

"Let me tell you something!" cried Colonel Ponde, getting to his feet. The noise subsided. "Let me tell you something," he shouted. "The Parish Council is dealing with an unreliable person! Is that quite clear? I'll repeat it if you like. I have heard the whole of the extended negotiations likened to a body of men trying to clear a lot of furze roots; but you can grasp a furze bush, I say, what? You can jolly well grasp a furze bush, although you expect to be pricked; but you can't grasp an eel, I say, what? Haha, erherher, an eel, what?"

The speaker sat down, amidst laughter, in which both he and Jonathan Furze joined.

"I reckon you've had more experience of eels than any man i' th' parish, Colonel," said Furze. "Although I've got a few in my pond—so the boys tell me when I give'm permission to fish," he added in a sort of confidential mutter.

# A DEMOCRATIC STORY

"It's the ratepayers' money that has to pay for all this irregular conduct," cried Charlie Tucker, threateningly.

Louder shouts and shriller yells showed that the men and women of the parish were "fully alive to the importance of recent events," as the local paper reported discreetly.

Encouraged, Charlie Tucker waved the lawyer's letter. "Yes, six-and-eightpence for this masterpiece, and who pays for'n, that's what I be asking! Why, the ratepayers!'

A roar of approval arose from the ratepayers. Charlie Tucker's wife was glancing round half proudly, half alertly, ready to take up any criticism from any other women present. Bale the trapper was bawling something at the top of his voice at someone across the room—it may have been the song he composed during the recent general election, and which he had sung to the Liberal Candidate, who had listened politely, and then politely congratulated the composer.

> Here's to good old Payto
> NAIL HIM DOWN!
> ## NAIL HIM DOWN!!

to the tune of the War marching song *Here's to good old Beer, Drink it Down*. Yes, Mr. Bale was shouting his anti-Tory election song, Mr. Peto being the prospective Conservative candidate; then he shook his fist at the far corner of the room where was sitting his father-in-law Ezekiel Goldsworthy, who the night before the total eclipse of the sun had gone to bed early with Bible and cashbox, and all blinds drawn in preparation for a possible end of the world. I heard Bale cursing genially but persistently against the uproar of the parish meeting.

Jonathan Furze sat still in a desk near the case of exhibits showing the life-history of the cotton plant from seed to handkerchief in seven stages.

His excitement increasing, Trapper Bale leapt to his feet and roared, as he might have roared when in action for the first time in the battle of Jutland—"I vote us all goes in a body and tears abroad *Mon Repos* and its bliddy new neighbour and vorces Varmer Vuzz to erect 'em t'other end of Netherhams!"

"Order! Order! Gennulmen please! Let us be orderly, please!"

Mr. Alford injected his pleas vainly into the mass of people now thoroughly enjoying themselves.

When it was quieter Arty Brooking the grocer and butcher got up and announced with a grin, "I've got a proposal."

He was dressed in smart new breeches, leggings, and boots. He had opened a branch shop in Cryde that morning. He seemed in no hurry to get on with his proposal, even when the Chairman, John Brown of Crowcombe, remarked that if he had any motion to propose, the Meeting was prepared to consider it. Arty Brooking scratched his head, and grinned. The Meeting waited.

"Darned if I knows what I was goin' to say," he announced cheerfully.

"Sit down, then!"

"Order!"

"Get to business!"

"Us can't bide yurr all night!"

"This isn't the Lower House!"

"I know it ban't th' Lower House," retorted Arty Brooking, changing his tone as he looked at Jonathan Furze. "I heard your remark, Mr. Furze. I'll trouble you to speak respectful to me. I could say something about something, you know, if I'd a mind to!"

"Arty Brooking!" said Jonathan Furze, "you'm only come over here to set up a row. I don't know whether you'll get any-one to second your proposal unless your crony do, that's sitting a seat or two from 'ee!"

"I be as good a man as you be, Jonathan Furze; if I have a bottle of stout or a glass of cider, I go in and have'n openly. Keep your mouth shut about me in future, or I'll shut'n for 'ee."

"Order, gennulmen! This is no place for personalities."

"Get on with your proposal, you dolled-up mommet!" yelled Bale, amidst laughter.

"All this is a waste of time and kids' foolishness," said

Charlie Tucker, rising angrily. "What I would like the meeting to know is that the ratepayers' money is being wasted because the Parish Council in the execution of its duty is unable to get Mr. Furze to abide by his pledged word!"

"One moment," cried Arty Brooking. He struck an attitude. "I didn't come here to be insulted, not by no man. I happen to know, and I can prove my words, but all the same I'll keep my knowledge and my proofs to myself for just as long or as short a time as it pleases me—"

"Order! Order!"

"Sit down, Butcher Brooking!"

"Go to Zomerset and taste some more hard cider."

"While I'm here," went on Butcher Brooking, suddenly very quiet-voiced, "I may as well say that the lies what some people are telling about the kind of mutton I'm selling here and at my new branch at Cryde are wicked inventions—" he stared at Jonathan Furze. "Just because I didn't buy a certain lot of sheep from a particular source, I suppose certain folks think they have the right to go spreading lies about the quality of the meat I sells—I buys only tegs and lambs vit for kiell—no sick or dead mutton in my shop—"

"One moment, please. This is not the place," said the Chairman, "to air grievances fancied or real. The meeting is concerned only with that which bears upon the subject of the proposed New Cemetery in Netherhams field which site, so I understand, is at this moment being occupied by materials for the building of a dwelling house, after the owner and the Council had agreed in writing to submit to arbitration regarding the price—"

"No!" said Jonathan Furze, rising. "Pardon me contradicting you, Mr. Chairman." He spoke in a slightly shaky voice. The schoolroom was silent except for foot-shuffling round the door where P.C. Bullcornworthy kept order, and the wriggling of people in the children's desks. He went on dryly, "I know it isn't customary for one man to contradict another at these affairs, so I won't introduce any bad habits."

A few, approving this sarcasm, laughed. Thus encouraged, Mr. Furze went on equably. "The point I wish to query, Mr. Chairman, in your statement is that any particular acre was stipulated."

"But you knew—" began Mr. Alford, indignantly.

"Business is business, gentlemen. I repeat that no boundaries were definitely laid down in any argument about any field of mine. If I receive a good offer before anything is settled, who is to compensate me—"

"You've got enough already!" cried the shrill voice of Mrs. Charlie Tucker, indignantly. "Why, it wouldn't hurt 'ee to give away an acre, you got so much already!"

"Well, that is a proposal I was going to make as soon as the more important proposals of more important speakers than myself had had their say," replied Mr. Furze, dryly.

Cries of "Not likely!" "You wouldn't give away two penn'oth of cold water!", "Talk goes away light!", "Vuzz by name and vuzz by nature", "A leary (unladen) cart maketh the most noise", etc.

"I was going to propose," said Mr. Furze, standing during the cries, "that the Parish Council accept as a gift from me in fee—which means for all time—an acre of ground for the purpose of converting it into a public cemetery."

He sat down.

The schoolroom was completely silent.

At length Mr. Alford arose, and after adjusting his spectacles on his nose, "Am I to understand, Mr. Furze, that you intend to *give* the land?"

"Certainly. I abide by what I said."

"Well," said Mr. Alford, looking around. He paused. "I hardly know what to say to that! I certainly think we should propose a vote of thanks—"

"I beg to second that motion!" cried Harry Zeale, rising and sitting down again in one breath.

"I rise to enquire about a point of order," interrupted Charlie Tucker. "As the Parish Council has already adopted the Burial Acts—"

"Sit down!"

"Order!"

"Aw, there ban't no sense in you, midear!"

"It is a question of procedure, of course, of course," said Mr. Alford, "I fully understand the last speaker's—"

"The acre of ground I offer to the parish," said Jonathan Furze, reaching for his hat, "is in my field called Croxton Park. It be level, there be the lane, and as you'm determined to have your cemetery near dwelling houses, there be some in the vicinity—just over a hundred yards distant, I reckon, and measured by the chain—Mr. Charlie Tucker will know all about its advantages, 1 reckon. Well, good night all."

"Witnesses! Witnesses! You heard the offer!" cried Admiral Bamfylde, excitedly. "You all heard! We'll jolly well keep him to his word this time!"

"That be all right, sir," retorted Farmer Furze, from the doorway, twisting his hat in his hands, "My offer is open for fourteen days from to-day. Good night all."

As Jonathan Furze left the meeting, Charlie Tucker cried,

"He can't give it! The Ministry wouldn't approve. The Parish Council has adopted the Burial Acts—"

Harry Zeale laughed. The Admiral looked pleased—for there had been talk of choosing a site in Mr. Furze's other field higher up the lane, adjoining the drive to Pidickswell Manor, where the Admiral resided. Bale chanted his Election Song. Charlie Tucker was red with rage. The field called Croxton Park was in Higher Ham, adjoining his field of building sites.

The meeting broke up in disorder.

# 16

An Extraordinary Meeting of the Ham Parish Council took place ten days later. After it had been decided to write a letter to the District Council calling attention yet again to the nuisance created in the village by the insufficient sewerage system, the matter of the Proposed New Cemetery was next on the Agenda, said the Chairman.

Admiral Bamfylde proposed at once that the very generous offer of Mr. Furze, of an acre of Croxton Park free, should be accepted forthwith.

"I need not remind you that only four days remain to accept this offer. Action is imperative. Delay is fatal. It was delay in getting the right kind of shell for our troops in France in 1915 that caused the tragic losses at the battle of Loos. It was the delay of the Government in tightening up the blockade that enabled the Germans to keep in the War after 1916. It was delay —I say almost fatal delay—in organizing proper counter-submarine measures that resulted in us nearly starving in 1917—" He had evidently been reading Mr. Winston Churchill's *World Crisis*, which I had lent him a week before.

"Farmers didn't trouble much, I reckon," interrupted Charlie Tucker grimly. "Butter at five shillin' a pound, rabbits four and five and six shillin' each, and potatoes a guinea a sack—"

"Order, gennulmen, order!"

"I've said enough to show that what is required is prompt and unequivocal action!" cried the Admiral. "Delay is—"

"Hear hear!" said Colonel Ponde.

"We should accept Furze's offer forthwith in writing. We should telegraph to-morrow to the Ministry of Health, demanding an official by the next train—"

"We'd be lucky to get an answer before three months," remarked John Brown of Crowcombe.

" I rise to a point of order," said Charlie Tucker. "It ban't necessary to go to all the trouble and expense over again. Mr. Furze said he'd give the acre, but what about disturbance of his tenant? And there be the question of compensation. Give the acre, yes, but there would be all the expenses we have incurred all over again, plus the expenses already incurred. Tidden sense, to my way of thinking, if you excuse my plain speaking. 'Tes quite simple, there be the adjoining vield, and the cemetery would look just so well in there as near the school, better, in fact, for the land rises thereabout and falls again slightly, and the cemetery would be out of sight of the village."

"Hear hear!" said Councillor Ponde.

"Gentlemen, the issue is clear," cried the sonorous voice of Chairman Alford. "Have we any authority in the matter, or have we none? The irregular procedure of Mr. Furze—"

"I rise to a point of order, Mr. Chairman. I claim that my motion has been overborne by the remarks of the last speaker, which are not relevant, therefore out of order. I hereby propose—"

"And I rise to a point of order, Mr. Chairman! And I didn't come here to be insulted. Us all be equal on th' Parish Council, whatever be our ways and means outside. For twenty-two year I've sat on th' Council and been Clerk for the past twelve—"

"No insult, my dear fellow, no insult intended," said the Admiral blandly, adjusting his monocle. "The matter of the Council's duty to the parish is in danger of being overlooked altogether. I wish to assure the meeting that there is rising among the ratepayers of this parish a feeling of criticism against us, due in the first place to the long time we've been about the whole affair, and also to a growing belief that our business is not conducted on the most economical lines, not to put too fine a point on it. I have even heard the word Squandermania mentioned!" The Admiral obviously read *The Daily Mail*. "I say without fear of contradiction there is an increasing feeling of impatience in the parish against this council, and now that we have had this generous offer of free land, why, the parish naturally looks to us to accept this way of avoiding the very heavy expenditure which is otherwise threatened!"

After this bout of eloquence, the Admiral was red in the face. He wiped his face, and re-adjusted his monocle—the same monocle at which he invited the parish to laugh when he played the silly-ass parts in his annual revues.

"And I repeat we can't do it—now!" cried Charlie Tucker, getting red about the neck. "It be too late. The Council be committed by arbitration to take an acre of Netherhams, and us can't get out of it now, not without the permission of the County Council."

Growing purple in the face the Admiral cried, "This Council is supposed to represent the interests of the whole parish and not of one individual member of it!"

"Order, order!" cried Mr. Alford. "No personalities."

"I ban't done with the subject yet!" shouted Charlie Tucker. "No man can accuse me of working for my own ends as Clerk of this Council for twelve year without justifying his accusation or taking the consequences! No man, I say, not if he were Mr. Stanley Baldwin himself!"

"Not twelve years, my dear sir," retorted the Admiral, in even tones. "I am referring only to this one occasion. Listen! Don't shuffle your feet when I am speaking! This is the situation! Furze offers an acre of Croxton! You object, as Clerk you say! Very well! But it is curious, is it not, that Croxton adjoins your field, where two of your cottages are already standing!" He sat down abruptly.

"And I'll tell 'ee something, Admiral or no Admiral!" shouted Charlie Tucker. "The new site will be tight up against what you'm pleased to call your drive, that's why you'm objecting, sir! And the lane to Pidickswell no longer is a private road, for when the last owner sold his estate he made it over to the Parish Council! Us all know there be one law for the rich and another for the poor!" He sat down violently.

"Order! Order!" cried chairman Alford, rapping on the table.

"How dare you accuse me of self-interest, fellow!" roared the Admiral, jumping up. "Damned impertinence! It shows the rotten state the country's coming to, that such infernal insolence should be permitted. I shall resign from the Council immediately!"

"Order, gentlemen," said Mr. Alford.

"And I be finished with the lot of you, too!" shouted Charlie Tucker, springing up.

"One moment, please, gentlemen. This is not the place—"

## A DEMOCRATIC STORY

Charlie Tucker strode from the schoolroom by the cloakroom door.

The Admiral strode out by the main door.

## 17

Soon afterwards bills calling for a Public Meeting were posted about the village, to be held at the unusual hour of noon, in the new Village Institute. Afterwards this was known as the Lawyers' Meeting, for both the solicitors of Mr. Furze and Admiral Bamfylde addressed the fifty people present. The theme of the double speeches was, Did the ratepayers realize what was about to be done with their money? Had they full confidence in their Parish Council? Did they know that the Parish Council was their servant, not their master? And that they, the public, had the right to attend all Parish Council Meetings? As for the field which the Council had made a dead set against, were the ratepayers prepared to be crippled by the payment for it?

Charlie Tucker got up and asked a lawyer if he knew where the field was. The lawyer, representing the Admiral, admitted that he didn't.

"Then what be the use of all this talking?" asked Tucker. The lawyer, a quiet and inoffensive fox-hunting junior partner of his firm, seemed embarrassed; so the other lawyer, Mr. Lamprey, a big-faced man, jumped up and cried, while pointing dramatically at Tucker:

"Ah ha, who is it asking questions, who is it I see before me, quibbling? Can it be the clerk of the very Council which has taken four years, four whole years, with expenses adding up all the time mark you, four years in which to demonstrate its inability to choose any but the most expensive site for its new cemetery! My dear sir, I suggest to you that it were better if you sat down, and allowed others to speak: four years, I think, is long enough for you to have said what you wanted to say—now is the time to ACT, not to TALK!"

Muttering that he had better things to do than to stay listening to such bimble-bumble, Charlie Tucker, scowling, pushed his way quickly out of the meeting.

The results of the Lawyers' Meeting, which had been arranged by the Admiral after conferring with Mr. Furze, was the Extraordinary Great Meeting which took place in the schoolroom three weeks later.

## 18

The schoolroom was packed with people. Clib the sexton had told me that there was likely to be a lot of hard words.

"I be goin', zur, I be goin'. Eight o'clock, zur, eight o'clock, that's it. Eight o'clock. My wife be goin' too, my wife be goin'. My wife. 'Twill be lively, her saith, lively. Her likes a bit of life, my wife saith."

Very gently, almost tenderly, the red-haired postman handed me an envelope containing some rejected MSS., as he had been delivering them to me for the past seven years. Perhaps he thought the bulky envelopes contained banknotes, for he was always hinting at the great wealth accruing from books which did not sell more than 300 copies each in America and England together. After a sweet word for the baby and another for the old spaniel, he went up the road, wheeling his bicycle, hastening because it was dimmit-light and his lamp was unlit, and he did not want to risk meeting Mr. Bullcornworthy the policeman.

In the porch stood Mr. Bullcornworthy, the policeman, in full uniform. He was, I observed, gripping his staff under his cape. He was surrounded by youths and men who had not yet made up their minds where to sit, or who were waiting for their friends and their girls. I went and sat quickly in the nearest vacant seat, not liking to be stared at.

This seat was a length of deck made to hold half a dozen children. It was already occupied by a small widow woman about whose case a question had been asked recently in parliament: for all her sons had been killed in the War, her husband had recently died, and she had no pension or any money to live on. Dressed in black, she sat in the desk as when she had been a child; but now so still, one who had travelled beyond grief, and found truth, or rest from strife, within her own tranquillity.

The desk was of pine wood, brown with age, scored and polished by the movements of the little captives who had been restrained there, to answer questions in sing-song unity, so to be prepared for a democratic, money-based life in the village. Every softness in the grain of the wood had been explored to the $n$th degree by the children who had sat in the desks; legions of pencils and nibs and nails had travelled along the worn ruts and grooves between the hard and resinous ridges of the grain, in and out of the initials, dates, faces, and animal-outlines crudely channelled in the wood, the work of minds or spirits avoiding the layers of words, words, words, which, like road-metalling and tar, would press the pasture of their minds to later barrenness and dearth. I recalled sounds I had once heard when looking through the doorway—the mass voices of children and the placid voice of the parson.

"Now, children, look to your front. 'I am, I ought, I can, I will.' What are you?"

"I AM A CHILD OF GOD, I OUGHT TO DO HIS WILL, I CAN DO WHAT HE TELLS ME TO, AND BY HIS GRACE I WILL," came the appalling massed shrillness in reply.

"Why ought you to do God's Will?"

Again the prompt response was like a shock.

"I OUGHT TO DO GOD'S WILL, BECAUSE I AM HIS CHILD, WITH A MIND TO KNOW HIM, A HEART TO LOVE HIM, A WILL TO OBEY HIM, A BODY TO SERVE HIM, AND A CONSCIENCE TO TELL RIGHT FROM WRONG, AND BLAME ME IF I SIN." Several children thereafter began to grin at me, so I hurried away before my guilty presence be seen by his reverence.

What were the children growing up to inherit, I thought to myself, as I sat at the desk: a world of which the present was but a preparation for war arising out of human chaos? I could see no alternative, except by revolution. These people were the world. All the world was like our village.

# CEMETERY OR BURIAL GROUND?

Mr. Alford had sat at one of these desks, and later, Charlie Tucker and John Brown, with Tom Gammon and his brothers, with the Loverings, Hancocks, Tuckers, Physicks, Treasures, Zeales, Perrymans, Goldsworthys, and Clibs. Perhaps Jonathan Furze, a very small boy, had sat here timid yet alert, before going to the school at Tiverton where Jan Ridd, hero of Exmoor's favourite classic (except the Bible) was educated.

A stir in the packed assembly under the great hanging oil lamp, for Admiral Bamfylde had arrived and with him, Mr. Jaggers.

Mr. Jaggers was considered in the village to be a semi-mysterious person. How was it, asked Mrs. Revvy, Mrs. Thunderbolt, Mrs. Clib, and others, how came it that *the* Jaggers of the famous JAGGERS' JAM, how was it that he was living with his wife and daughters in a bungalow he had made himself: a bungalow, moreover, made chiefly of wood and tarred felt? Tom Gammon, who with others had strolled that way on Sundays, just to see something interesting, had christened the structure *Orange Boxes*, and by that name it was known in the village. Once or twice Mr. Jaggers had preached in various chapels in the district, and his sermons were discussed for weeks afterwards; by some he was considered a man of exceptional spiritual powers, who had renounced a great fortune in jam for the sake of the Lord. As a fact, Mr. Jaggers had no connection with JAGGERS' JAM.

The Admiral and his companion having arrived, John Brown took the chair, and declared the meeting open.

After a stir of expectancy, Tom Gammon got on his feet.

"We're all here," he began rapidly and truculently. "Poor unfortunate ratepayers—"

At this Mr. Alford bobbed up hastily crying, "Order! Order! I rise to a point of order—must sign minutes of last meeting—merely rise on a point of order."

"Sit down Rabbiter!" said Bale the trapper, amidst laughter, for Tom's two lurcher dogs, Spring and Caesar, were well known.

After the reading and signing of the minutes, Tom Gammon

began rapidly, "Us poor unfortunate ratepayers have got to pay pension money, so I understand to—"

Immediately Charlie Tucker jumped up. "I don't want no personalities bandied about by anyone!" he cried. "I've served the Parish Council as clerk for over twelve year and I be as good as any man present, and I'm not going to hear slighting remarks about the pension I'm entitled to—"

"Order, gennulmen," said John Brown mildly.

"This ban't the Ministry of Pensions!" remarked Bale.

"Nor yet the Lower House!" retorted Charlie Tucker.

"Write to Mr. Baldwin about it!" sang out John Tucker. "That's the only way to get your rights. They'd do a man out of his breath if they could. You write to Mr. Baldwin and demand your rights."

After much business with papers Charlie Tucker said, looking up with a smile on his face, "Before I read the correspondence I've an announcement." His face beamed. "My wife is going to put up for councillor at the next election."

There was a stir in the schoolroom, for this was a revolutionary announcement; but the amazement changed to laughter when a sepulchral voice exclaimed, "Aw don't 'ee put 'er up, vor I don't like 'er, and there's an end to it." The speaker, hidden away among several ample women, was the small body whom I had observed most days making journeys to and from the Lower House, carrying a rush bag.

A mournful-looking man, a gardener of Admiral Bamfylde's called Matthew Hammett, arose and said, "I'd like to ask what we would prefer, a dear relative to be laid in rock or down in a swamp, where after twelve month they would all be gone? I'm only saying what I've heard tell, but if the new site I've heard about be in the swamp, I'd like to say it shouldn't be allowed."

A murmur of agreement arose; and then Alfred Rodd, a small bow-legged farmer, owner of the field opposite the entrance to the old drive to Pidickswell, got up and said, "I should like to inform the meeting that there be rock ten to twelve inches under my field Mr. Hammett be referring to."

## CEMETERY OR BURIAL GROUND?

"But the minister, when he came around, satisfied himself, by looking down the well dug by Mr. Charlie Tucker for Mr. Walker's bungalow. I say that no trial pits were dug." Mournfully the speaker, perched on a desk against the wall, put his pipe back between his blue lips.

"Mr. Chairman, Mr. Chairman!" said Mr. Alford, to whom the vast bundle of papers had been given by Charlie Tucker. "I rise to a point of order. All the foregoing is out of order. The Parish Council has called this meeting in order to prove that it has acted in the only way possible, I said the ONLY WAY possible, please don't interrupt over there, one speaker at a time please, fair play, be British! I said the only way possible in the circumstances. I have here proofs, proofs I said!" He rustled the bundle of papers, and looked around the room over the steel rims of his spectacles, "Proofs! Now as Chairman of the Parish Council I am going to summarise what has been done about the acquisition of the site for the proposed New Cemetery, and if afterwards you approve, as I hope you will, you will show your approval when the acting-clerk calls for a show of hands."

Mr. Alford adjusted his glasses, and prepared himself for half-an-hour's speech to the ratepayers. He began at the beginning.

"Now the ratepayers adopted the 1875 Act in order to—"

"Just a moment!" said red-faced "Champion" Hancock, springing up. I had noticed a signal of a lifted finger from the Admiral a moment before. "All us wants to know, maister, is just why the ratepayers are faced with a bill for £347 for one acre of ground for a new ceme-tery."

A murmur, a few shouts of approval.

"I am about to explain—" began Mr. Alford; but the other interrupted—

"Now eleven sites were picked out four year agone. They were reduced to three." The farmer looked down at a paper in his hand. "The glebe was valued at £120, Mr. Furze's field at £80, Mr. John Brown of Crowcombe's at £100. Then why—"

"I see what you're getting at, and I'll answer!" cried Mr. Alford. "The valuer came down and picked Mr. Brown's field,

172

but there were objections. So we wrote about Kennel Field, and the Ecclesiastical Commissioners demanded £240, in addition to £21 lawyer's fees, and compensation for the disturbance of tenant. Then we wrote to Mr. Furze, who didn't reply."

"I protest!" exclaimed Mr. Furze. His voice shook. "The valuer viewed all three fields. All were agricultural land, so an agricultural value was put on. My field at Netherhams, situate where it be, is much too valuable for a cemetery. I said so, but they were determined to push the site on me. As for Kennel Field, £150 ought to buy the whole field, no value at all as building sites. However," he went on, smiling, "The Parish Council has pushed the site on me, as I said, and also made me a present of £210 over and above what the valuer put on it. Thanks very much for the nice present! Then what happened? I offered to give land free elsewhere, but it wasn't accepted. The Parish Clerk's house was near, you see!"

There was laughter.

"Don't you go reeving up all they old objections!" shouted Charlie Tucker angrily. "It ban't the whole truth you'm telling! Once the Parish Council had adopted the Burial Acts—"

"Oh, go to Halifax with your Burial Acts!" cried Furze.

"I tell you there's a conspiracy!" burst out the Admiral. "There's an infernal air of secrecy about the whole business! Mr. Furze has told you that he offered to give land FREE to the parish, and here is the Parish Council asking for your vote of confidence so that it can saddle you with £347 for an acre of unsuitable ground! Now listen to this!" He waved a letter. "I have here a Zinovieff letter! Listen!" He then read a letter from the lawyers acting for the Ecclesiastical Commissioners stating that they were prepared to let the Parish Council buy an acre of the glebe called Kennel Field for £200. "What about that? Haha! you're blustering, are you?"

"One moment! one moment! one moment!" cried Mr. Alford, raising his voice vainly against the flood which was beginning to swirl about him. "One moment! We were asked by the Church Council to procure—"

"Withdraw your insinuations!" yelled Charlie Tucker to the Admiral.

"I won't withdraw!" roared the Admiral from across the room.

"Here's to good old Payto, NAIL HIM DOWN!" sang Bale, behind me.

"One moment! one moment! one moment!" cried Mr. Alford. "Give me a chance, please. Give me time—"

"Here's a man asking for more time!" said the Admiral. "He's had four years already, and wants more time!"

"You should use some of the time you spend in the Lower House!" remarked Mr. Furze.

"But never at your expense!" cried Mr. Alford. "Gentlemen—"

Then Mr. Jaggers uprose, and folding his arms, gazed around with set face. Mr. Alford's voice faltered. Mr. Jaggers, preaching in the Chapel about Hell and the Devil, had made a deep impression on Mr. Alford's consciousness. Mr. Jaggers held up his right hand. There followed silence.

"Mr. Chairman, ladies and gentlemen—" said Mr. Jaggers.

"And Orange Boxes," muttered Tom Gammon, audibly.

Mr. Jaggers' speech, or harangue, was like the cloud-burst which roared through the village three years later, sweeping away walls, culverts, iron harrows and rollers, flat stones weighing a quarter of a ton, scouring many gardens till only the rock was left. Like the flood, the speech went on while time passed unnoticed.

The address began without any warning. The orator announced intensely that he had read all the Burial Acts. There they were, in his left hand, in case the Council wished to dispute them. There they were, FACTS! He shook them at Mr. Alford. Why, the Chairman of the Parish Council couldn't even quote the dates rightly!

"One moment! one moment—"

Vainly Mr. Alford tried to stand up against the torrent of oratory. Mr. Jaggers' stertorous words were declaimed with frequent percussions made by a hand smacked down on the clutched Burial Acts. It had been inferred that the adoption of the Burial Acts was an act which they could not renounce, an Old Man of the Sea round the ratepayers' necks. Nonsense! RUBBISH!! FLIM FLAM!!! The Old Man could be got rid of by a simple procedure, a vote of no confidence in the Parish Council! They had had four years to do their work in, and what was the result? £347 for an acre of ground! That was a FACT!! And was there a clear record of how that result had been attained? The Burial Acts were muddled by the Chairman, but what about the Clerk? Those two responsible authorities? Why, the Minute Book was incomplete! Pages had been cut out. Ah why? The Clerk, seeing the game was up, had resigned: and the book he had handed over was deficient of several pages! The sacred Minute Book, with pages of perhaps crucial importance, calmly removed by a knife! Ripped out with a knife! The book of FACTS, belonging to the Ratepayers, mutilated by the man who now demanded a Pension! A PENSION!! That was their Parish Clerk!!! £347 for one acre! Did they think they were buying Devonshire House, or an acre in Piccadilly? The speech roared through the Parish Council, uprooting the work of committees, valuations, arbitration; a torrent of repetitions, crescendos, froth in the corners of the speaker's mouth; terrific and dramatic palm and fist strokes on paper and desk. The audience laughed as one person, cheered as one person, growled indignantly as one person, and at the end stamped feet, waved arms, and poured derision upon the Council.

At last the flood passed. Mr. Alford sat speechless before the ruins of his Council. His face was pale as his bald head. He stared on the floor. I dreaded lest a stroke be imminent.

After a murmurous interval, the Chairman said the motion before the meeting was that the ratepayers repudiated entirely the work of the Parish Council, and moved a vote of no confidence. Those in favour, would they please put up their hands?

Slowly they were counted. Ninety-seven. Charlie Tucker, bobbing about uneasily during the counting declared that the

Chairman was not reckoning correctly. This almost developed into a row; and the schoolmaster, who had been a neutral non-voting spectator, was asked to recount. Ninety-seven for the motion.

"I for my part shall only be too glad to hand in my resignation," declared Colonel Ponde. "I'm sick of wasting my time on behalf of a lot of—"

"Eels," suggested Tom Gammon.

"By Jove, you've said it, Tom Gammon," cried Colonel Ponde, laughing to himself. "You've said the very word! Slippery eels!"

Against the motion. One. There was laughter, and Mrs. Charlie Tucker, red-faced, shifted uneasily in her narrow desk.

"Have a recount," suggested Tom Gammon.

Jonathan Furze laughed.

Charlie Tucker sprang up and shook his fist under Furze's nose. "I can do without the parish!" he yelled. "I don't look to no man for anything! I've got more property than anyone in the parish."

"Really," said Mr. Furze, smiling. "Well, you'll have more time to attend to it in future. Good evening all!"

# 19

But all was not done. As the ratepayers and non-ratepayers (Mr. Furze, being one of the farmers who were, according to some newspapers, "hard-hit by bad times", did not pay rates) were going out of the door, the figure of the Rector arose, and his voice said, very calmly, very placidly:

"One moment, please!"

The shuffle of feet almost ceased.

With the placidity of a corpse, the figure spoke again.

"I have an announcement to make!"

The shuffle ceased obediently.

"Will all who are members of our Church please wait behind as I have a special message to deliver! All who are not members of our Church are welcome to remain, but they must please understand that it is a Church Council meeting."

The Rector waited, with composed face. Two women sitting near him took stealthy glances at the hair at the nape of his neck. Was it a wig, or his own hair, they were obviously wondering.

"Come along Tom Gammon, either in or out!" the Rector endeavoured to make his tone light. "This is not—"

"—the Lower House," muttered Tom, sitting down. "Beg pardon, y'reverence."

After sucking a tooth the Rector began his address.

"Now I want to say a few words to those interested in the burial of their loved ones—when the time comes, I mean. I want you all to consider very carefully if it is seemly that such horrid bickering should precede what will eventually be the consecration of a fresh acre of ground into a new Acre of God. It has, believe me, been very painful for me to stand by and observe the way in which the whole business has been carried out. Many summer visitors—and I need not remind you how in our beautiful village of Ham Saint George we depend on summer visitors to tide us over the dark and dreary months of winter—I repeat, many visitors have remarked to me that it is such a pity that the inhabitants of our beautiful village, with its beautiful scenery on hill and dale, lane and sea, that the inhabitants among all this beautiful countryside are apparently such a grumpy lot, unable to agree among themselves."

The Rector paused, and looked around. He pressed his lips together. He went on in a changed, a very decided voice:

"It has gone on long enough. It must be stopped. It must end. It is time that it ceased. There should be a termination. It must not happen further. It is disgraceful, the way the actions of our Parish Council have dragged the name of our fair and beautiful village throughout the length and breadth of England!"

"If you please, sir, I rise to a point of order—one moment, sir—"

"This is not the Parish Council meeting," replied the Rector, firmly. "You, Mr. Alford, have no right to interrupt this meeting; especially so, when you hear what I am going to say! Now I know very well that in this age there are many ideas going about, but let us not descend to the low measures of those who serve anti-Christ, let it never be said that we in Ham Saint George acted as Soviets, stealing the land of one of our neighbours! Let us not be as thieves, who come in the night! After learning to-night of what has been going on here during the past four years, I am ashamed to think of how the good name of Ham Saint George has been dragged in the mud by the Parish Council!"

"I beg pardon, Rector, for interrupting. One moment, sir—"

"We in the Church Council have been considering the matter," went on the parson, with a flat calmness of voice. "And we have decided to take charge of the matter, and so to solve the problem that others have found too hard to solve. After consultation with the wardens, my own warden and your warden, I have decided to write to the Bishop and get his blessing before applying to the Ecclesiastical Commissioners, suggesting that we, the Church Council, are prepared to extend our Burial Ground into that area adjoining the churchyard, roughly an acre of ground lying to the west. You all know it, for certain. It is where the rooks are beginning to build again. I am sure you are all pleased that the rooks are returning. A rookery is such a social thing in a village. We all love their cheerful cawing, do we not?"

I had seen both Charlie Taylor and Charlie Tucker shooting at them only the day before—casual shots when returning from rabbit shooting. I had hit Taylor with a potato on his prize-fighter's head.

"Yes, we will extend our Burial Ground into the Church's glebe land!" intoned the Rector. "And save what is left of the good name of Ham Saint George!"

A stir and buzz of approval greeted the announcement.

"We, members of Christ's Church on earth, must act as the peacemakers—it is our duty," concluded the Rector as he sat down.

"But Rector," stammered Mr. Alford, getting on his feet. "It was the Church Council in the first place who refused to extend their Burial Ground! It was the Church Council who asked the Parish Council to acquire a New Cemetery!"

Thin and tired, like something that was worn out, the old man went away, in silence, and alone.

## Chapter Twelve

## BILLY GOLDSWORTHY'S COW

At the seaward end of the village—called West End—a short lane dips into and rises out of the hollow of the valley round which the cottages cluster. This lane, called Zeales, is about seventy yards in length, and steep at both ends. Four cottages stand beside it, two on each side of the lane; the stream goes under the road at the bottom of the hollow, running down the valley to the sea.

One of the cottages was owned by Billy Goldsworthy, a small dairy farmer. Like most of the villagers who did not go to the pubs, he was semi-solitary. I had seen him about in the village some years before I learned his name. He had lived in the same cottage with his mother since boyhood. From glances I had had through the open door, when going there to buy pears or cabbage plants, it looked as though the place had never been painted or papered since his boyhood; yet neither wall nor woodwork of the dim room was dirty, but a kind of worn-out drab hue, in keeping with the early Victorian clothes worn by ninety-year-old Mrs. Goldsworthy—ballooned and pleated sleeves, wasp-waist, and swirling skirt-hem—all drab and frayed, and like shadows made animate. Shadows absorbed in themselves.

Farmer Goldsworthy owned four acres of land, and rented another four of pasture—a field called Rock Park, poor stuff, soon drying up in summer, since the grey shale rock lay close under it. He kept two cows, and never wasted money on drink or smoke. A pear-tree was trained—rather it grew—against the south wall of his cottage; an old tree, full of dead and "wild" wood, bearing cankered small pears which he was wont to take round in a basket every September, offering them for a half-penny each. "'Tis a fair price, don't you think? I'm selling them for a halfpenny apiece. They'm dearer to Town or Combe: they'm asking so much as a penny or dree-'apence, so I'm told. They'm quite sweet and juicy." All this in a semi-confidential voice. He was entirely truthful.

The tree was never pruned; it was gnarled and brittle with old blights. If tree and man could exchange spirits, neither would be altered much.

For years old Mrs. Goldsworthy and her son had been doing the same things. Farmer Billy seemed always to be going about a job—carrying straw, chopping wood, tilling his garden—but I seldom saw him actually doing it. He never seemed cold, never sweating. He passed up and down the lanes more or less regularly, except on Sundays; yet he never went to church or chapel. Nor did he rest; he was always thinking about his be-longings. Often he worked at night in his barn by lantern-light, generally some work which was done with a great deal of knocking and banging, such as splitting dry elm-logs. A more methodical man would have split them when wet and sappy, but not Billy Goldsworthy, who loved to hoard and think about his property.

For one so old, Mrs. Goldsworthy was active and upright, carrying her ninety years as steadily as a poplar tree bears its almost leafless branches. She had been a good maid, a good and steady wife and mother, always finding work to do in the house, and sometimes needlework for poorer neighbours; and her son had grown up like her, except for his sense of what is called the world: he had his decided Liberal convictions about the land, which meant not so much that he imagined a fairer or more liberal world, as that he had a perpetual half-grudge against those men who owned much more land and house property than he possessed. Sometimes his voice would be heard, in odd corners, quietly arguing hour after hour—or rather ranting passionlessly; but it is doubtful if after a "talk" he had learned anything, that is, had absorbed anything to widen his personal and impersonal sympathy.

Billy Goldsworthy's mother seemed tranquil and passionless as her shadow; an old woman with the scanty hair of her small head bound in a black string net, under the same black bonnet bearing a few tags of stuff like the topmost leaves of a poplar persisting in November. From the scanty words I exchanged with her, and the few glances I took, as she followed slow and silent after her two cows idling along the lanes from milking, I used to imagine that she was a child grown old without essential change. The turmoil that wears and wraps our common life seemed to have passed her by. That vision of a child in its solitude dream of green leaves and the sky—which lies within the shadow of a tree in a sunlit mead: the essence of Life, that all of us know in rare moments—had been with her along the hedgerows all the years of her gentle life. Had she taken this essence from the sweet air until it had become part of herself, or did she unconsciously perceive it, rest tranquil in it, because she had been born with a fine balance of instincts and their servant senses? (Has not the green earth made the Mind of man, essence of all joy that has been perceived through the ages in which he has conquered, and become calmer?)

Such an attempt to describe the unseen Spirit of the earth-life might have puzzled old Mrs. Goldsworthy—the written words attempting, vainly, to indicate it: for she could neither read nor write—but sometimes, as we passed in the lane, the calm of her innocent old eyes would inform me of the truth in her before I could formulate any thought about it. She might say, "Butiful weather, midear," but her inner being left its home by the door of intuition. It knew the air of Shelley's skylark, I would think to myself, in those days before responsibilities made such thoughts to seem both facile and idle.

# BILLY GOLDSWORTHY'S COW

In her heavy boots, and always with a black shawl over her shoulders, and a stick in her right hand, Billy Goldsworthy's mother had followed the cows upalong and downalong the lanes with their ferns and their flowers coming faithfully in their seasons—hart's-tongue, wall-rue, brake-fern, celandine, campion, speedwell, stitchwort, hawkbit, ground-ivy, a hundred more. All the while she had been lingering behind the cows grazing on the lush grasses by the wayside, the wandering air of the sunlit fields had ever renewed their inner essence in her mind. Her eyes were tranquil as water in a wayside well.

I remember vividly the last time I saw her. It was early one autumn evening. For an hour or more I had been impotently groaning in my writing-room because two voices below in the road had been mumbling on and on and on about the foolishness or the rectitude of the Parish Council in its prolonged conflict over the problem of the New Cemetery. I had been cursing the wraiths of the speakers in my mind, and using up all my stock of swear-words and oaths in order to rid my mind of the Stroyle George—Billy Goldsworthy octopus of garrulity. At last they parted, but the tentacled wraiths remained, and in irritation and despair I had left the rewriting of *Tarka*, and gone down to my lukewarm tea.

The meal had hardly finished when there was a knock on the door and the voice of the milk-girl from the farm in Higher Ham said breathlessly, as she handed the can over the cottage threshold,

"Have you heard the news about Mr. Goldsworthy's cow? Her have just a-go! Her be lying in the road down to Zeales! Her just dropped down outside the house! 'Tis a loss, idden it?"

A cow recently dead! Here was excitement. I put on my leather jerkin, seized my stick, and went out into the lane.

I stepped cautiously towards Zeales. The night was so dark that the firs in the garden on the rising ground before me could not be seen against the sky. I scraped my stick on the stone road, for my rubber shoes made little sound; and men standing in the road were wont to cease talking when another approached at night, thus having the advantage of the new-comer. It is startling to bump into a silent man at night. It was very dark and quiet before me; the tops of the firs were without sound. I moved on, over the little ridge where the red ironstone metalling was worn down to the grey rock by wheels, and down the slight slope to the three cottages of Rock Park, which stand up above the lane called Zeales. A short cut to Billy Goldsworthy's cottage—it saved ten yards or so—lay through a gap in the wall, and down over the steep rock. I stepped slowly and cautiously, where men who knew the way would have taken easy strides on known and worn footholds. The darkness was thick and heavy.

The flame of a hurricane lamp, held low, just revealed boots and trousers and skirts. I heard the murmur of Billy Golds-worthy's voice. It ceased as I arrived, and bade me a very sub-dued good evening. I replied that I had just heard about his cow. "It's bad luck," I said, exaggerating, as most of the vil-lagers did, in their voices, the effect of another's misfortune. "Dear me, it is a loss. Good heavens."

"Aiy, 'tis that," he said.

About a dozen people stood there. A faint noise of hissing came from among them—a strange and puzzling noise.

Peering over the small shoulders of Billy Goldsworthy, I saw the shape of a cow, lying on its side. The hissing came from its great swelled body. The swinging gleams of the hurricane lamp showed a staring eye, and froth and cud on greyish lips.

"'Tis a loss, idden it?" said the voice of Mrs. Zeale, singsong with exaggerated sympathy. Farmer Goldsworthy stared at the hissing carcase.

"Aiy, 'tis a loss," he replied. There was a long silence, and the steady hissing of escaping gas.

"'Tis turrible sudden it were took bad, too, weren't it?" remarked another woman. This woman had a thin pale face and reddish hair disordered like an old haystack in a gale. She lived in one of the four cottages in Zeales; a cottage which, being lower than the lane, was splashed with red mud by every wheel passing in wet weather, and flooded out at least once every winter by the stream.

"You'm right, missis, 'tis a loss."

Billy Goldsworthy looked more shrunken than ever beside the monstrous hissing body of his cow. I asked if it were quite dead.

"Aiy, 'tis dead, surenuff, more's the pity," replied his dismal voice.

"'Tis a loss," came the chorus of Mrs. Zeale and the red-haired woman.

In the quietness of the night the rapping of someone's knuckles in curiosity on the brown hairy hide seemed loud and hollow. Everybody watched the action.

"H'm, I reckon her won't give no more milk," said the knuckler, after consideration, looking at Mr. Goldsworthy.

"Noomye!" declared Farmer Stroyle George, decisively. "You'm right there. Her's dead as a bit o' dung!"

"'Tis a loss," declared the women. There was another hissing silence.

"Pity 'ee couldn't stab 'er sooner, Farmer Billy," said a new voice.

"'Twas dark: twadden as though 'twere daylight you see," replied the depressed owner of the inflated corpse.

"Her dropped just here, didden 'er?" enquired another woman, Mrs. Tom Gammon, whose face, peering in the lamp-light, wore its permanent expression of sympathy and amazement. Mrs. Tom knew the answer; she had heard it several times already; but she asked the question out of sympathy for Billy Goldsworthy.

"Aiy," replied Billy Goldsworthy. "Mother here, her was a-fetching of'n from Rock Park and 'er seemed all right then. Isn't that so, Mother?"

"Aiy, her seemed all right then," said the placid voice of old Mrs. Goldsworthy. She was a shadow with pale glimmering face by her gate.

"Ah, her seemed all right to Rock Park, did her?" asked Mrs.

Tom Gammon, peering forward, as if unable to believe her ears. She wanted to enjoy the drama and suspense of the story as many times as possible.

"The first Mother knew was when her dropped down, and started belving and kicking."

"Aw, 'tis a loss, you know," declared the voice of Mrs. Zeale, from out the darkness.

"It is, idden it?" said the red-haired woman, turning to her, as though profoundly affected by the thought.

"So that was the first your mother saw, was it, when her dropped down and started belving and kicking? Well, I never did hear!"

"Aiy, 'twas a stoppage, you see. 'Twadden no time vor to do anything. 'Twas all so sudden like. Tidden as though it were daylight, you know." Billy Goldsworthy was the chief actor; all were playing up to him.

"But you was late with the milking, wasn't you?" asked Mrs. Gammon dubiously. "'Tis after six o'clock."

The others seemed to become very silent at the question.

"That's so," said Billy Goldsworthy, bending his head, covered with the perennial cloth cap, over the motionless and sibilant corpse. Mrs. Gammon had, quite innocently, asked an awkward question.

"But perhaps you was away working?" asked Mrs. Gammon, still more dubiously.

"Aiy," he replied, in a more subdued tone.

I asked what had been the cause of the stoppage.

Billy Goldsworthy did not answer for a moment or two.

"My dear soul, a man can't be everywhere to once," said Billy Goldsworthy, a little apologetically.

"I meant, what caused the stoppage in the cow? A flake of mangold?"

"Maybe anything," said Billy Goldsworthy. "Maybe a bit of wet grass, 'tis the wet you see sir, a bit of old wet stuff that can't pass out of the first belly on'm, and not seeing it in time vor to stab the poor baste, 'er blew all up and the wind pressed on the heart, and there you are! 'Twadden as though it happened in daylight, you know!"

"Maybe a bit of wet grass, you say? Or some old wet stuff?" The head of Mrs. Tom Gammon craned over the barrel body, and then looked up like a doleful plucked hen. "You didn't see it in time vor to stab the poor old cow! Well, think of that now!" She clucked her tongue.

Billy Goldsworthy seemed to be thinking of nothing else.

"It pressed on the heart, you say, and that did it? Well, I never did!" Mrs. Tom Gammon looked at me, to pass on the emotion of her lugubrious amazement.

"Was the cow insured?" I asked Farmer Goldsworthy.

Often in the local paper I had read paragraphs, obviously paid advertisements, hidden amidst news-items headed with the name of a village, and containing the name of a farmer, and the same stereotyped words, such as—

> Last Monday, Mr. Dawbake of Zamzawed Farm, Stroyla-combe, had a sheep destroyed by lightning. It was, however, insured through the agency of Mr. Castel Wrey, Insurance Agent, Barum.

"No, zur," said Billy. "Us poor volks can't afford no such fancy work. That sort is only for the big high-up volks, I fancy." He looked round for approbation. There was a general murmur; while the corpse hissed on steadily.

The noise of boots, clattering down the rocky way I had come, made them all turn their heads together.

"Ullo," cried a voice I knew.

It was Revvy the labourer. He was panting.

"Be the coo dead?" he asked, anxiously. Here seemed, in honest old Revvy, a genuine feeling.

"Aiy," replied Billy Goldsworthy, shortly. "Her's dead enough, I reckon."

Revvy hurried up, and stopped with the light of the lantern on his legs.

"Stan Zeale told me," he panted. "I only just heard about it.

Dear'm me. 'Tis the li'l ol' brown coo, too! Poor li'l dear. That be the li'l ol' brown coo us raised young Ernie on. Dear, dear." He stared sorrowfully at the ground.

"Aiy, I minds it," said the voice of the shadow by the gate.

"Wadn't no other would suit'n'," said Revvy, speaking thickly, with feeling, towards the voice. "Until us tried—until us tried—the mulk o' th' li'l ol' brown coo! Young Ernie never looked back once 'a'd giv'd 'n zuck to th' mulk o' thaccy coo!"

Whenever he was angry, or excited, Revvy's words lost shape and thickened in his mouth. Suddenly I remembered; and the dead animal changed for me. I saw it through Revvy's eyes. He had told me of the little old brown cow and its milk before; and I knew he had always regarded it with grateful affection. It had saved the life of his first-born.

"'Tis a loss you know," both Mrs. Zeale and the red-haired woman informed the air together. And turning to each other, they said, "Yes, idden it?"

"Poor baste," said Revvy. "Didden 'ee put a reed-mott in when 'ee stabbed her, Billy?"

"'Twadden no gude," said Billy. "It all happened in the dark, you see."

He repeated to Revvy what he had told the others, amid the sympathetic chorus of the neighbours.

"Aw, pity 'er weren't stabbed in time," said Revvy.

Sometimes in cases of colic it was possible to stab the animal a hand's-breadth back from the point of hip, and to thrust into the small wound a quill or a reed-mott (length of unbruised wheaten straw). It had to be done quickly, for the surprised cow, feeling the stab, usually bucked and kicked, and galloped away.

"Poor ol' coo," said Revvy. "I liked that li'l ol' brown coo, I did!"

Other people came up. Each newcomer out of the darkness agreed with the women that it was a loss. For a quarter of an hour we stood there in the cold damp air, while the hissing never ceased, and the smell of cud spread over and filled the air in the hollow.

When Stanley Zeale came back with a rope, it was hitched to the horns, and the soft inert mass was dragged by half a dozen men, a few inches at a pull, into its shed at the back of the cottage. Billy Goldsworthy thanked his helpers; they replied that he was welcome; and they went off home, talking about the death of his cow. I saw the glimmer of Mrs. Goldsworthy's face pass away from the gate.

After supper I tried to write in my gable-end room; but hardly had I started when a dull bump-bump-bump came through the far wall of my cottage, and along the floor, with dreary monotony. Ten o'clock struck, and still it went on. Billy Goldsworthy was splitting, or trying to split, more of his seasoned elm-logs, with their grain like that of leather. My wife entered. "I hope the noise won't wake the baby."

"He's thumping away his grief," I replied. "Otherwise I'd ask him——"

The night beyond my window was clear and starry. Orion was rising over the cottage roofs, shaking his coloured frost-glitters. I decided to go for a walk as far as the sea, for the still air was roaring with the noise of waves on the sands of Cryde Bay. As I passed by Zeales I saw the light of a lantern by the pump, and heard excited voices. I went down to find out what had happened. Mrs. Zeale stood there, with the red-haired woman, and two others. Mrs. Zeale cried to me: "Where be Billy Goldsworthy? My dear soul, what do 'ee think has happened now? Aw dear'm me, troubles never come singly!"

"What's happened?"

"Old Mrs. Goldsworthy be lying dead up auver!"

In the following words Mrs. Zeale repeated the story of her discovery to every one in the village; and so I was enabled to learn them by heart:—

"I went in vor to say good night to the old leddy, and her were making chiel's frock. And her scatt'n down on the table, and said, 'That's all I be g'win to do to-night.' And her looked

# BILLY GOLDSWORTHY'S COW

at the clock, tho' (then). And her said, 'I must put me bread
goin'.' (Butiful plumm bread 'er always 'ad!) And I looked up
to the clock, tho'. And I said, 'Well, midear, I must be g'win.'
And I went into me own house. And I went auver the stairs
and brished me hair, and I was goin' to get into bed, but I
hadn't took off me stackings, when there was a knack on me
door, and Zilla here said, 'Liza, come yurr, quick!'

"I heard the ould leddy knacking, yess, I did!" explained
Zilla, breathlessly. Her red hair looked more dishevelled than
usual.

"Well, I put on me clothes," went on Mrs. Zeale, "and us
went over to the house together, and us went vor the bottom of
the bed, and Zilla looked in upon her, and her said, 'Mrs. Goldsworthy!'"

"And her didn't spake!" said Zilla, more breathlessly.

"And her didden spake! And us went for to the tap (top) of
the bed, and us looked in upon her, and us said together, 'Mrs.
Goldsworthy!'"

"And her didden spake!!" said Zilla hysterically.

There was a pause.

"And us zaid again, 'Mrs. Goldsworthy!'"

" And her didn't spake!!!" Zilla screamed faintly; and choked.
Pause.

"And her was a-go!"

"Her was a-go! Dear'm me!"

The next afternoon I saw the solitary cow coming along the
lane leading from the little field called Rock Park to her milking
shed. The cow passed with slow-swinging milk-bags, and after
her shambled the owner, moving his long neck this way and
that as he glanced under his cap-peak at stones and weeds by
the road. Sometimes he touched a weed with his stick—the
stick his mother had used for so long. He barely looked up as
I passed.

When I next saw him, three days later, he was standing outside his gate, beside the coffin-stools, waiting for the bearers to
come out of the cottage. In answer to something I said, he

replied, "Aiy, her was a good mother to me. Aiy. Her was that."

He stared at the road between his rough-polished boots. "Well, us have all got to go sometime, midear. 'Tis natural."

He was wearing a bowler hat of unfamiliar shape. It had belonged to his father, the usual black, pot-shaped object worn in the village for births, marriages, deaths, and general elections.

"Mother loved that li'l ol' cow, in a manner of speaking. 'Twas a dumb creature, I know, but 'tis my way of thinking there's a butiful nature in a dumb beast."

He glanced at the stark pear-tree. In a low, almost meditating voice, he said:

"'Twas a loss, you know, 'twas a loss."

I withdrew from him, for the leading bearers, awkward with shuffling, were coming through the doorway framed by the black and twisted and inter-grown branches of the pear-tree. Billy Goldsworthy shook his head slightly; in a voice of resignation, like a sigh, he murmured to the approaching coffin:

"Aiy, 'twas a loss, th' li'l ol' brown cow. Aiy, it was." I went away, feeling this man knew that harmony which I aspired to, but could not yet attain.

*Chapter Thirteen*

## THE ZEALE BROTHERS

One Saturday evening in late spring when I went up to the Higher House to get a game of table skittles I saw Sailor sitting heavy and moody under the clock. A pint glass of sixpenny, from which he had taken a couple of gulps, stood on the long table before him, halfempty. He was talking to Albert, and I had entered during one of the long, meditative pauses in the conversation. He pulled at a clay pipe with a shortened stem; the smoke came with an air of dejected disgust out of his down-curved mouth. He lounged on one elbow; the hair of his big head needed cutting. He eyed me, and gave me a reluctant good evening.

I had not seen Sailor for at least a couple of years. Of late his visits to the village had grown more and more infrequent. He used to live in the cottage by the pump in the lane called Zeales, with his married elder brother, who owned it. Many generations of Zeales had lived in that cottage by the pump; but being jovial men, fond of company, no one Zeale had saved enough to buy it—if indeed it were possible to save any money in the past, if you were a field labourer with a family.

The present generation of Zeales, however, had produced one man of thrift and ambition, the elder brother. His name was Sidney. He worked hard on his two acres of well-tilled garden, and did various other jobs, one of them quarrying stone for building.

When his younger brother was pensioned from the Royal Navy, Sidney gave him a home, and took him to work with him. Often in my early years in the village, after the War, I used to see the brothers working together in the quarry in the oakwood valley, breaking abroad the ironstone with bar and blasting powder.

Once a month, having drawn his pension, Sailor used to go to the Higher or Lower House with what money remained after paying his sister-in-law for the previous month's board and lodging. There he would enjoy himself in his slow, rather ponderous way. Perhaps he would desire a wider range for his enjoyment, and then he would hire the car of the Lower House, and with the landlord as driver tour round the country to various houses of call; his range of country being bounded on the east by Town, and on the north by the popular summer resort of Combe. On returning to the Higher or Lower House his eyes were likely to be slightly bloodshot, his dark hair ruffled, his speech slower, and the "Heys?" accompanying his heavy repetitions more frequent. In the village expression, he was mazed drunk—a good-natured, lumpy sort of drunk.

# THE ZEALE BROTHERS

Towards the end of his motor touring, when the constant spirituous stimulation had worn the nerves of his driver to the point of irritability and rage, Sailor was liable to be quarrelled with, and then he swore all the oaths that had been burnt into him in the glare of stoke-holds. It would be in the bar of the Lower House, probably, and the landlord's wife would exclaim at the shocking words: at which her husband would rise hot with rage and condemnation. Invariably, in these moments, a look of heavy and helpless amazement and un-understanding came over Sailor and settled in his eyes. "Hey? Hey?" he thickly articulated, on being told to take himself off quick.

"Out of it, d'ye hear? OR SHALL I PUT YOU OUT?" the landlord roared, flushed with sudden rage.

"Hey? Right. Hey? I'll go, 'at please ye? Hey? Hey? Certainly. I'll go. I'm as good a man as you are, hey? Hey?" And Sailor's big semi-shaven face swung round with an expressionless stare of brown, bloodshot eyes, and he remained where he was a few moments; until, getting all his body into the control of his mind, he would express himself unconsciously by the working of his mouth; and suddenly a squirt of brown saliva left his lips and splayed itself neatly on the floor. "Ye want me to go, hey? Is that it? Hey? All right."

Gathering himself upright, he pulled open the door with a crash, and lurched off the threshold.

Sometimes his brother Sid would have a few pints with him. They seldom spoke to each other in the inns, like most—if not all—of the brothers in village families when up to pub. In drink, the elder brother was sharper, angrier, like a bramble talon which his nose resembled. One Saturday evening, some years before, I had told him, in casual conversation in the Higher House, that I disliked eating meat, chiefly because nearly all the beef in the village seemed to be that of very old cows, and he invited me to go home with him after closing time, and have supper with him. His wife, he said, was a proper little cook, and no one wouldn't want for a better bit of grass-fed bullock beef in all the parish.

The four of us—Sidney, his wife, Sailor and I—sat down to table about half-past ten of that Saturday night. The brothers had had a fair quantity of beer in the Higher and Lower houses —perhaps a dozen pints each. In addition, Sailor had brought home two quart bottles of ale. His monthly celebration—they were as regular as the spring tides at the full of the moon—was almost at the ebb; within two days he would be working again with the iron bar in the quarry at Anneswell. He began to sing, and Mrs. Zeale said,

"Oh, stop your rattle, Sailor! Us don't want all the neighbours to know you'm mazed drunk. And before this gennulman, too!"

"Hey?" said Sailor, thrusting his head sideways at his sister-in-law, and partly closing the near eye. "Hey? Can't a chap enjoy hisself, hey? When he likes? Hey? And this gennulman, I've heard him zinging before now."

"Aw, don't begin it all over again. Us don't want no more trouble. Us'v had enough. Why don't you shave yourself, going about like a proper old moucher, you be."

"Moucher, hey? Moucher? Can't a chap—"

"Don't say naught about it!" suddenly cried his brother, regarding him sharply. "Don't say naught about it, my friend. Us'v just about had enough of your rattle!"

"Hey? Rattle, hey? Me hey? What about yourself?"

"Aw, stop rattling, and ait your meat up, both of you," suggested Mrs. Zeale.

Sailor grunted; then pulling the cork out of a bottle, held it up to his mouth. The bottle gobbled the air, and the beer sank down rapidly.

"That's a nice way to drink with a gennulman present at table," Mrs. Zeale reproved him.

"What's up with you now? I ain't spilled any, have I?" grunted Sailor, putting down the bottle.

The beef was excellent. Sidney Zeale carved it with care, in thin and even slices, using a knife whose edge he had touched up on his boot, and finished off on the hard palm of his hand.

"My advice to any man, Mr. Williamson," said Sidney Zeale, after the meal, as he loosened his waistcoat, thrust his hands into the pockets of his flapped breeches, and eyed me sideways, "is this. When a man marries, let him choose a maid he's known all his life. Let him look around a bit, until he finds one that will suit him best. That's my advice, and I defy any man to say it better."

Sailor grunted, and turned the quid of tobacco in his mouth.

"Now take the case of 'Liza," Sidney Zeale jerked a thumb out of his pocket, and then re-inserted it. "There's as neat a little woman as ever boiled a tettie. Me and 'Liza have never had a bad word between us since we were boy and maid to school together. I won't say," he added meaningly, "that we aren't better off together when we're alone in our own house."

Sailor grunted again, and squirted skilfully between the bars of the black and shining kitchen range.

"Aw, stop it, you two, do," said Mrs. Zeale. Having cleared the plates into the backhouse, she was now sitting on a chair before us, upright in her corsets, like a big doll filled with passive kindness. She sat quite still, attentive to and pleased by every word and gesture of her husband. Her feet were close together. In imagination I saw her as a good little maid, quiet and neat, that had sat by and watched the virile Sid fighting or kicking his boots out on stones in the worn playground: who had grown tall, and had filled with love for him, and married him: and all the while she had been the same little maid, always doing what she had been told to do. The grandfather clock in the corner ticked on unsteadily; it was half-past eleven. I was about to get up in preparation for departure, when my host addressed me in a way that was both significant and a little disconcerting.

"Personally," said Sidney Zeale, looking sideways at me. "Personally, midear, I like a neat home, and everything regular. But when you've got someone always about who doesn't care a booger for tidiness, well, personally—I'm telling *you*, mind—personally, I don't care very much for that someone."

"Hey? You don't ever take a drop yesself, hey? Now and again? Hey?"

The elder man went on in an ominously quiet voice: "Even —even—I'm telling you, mind—if that person were my own brother, I'd still say the same thing. Me and 'Liza are perfectly happy by ourselves. Isn't that so, 'Liza?"

"Yes," said Mrs. Zeale, "but don't keep on so, you two."

"Who's keepin' on? Hey? D'yer think I care a booger what's being said just now? I have a drink sometimes, but I allus pays my own way. Isn't that so? Can anyone say anything against that?"

"Don't you worry yourself about that, midear. There's something coming to you very soon, that's all I say at the moment."

Sailor grunted again, and then turned to me.

"You know about birds, don't you, old cock?"

I was about to say, "Not much"; but he went on,

"'Ow is it a goldfinch with white legs will allus build in a pear-tree, hey? And a goldfinch with black legs will allus build in a blackthorn tree? Hey? Can you tell me that, hey? And why is it that goldfinches that build in a pear-tree allus makes the best singers? Hey? Can ye answer that?"

His gaze made me feel uncomfortable; but before I could reply that I didn't know,

"The subject ain't exactly goldfinches," said Sidney, filling his pipe; and the flare of the match revealed a sardonic expression on his dark face.

"Can't I ask a question if I like, tho'?"

"You can ask as many bliddy questions as you like, midear. I'm saying naught against that."

"Well then, what's all the —— trouble all about, tho'?"

"Oh!" exclaimed Mrs. Zeale, her eyes and mouth and face all becoming round.

"If you want to use that sort of filthy language you can, but NOT IN MY HOUSE, d'ye hear? Is that plain? Or shall I have to put you out?"

"Put me out, hey? It would take a man to do that, I'm telling you. But it would take a better man than you to do it, hey?"

"Aw, stop it," suggested the amiable and pretty Mrs. Zeale.

Sidney Zeale glanced at his wife. "You think you're someone, don't you, my girl?"

"Aw, you'm both mazed drunk, that's the trouble with you. You ought to be ashamed, both of you, talking like that before a gennulman."

"Well, it's you I'm thinking of most, midear. You'm of a mind with me about your own house, I fancy."

"There's times for everything."

Sidney Zeale leaned forward, took the pipe from his mouth, and said unexpectedly:

"Well, then, it's time for the gennulman to see your beautiful hair, midear."

Sailor grunted and spat, and reached over for the bottle.

"Come on, midear, don't 'ee be shy. It isn't the first time this gennulman's seen a woman's long hair, I'm thinking. Mind you, I'm not giving no names, but that's what I'm thinking. What was it poor old Tom Fissick used to say? 'Over them boogerin bannisters next time,' wasn't it? But there, us'll say naught about it."

Mrs. Zeale giggled. I tried to accommodate my expression to the occasion. I had a reputation for being one for the girls. One morning I had gone to see some friends of mine lodging in old Tom Fissick's house, and had just tapped on a bedroom door— it was 9 a.m. and late, I thought, for anyone to be in bed—when Tom had come along and asked me to wait downstairs; which I did, thinking no more about it.

After further encouragement from her husband, Mrs. Zeale put her hand to the round loaf-shaped mass of hair at the back of her head, pulled out some hair-pins, and put them, one after another, between her lips.

While she was doing this, Sailor swung his head at me, and said, with a series of grunts,

"I axed a civil question, didn't I, hey? Do you consider I axed a civil question?"

"About the goldfinches?"

"Certainly, about the goldfinches. I thought as how you would be interested."

"I am, Sailor."

He moved his head up and down slowly, while shifting the quid in his mouth. "That's all I want to know. You got me? Hey? I'm asking just that one question, understand."

"Why are you so interested in goldfinches all of a sudden, tho'?" enquired his brother, in a manner that seemed to me to hold an almost sinister intentness. "Trying to talk big, is that it?"

"Well," said Sailor, making a whirlpool of the tobacco juice in his mouth, and speaking to me, "Well, that's my experience. A goldfinch with white legs will allus build in a pear-tree." He belched, spat, and seized the bottle. After a long pause he added, holding the bottle in his hand, his weary eyes staring unseeing before him. "And a—hic—goldfinch with black legs will allus build in a blackthorn tree."

Mrs. Zeale shook her hair free, and smiled bashfully. She sat still on her chair, obedient and expectant, her feet close together.

"There, what d'ye think of that, eh? Idden it butiful hair? I wager you won't find a better head of hair in all the parish, not even if you was to include the gentry, neither! Stand up, 'Liza, and turn round."

Mrs. Zeale stood up and turned round. The hair hung to her waist, the colour of faded straw. Once, I could imagine, it had had the colour of oats grown on good land—dark gold, and rich-looking—but now the hair was thin, dislustred, faded like weathered straw. As though reading my thoughts, Mrs. Zeale turned round and said, "Aw, tidden nothing now to what it was when I was a maid."

Sailor grunted, and stretched out his huge brown hand, with its swollen fingers, chipped and scaly, and grabbed the bottle.

"Aiy," he said, sucking his upper lip. "A goldfinch with

white legs will allus build in a pear-tree. Am I right?" he shot at me.

"I don't know. I expect you're right. The only nests I've found have been in apple trees and sycamores and elms—high up on the slender branches. Last year, I—"

I could see that he was not listening.

"Am I right, 'Liza? Hey? Can you answer that one? Hey? A goldfinch with white legs will allus—"

"Aw, stop it, Sailor. Don't keep on so."

"'Tes a butiful colour on the wings of the goldfinch," mused Sailor. "D'ye mind that one I gave 'ee once, 'Liza? It 'ad white legs, and I don't care who hears me say it, but 'twas the best singing goldfinch in the parish. And it 'ad the whitest legs I every zeed on a singing bird."

His eyes were dull; his hair dishevelled. He swayed, and his lips worked, as though chewing the cud of some far-off memory.

The deeper voice of his brother persisted in my ear,

"Answer me, midear! Don't 'ee think my wife's got the most lovely hair? Can you beat that anywhere?"

"Don't talk so mazed, Sid. The gennulman will laugh at 'ee."

I replied that I thought it really was very fine; but it must have been "perfectly marvellous" (unconsciously I used a modern, usually meaningless, slang phrase) about the time that Mrs. Zeale was married.

"My friend, you've said it!" cried Sidney Zeale, his dark eyes lighting up, but sinister still in the intensity of his expression. Was it the light of a long-smouldering jealousy? I glanced at Sailor, who was leaning forward, nodding to the clock, and blinking his ox's eyes. Did Sidney Zeale read my thoughts? Probably not, for his face was still darkly lit by an inner exultation. He slapped his knee, saying harshly, "You've said it! 'Marvellous' is just the word. That's what education does— the very word for everything. You heard what the gennulman said, 'Liza? 'Perfectly marvellous.' I couldn't have thought of that if I'd tried."

"Per-fer-kly maar-vlous," mimicked Sailor, and his mouth began working. A suggestion of a smile worked itself into his lips. "Well, Sid—it's time you cut—'Liza's 'air off. 'S—ol' fashioned, mi-dear."

"Nowhere in the parish will you see hair like my wife's," cried Sidney Zeale, grim and dark, ignoring his brother's remark. "Nowhere!"

The grandfather clock in the corner made a slight whirr, followed by a click; then it settled again to its slow *tick-tock*. It was preparing to strike. Three minutes to twelve.

"Yes," said Sidney. "It's nearly Sunday, midear."

"I really must go," I exclaimed, rising from my seat again.

"What's the hurry, hey?" asked Sailor.

"No hurry for you, perhaps," said Sidney, "but other folks isn't so bliddy lazy, perhaps."

Sailor worked his mouth, leered sideways, and replied, "You fancy yourself a bit too bliddy much, that's my way of thinking. Hey?"

"The trouble, you see, midear, is that 'Liza and me gets on very well together, do you see. But when there be a dirty drunken loobey spreading himself about the house—"

"Talk goes away light," grumbled Sailor, looking up at Mrs. Zeale.

"Aw, stop it, you two. You'm looking black as the ace o' spades, Sid!"

"That's all right, midear. This is between us two—no need for anyone to interfere, I fancy."

"You think you cut a bliddy fine figure of a husband, hey?" exclaimed Sailor, truculently.

"My friend, be careful! Be very careful! I wouldn't like to say what's coming to you very soon if you're not very careful!"

Sailor put his hands on his big thighs, and nodded, leering, at the clock; the elder man stood over him, like a sickle about to slash at docks. Sailor swung round his head, his lips working heavily at the words he wanted to say.

"You think I'm scared by a lump of —— like you! Hey?

Think you'll put the wind up me, straddling me, hey? You can pull the head off a bliddy goldfinch, but by Jesus! you don't put the heavy stuff over on me this time! You great bastard, you!"

"Aw, stop rattling, why can't you?" said Mrs. Zeale. "It's time you was both in bed. To expect sense from either of you 'tes like trying to take a cherry out of a pig's mouth."

"The bliddy bird was choking itself, I tell you. Are you going to stop wagging your wab, or do you WANT ME TO PUT YOU OUT?" shouted the husband.

"Hey, HEY? By Cripes, you—"

Sailor's voice thickened and ceased, but his lips were working violently. His bloodshot eyes rolled. Ejecting the quid in his cheek, together with a mouthful of juice that slid and sizzled on the iron of the stove, he seized the neck of the quart bottle and raised it above his head, just as the grandfather clock in the corner clicked and buzzed and whirred, and began to strike.

"You great son of a bitch, you!" shouted Sailor, whirling the bottle round his head. "Think you can put me out, do you? Hey? Put me out, will you?" The bottle swished near me and I started back. "HEY?" bellowed Sailor, his nostrils opened wide. The weights inside the clock-case knocked and bumped, and the works groaned before each rattling strike. "OUT? ME? HEY?" he roared, turning towards the clock. "PUT ME OUT, WILL YOU?" and he flung the bottle at the square glass face, where it crashed and fell with noise of glass. Blinking and grunting and swaying, Sailor stood there; and then he sagged, and muttering, "I don't give a flip for no one," he sat down suddenly in his chair.

His brother, now animated by a suppressed fury and violence that made his muttered words as harsh as the noise of thorns in a fire, went forward and caught hold of his coat collar. Mrs. Zeale cried out to him not to hurt Sailor; her husband answered that he would not hurt him, no, he would not hurt him, O dear no: there would be no chance any more of anything, hurt or otherwise. He would find out that he got from him more, O, much more, than he bargained for.

And the younger man, half passive and half struggling, was dragged to the door, and pitched outside.

"Well, I think I'd better say good night. And thank you for the excellent supper," I said, when Sidney Zeale had used up two matches vainly trying to light the ashes of his pipe.

"Don't say naught about it, midear," replied Sidney Zeale, sardonically pleasant, as he opened the door, closing and locking it behind me.

It was a clear night, with a moon. Earth and sky were silent, except for the wabble of the stream in the culvert below, and the noise of Sailor getting on his feet.

" Fine," he said, and swayed towards his dim shadow beside the pump-shadow. There he rested awhile, before looking up and saying:

"I couldn't be better pleased, hey?"

He started to walk up the short steep bit of road that led to the school and the sea on the west, and the other way to the moon over the battlements of the church tower.

At the top of the slope he stopped, and fumbled for stick of tobacco and knife. I considered asking him to sleep on the spare bed in my cottage; but at that moment he belched, and I said:

"Shall we sleep on the haystack at the top of Netherhams?"

He grunted, and shrugged his shoulders. "Anywhere as you likes. I don't trouble."

I suggested I should go back and get some blankets I had scrounged from the Army, and that he should await my return.

When I came back the moonlit wall on which he had been leaning was vacant. I searched around, and could find nothing. Could he have gone back to the cottage? I crept down, saw the small window of the left bedroom lit by a wan yellow opaque square; the right window, of Sailor's room, was dark. I listened a moment, and returned. Snores came from the lime-washed wall in front. A white wooden door cast a narrow triangle of shadow. I opened it, and looked in. I spoke, and getting no answer but a snore and a double grunt, I struck a match.

Sailor was inside, lying on fresh straw, back to back with an immense black sow, asleep. Both seemed happy, so I left them, and in the bright and wonderful moonlight I walked over Netherhams field to Farmer Furze's thistly haystack. I would like to say, however, that it was not I who broke his ladder. Besides, the ladder was worm-eaten, and quite rotten with several rungs missing; and such ladders should not be allowed near romantic trysting places.

The next day Sailor left the village. He returned several times during the summer and autumn, always at the beginning of the month; but after the first year his visits became fewer, until they ceased. And now, after an interval of two years—twice the apple-blossom and the goldfinch song without him—he had come back. Sitting there at the long table of the Higher House, he looked just as he had looked when first I had seen him after the Great War, except for the grey hairs now in his head and unshaven chin. He looked lost. Perhaps he had never found himself. What life had he had, outside the stoke-hold of the ships he had served?

I lingered in the room, wishing to show I was glad to see him, but our talk was a failure. He took gulps of his beer between long intervals of moody silence. I had not long risen from my bed, after a feverish cold; and so, perhaps, I exaggerated his loneliness. This, I thought, was his home—he had no other place in the world. We played a game of table skittles, but he was worse than I, and we gave up after the first "leg", or up-and-down pegging on the score board. About a quarter to eight, as I was about to leave, his brother came in, and I stayed.

The brothers did not speak. After awhile Sailor called for drinks all round—six of us were in the bar then. Albert quietly took our orders, all for beer; but when he came, with an extra softness of voice it seemed, to ask the last man, Sidney Zeale shook his head and said with quiet distinctness, "No, thank you."

Sailor spat on the floor. The drinks were brought, paid for, and partly swallowed. Sidney Zeale continued to talk amiably with Farmer Stroyle George about the burial ground being extended on Church land. Both were in agreement about the cunning of Farmer Furze in erecting a house on the requisitioned site, and so not many words were passed. I stood the next round of drinks, and again Sidney Zeale refused. He was about to go home to his supper, thank you. It was then about twenty past eight; and he stayed until half-past nine. Sailor watched him empty his fourth glass, and then moved over to him.

"Won't you have a drink, Sid?"

"I told you before, I don't want anything more to do with you."

"Hey? I'm as good a man as you be, I reckon."

"Us'll say no more about it, midear."

Sailor stood near him, his mouth working, then he held out his hand.

It remained unclasped.

"Good night, all," said Sidney Zeale, and rising he opened the door and went out.

I went for a walk, for the evening was beautiful over the fields of Higher Ham, with the voice of the corncrake in the tall grass, the white owl wafting its silent way down the hedges, and the sunset beyond the sea and Lundy. As I came down the lane from Ox's Cross, in the dim light, I passed a slow figure trudging unevenly up the hill. It was Sailor. We stopped awhile, but as before, we had little to say to each other; and with a "So long," he went on his way up the hill. Having exhausted his money, he was walking back to Combe, a distance of eight miles, whence he had come by car in the afternoon. Albert Gammon had long ago told me how he had left home as a youth, and joined the Navy; how before then he had been courting 'Liza, but when Sidney Zeale had come home from working on the railway, there had been tears, and quarrelling between the brothers.

"Sailor and 'Liza was quite happy, if you understand my

meaning," said Albert. "But Sid, he was always a turrible jealous chap, and couldn't abide his brother having what he hadn't got."

He had made plain to me, also, the references to the gold-finch, which had been found dead in its cage—gift of the younger brother to 'Liza. "I minds the time he got it from Billy Goldsworthy's pear-tree," said Albert. "Although the tree belonged to Billy's father in they days. Yes, that's it. Turrible jealous chap, Sidney Zeale always was; very masterful in some ways, but no more heart than a goose-chick."

I listened to the footfalls until they were·gone through the trees on the skyline: then the lane was dark and lonely, and filled with the sadness of all human farewells; and I hastened down the hill to the village, longing to see the light in the window of my home, where my little boy lay sleeping.

## *Chapter Fourteen*

## THE LINHAY ON THE DOWNS

On the high down above the sea, in the corner of the last rough grazing field, stands a linhay, half fallen into ruin. It is built of boles of spruce fir, unhewn but barked, and boarded with rough wooden boards. It has a roof of corrugated iron. The roof is intact, but many of the wooden boards have fallen with the rusted nails. Those boards remaining are green and damp, and shaggy with grey lichens.

The linhay had been built with its eastern end open to shelter bullocks in stormy weather, but the gentleman farmer had sold the down with his other land after the Great War, and the new owner, a native farmer, had let it fall ruinous. Battering winds and rain straight from off the Atlantic, and the hot sun of summer, had warped and rotted the boards and opened two other walls to the weather.

# THE LINHAY ON THE DOWNS

On windy days buzzard hawks lie over the downs on crooked wings, watching for rabbits in the heather slope below; or turn and glide over the line of the hill. It is a beautiful and desolate place, where the spirit can spread itself wide and airy as the sea and the sky.

One morning between winter and spring I set out to picnic in the linhay with a companion. As we climbed the road to Windwhistle Cross the wind blew harder, and found cold places in our clothes. Past the beech plantation the way lay over fields, cutting across the broad and rushing gale. I was more hardened than my companion, who covered her face with her gloved hands and walked with bowed head. After awhile we reached a wall of stone and earth, tunnelled by rabbits, and fallen in gaps. The wind, seeking to level all things, was whipping up bits of stone and earth over the wall, and we had to shield our eyes. Plants growing on the crumbling riband of earth remaining on the top of the stones were pressed tightly down, guarding their leaves among the mosses from the stripping storms. White splashes marked the stones, where in still weather the buzzards had waited and watched for rabbits to lollop out of their buries in the wall.

We reached the linhay, and knew immediately that it would give no shelter for a fire as in other expeditions. The hollow was frigid in shadow and scoured by the wind. The last stone wall before the heather and brambles of the wild seaward slope stood a few strides away, and behind this we sat down and rested out of the wind. An easy matter to break the old boards with a fifty-pound slab of ironstone fallen from the wall, but not so easy to make a fire. Half a box of matches and chips sliced with a knife, however, changed the acrid smoke of deal-wood into flame, and the flame into red and black brittle embers, which wasted in sparks over the grass. The wind was too strong. There was no contentment in such a fire.

While we were munching our sandwiches in the sunshine my companion, who had been staring into the shadow-cut interior of the linhay ten yards away, asked me if I saw anything above a stone against the inner wall. Yes, I saw a pair of ears upraised, and a dark brown eye below them.

I stood up, and the ears went down flat; but the brown eye continued to watch. A rabbit was squatting there.

I sat down out of the wind, and soon afterwards the ears were raised again. The wind tore at the flames and rocked a loose stone on the wall behind us. It was blowing harder. We moved away, spreading a raincoat before a derelict plough which old grasses had partly covered. Seagulls, shifting and slanting in swift uneven gliding, began to appear above our heads, first in pairs, and then in many numbers. The sunlight was put out, and the wind was trying to crush us with cold. I got up and looked over the wall.

I saw a grand and terrible sight. The headland which lay out into the bay, dark and puny under the vastness of sky that seemed to begin just beyond my feet, was blurred and lost. Beyond, a mile of two from the extended sands below, where hundreds of gulls were standing still and tiny as scattered whitish seeds, all was chaos. It was as though the sky was falling, as though a monstrous dark spectre had risen out of the sea and was moving to overthrow the land.

We picked up our raincoats, gathered them back from the wind, and allowed ourselves to be billowed into the linhay. The air-blows thudded against the boards of the intact side—the shippen was open west, south and east, except for the round support posts, gnawn with damp at the base, which remained upright. Wind rebounding from the single wall flung over us like a comber, dropping dust and straw-specks in our ears and the corners of our eyes. It was cold on the rough trodden floor, whereon lay flakes of frayed board and dried dung of bullocks. Slabs of stone lay against the wall, about six inches from the bottom board, and in one space the rabbit was still crouching, its ears pressed on its shoulders, its life quivering behind the staring dark eyes.

The headland was gone; the sky was falling. Beyond the forming ridges of distant waves the sea seemed to be taking on a wrinkled dull grey skin, like molten lead in a trough; and as we watched, the falling blackness was riven, and in the rift a snout arose, and spread upwards into the shape of a funnel as it travelled over the surf to the shore. It was a waterspout. We saw the tiny white seeds sprout with wings, and settle on the sands again. The open linhay trembled, and we buttoned our coats to the neck.

A ladder was fixed to the middle post of one side of the linhay, leading to the tallat, or loft, through an open trap-door seven feet above our heads. We climbed up, and were in an open space crossed by rafters under slanting corrugated iron sheets, lit at the seaward end by a window frame without glass. The floor was rotten in places. Wooden pegs of snares, some with tarnished brass-wire loops, were thrown in one corner, with a sack. The skull of a mouse, with brittle bones interlocked in greyish fur, lay on one beam, where an owl had roosted. I looked through a break in the floor; the rabbit was still beside the stone.

Wind-noises ran through the bleak tallat, coming in at the eaves, the floor cracks, the window frame stripped of putty and paint, where owls had perched. They filled the loft, like the hollow and curious voices of straying things never of the earth or its life. We stood close together, while light rapidly drained from the rafters, the floor, each other's face. We waited, a little fearfully, for the storm to reach us, awed by the mysterious noises of the wind, which were changing every moment.

The plaining voices were lost in the buffets on the iron roof. The skull of the mouse rolled on the beam, and the bones fell aslant, joining a trickle of broken straws along the floor. My companion wrapped her coat closer round her legs. I peered through an empty square of the window, and saw greyness rushing up the heather slope of the down. I saw the fire by the wall, already gutted of embers, kicked as though by an invisible foot. The charred lengths of board, flecked with yellow and red points of flame, rose up and flew yards, and fell flat, smoking violently in the grass.

# THE LINHAY ON THE DOWNS

Voices wailed and shrieked, seeming to dissolve the substance of the tallat in a pallor of darkness. Straw specks and mice bones whirled on the floor, suddenly to rise up and scatter. The linhay was shuddering in the wind. Would the inner core of its uprights hold in the storm? I trod a careful way to the trap-door, and the wind instantly threw up the wide skirt of the raincoat into my face.

We waited, our backs to the screaming draughts racing up the corrugations of the iron roof. Suddenly a hatch in the walled angle above the trap-door burst its wooden latch and flung half open, before wedging against the floor, and shaking on the ragged grass background of the field below. An amazing object moved slowly across the grassy rectangle cut by the lichen-frayed door! My companion also saw it, and clutched my arm.

The object moved on three thin legs, with a hop that threw its head up and down in alternate roll and flop. It paused, got its hind legs under it, and took another hop forward, dragging something on the ground. Each forward movement, which needed about five seconds to prepare, took it perhaps six inches nearer shelter. By its head and tail it was a fox—but was it a fox? The tail hung like a piece of old rope, the small head was almost without hair, the ribs showed under creases of skin muddy and stuck with tufts, through which the sharp points of shoulders and hips seemed about to break with the weight of the swelled body. I had just turned my glass into focus and seen that it was a vixen dragging the chain and iron peg of a rusty rabbit gin clamped on its foreleg when the first hail smote the roof with an immense clattering crash, and the linhay rocked with the hollow thunder of the wind. I feared it would turn over, crumple, and be carried over the stone wall immediately behind. The field space below the door was a grey blank; the day was torn up and hurtling past us. Jets of icy air were driven through the floor and up between body and clothes. The sack slid over the floorboards, reached the square of the trap-door, jumped to the rafters, on which it moulded itself before falling. It was snatched through the hatch. I yelled in my companion's ear that it would be best to stand by that hatch, to jump clear when the linhay should buckle and rise. I took her by the hand, cold as stone, and guided her along one of the joists lest the floor break under our tread.

We had reached the eastern end when the black of the storm descended on the down. Immediately we were under a torrent. I saw alarm with the misery in the dim face beside me. The linhay was lurching under the flood. Skits blown in from the open window tasted salt on my lips. And the sea was a mile away, at the end of a downward slant of fifteen degrees!

The earth under the linhay was awash. Water moved there in wrinkled sheets prickled with rain. I could see nothing of fox or rabbit. The smashing of wood for the fire had given me warmth, but this warmth was used and gone after five more minutes in the loft. My companion was rigid, as though being enclosed in an icicle. Her teeth chattered. The wind pushed its thorns under our nails and in our jaw-bones, and drew its brambles down our ears and cheeks. Our toes were broken in glacial gins.

There was no grandeur in the elements now; imagination was disharmonized from the sun. Nature was indifferent to the sufferings of all life. I could bear the screeching icy jets with fortitude, but my companion suffered, having no dolorous background in memory to make the present ineffectual. In that background were days and nights in water and yellow clay sludge to the waist, with death above the leafless winter hedge shot stooping-high: days and nights without sleep, weeks and months without hope, without liberty—life with neither present nor future, worse than death, for death was release—life more terrible than being in a gin, for God has blessed Man with the power to reason, and the seventeen-year-old volunteer knew that if he sought release, and failed, or escaped from killing men he did not hate, nor had ever seen before, he would be caught and shot before sunrise in peace time clothes, with a bandage over his eyes and a white paper mark pinned opposite his heart still joined in spirit to the mother who bore him in pain and after-joy, and his name and regiment would be read out on three successive parades to every soldier in the British Army in that alien country. The pain as of thorns pushed under finger nails was nothing—it would pass.

The linhay withstood the storm, as it had others, held by the stout cores of its upright posts. The day began to grow again in the twilight of the loft. Old boards grew swiftly green, the battering on the roof suddenly ceased with a few lingering taps against the iron sheets. Drops falling by the empty squares of the window were white, they glittered!—and blue and white sea and sky were beyond.

Kneeling down and moving my face to a crack between the floorboards I looked for rabbit and fox. Sight was limited, so I crawled stiffly (sometimes blowing through my half-clenched hands for warmth) to the trap-door, and peered over. The floor of the shippen was like the Ypres Salient in the winter of nineteen-seventeen, seen from a low-flying aeroplane. Hoof-holes, shapeless and trodden into one another, were filled with water to their broken edges. Wind wrinkled the sky-gleams by the posts.

Against the inner wall sat the vixen, on one of the slabs of ironstone. Her back and neck were curved like a snail-shell. Her nose touched the mud. She was shivering with every breath. The foot of the broken foreleg and the gin that gripped it were in the mud. Beside her on the other slab, about eighteen inches away, sat the rabbit. It looked about it with the relaxed movements and expression of an animal at ease. I had heard of timid and preying animals sheltering together innocently during a storm, but this was the only time such a pleasing sight had been witnessed.

A sound from above, from my companion, made vixen and rabbit look up together. We kept still and they relaxed again. I saw the vixen turn her mangy head towards the rabbit, which continued to nibble its fore-paw. The narrow head began to droop in sleep, or weariness.

I watched for some minutes: until a patient voice above me

begged to be allowed to get down. I had forgotten those bluish hands, rough with chilblains.

As I climbed down the ladder I saw, from the tail of my eye, the rabbit in a series of splashes crossing to the grass beyond the round posts. It disappeared. The field was a brilliant green, steaming in the hot rays of the sun.

The vixen was sitting on the stone; her mouth was open, showing her teeth. She stood on three legs placed close together, swaying to keep balance, her brush pressed against the wall. She tried to stay herself with her broken leg, but it gave no support, and each time she nearly tipped into the mud.

There used to live in the village an old trapper who nearly died of the effects of a fox's bite, which festered and made his hand swell, and his joints painful with inner corruption. This animal must have been feeding on slugs, beetles, and carrion left by magpies and buzzards—rats thrown out of gins in corn-fields, broken carcases of rabbits—and its teeth were probably more dirty than those of a healthy fox. How else had it survived, limping for weeks, or months (long before clicketting time, perhaps), dragging the gin clanking on every stone, and rattling on the hard ground? I was afraid of its bite, having seen some years before a fox dead in a gin with lock-jaw. Better to kill it and so put myself out of my misery, for it was a woeful sight; and although the poor beast might have been used to its slow and crippled ways, there were the cubs soon to be born. Better to knock the vixen on the nose with my stick and bury her under a heap of stones.

My companion and I ran over the grass in the wind and the sunshine, swinging our arms and laughing ruefully at each other with the pain in thawing toes and fingers. We had a warm, dry cottage in the valley over the down, a garden filled with vegetables, fruit trees, stores of apples, potatoes, and wood for firing; shelves of books to read, clothes to wear, and flowers to tend in the coming spring and summer; we had been married less than two years, but already we had one merry little babe with six teeth, who watched the rooks flying over the roof with sticks for their nests, and shouted "Dukaduk!" to them. So when we were warm again we returned with a sack to the linhay, and putting it over the head of the vixen held her easily in her weak struggles, carried her into the field, trod on the steel spring to open the iron jaws of the gin, and lifted out the paw. An easy matter to snick with a knife the frayed tendons, and to bind the stump with my tie, securing it with string. Then the sack was pulled away, rolling over the vixen. She kicked and scrambled on her three and a half feet and faced us, snarling, with arched back and ears laid flat. I tapped the gin beside her with my stick, and she snapped at it. Pushing the end of the stick through the spring I drew it away; she lifted the stump and made the other foreleg rigid, as though to resist. Slowly we walked backwards, drawing the gin over the wet grass. She whined, holding out a quivering stump. Five yards, ten yards, twenty yards—slowly we drew away from her, while she watched with raised ears and shifting feet.

We stood still. She rose and hobbled on, as though still dragging the iron. We watched her to the grass-tied plough under the wall. Here she smelt food, and down went her nose, searching for scraps of bread and boiled bacon left by us for the birds. She rolled on her back in the sunlight and then disappeared through the gateway to the slope of furze and heather.

The daffodils in the garden broke yellow and danced for weeks in the wind until their blooms were frayed; sandmartins and the chiff-chaffs came back to the headland; our baby began to pull himself, totteringly, to his feet beside my chair; rooks were sitting on their nests above the graveyard; the church was decorated with flowers and budding willow-wands at Eastertide.

When next we walked to the linhay, we saw the first swallows flitting over the seaward slope of the down. A trapper called to us from the bank, stopping his work to tell us of what he thought was a very strange thing. That morning, visiting his rabbit gins in the sandhills below, he had seen the prints of a limping fox, the marks of scurry round the gin it had sprung, and the trail leading away. How the bit of raggedy stuff had gotten in the gin he couldn't think. Raggedy stuff? Might I see it? The trapper was sorry, he had "drowed'n away, not thinking much of it at the time; 'twas a bit of old raggedy black stuff, with yaller stripes on'n. Aiy, like a wasp!"

I knew that regimental tie.

## Chapter Fifteen

## THE FOX IN THE MOONLIGHT

One candle was burning in the room. This night was no longer a routine occasion for drawing curtains in the little room of ship's-timber and plaster and sagging ceiling, for putting more logs on the fire, for reading the daily paper, for finding any reason why work should be put off till the morrow, for smoking too much tobacco, for sitting before the fire and becoming tired and irritable—no longer merely the latter part of a useless day, when talents were buried yet deeper by indolence—the night was Night, with the moon so white and quiet above the dark, as if sunken, village, above the dark thatches glistening silver where dew-drop or wet fern held the mystic fire. In my room was a wireless set, and from the Queen's Hall came the green-corn music of Delius, akin to the green-corn spirit of Jefferies: men who strove to dream themselves out of the present, whose desires arose like mayflies in ancient sunlight. The ancient moon shone over the village, the sad ecstasy of *Brigg Fair* floated from the dark alcove above the fireplace, the candle flame wavered as the slant of pallid light moved across the floor; and it seemed, as when I first came to dwell here, nearly ten years ago now, that the night was immortal, of interstellar Truth, the celestial strength behind the temporary nights of the solar system; that Life was a spirit of

213

harmony behind its outward forms of life. Idolised in the New Testament were incidents in the strivings of genius to reveal this immortality of Night; religion, poetry, music, all art was of this starry stream which poets saw in moments of exaltation, but not with their eyes.

The music ceased, the white Night remained. Almost I could hear the breaking of the leaves from the churchyard elms, distant by a barn and three cottages, the slow flitter down to the shadowy gravestones. Looking out of my window I could see the new poster, and its brown letters, white among the older bills and notices on the doors of Billy Goldsworthy's barn below my window.

THE HARVEST IS OVER

SUMMER IS GONE

AND WE ARE NOT SAVED

The harvest was over, and summer was gone—after the sheaves had lain sodden for weeks, and before that, the hay lying sodden in swathe and cock for weeks, or as it seemed, for months; some fields of it still lying there under the hunter's moon, with new leaves of dock and green sprays growing through the disappearing layers, where the black slugs glistened as they fed. About one-third of the hay crop was not saved, and much grain had grown out of the corn sheaves.

A woman's rapid footsteps passed in the lane outside. She panted, rather than breathed. I recognized the wheeziness of Mrs. Smalldon, the short plump little woman who passed under my window several times each day, always with a rush basket, on her way from her cottage to the inn. Up the lane she encountered another woman, and said breathlessly:

"They'm come! George said there be seven lamps stack up on seven girt tall sticks!"

"Where be'm to?"

"Up Higher Ham, outside Jonathan Furze's. Listen! They'm zinging!"

I too heard singing. The air seemed more still outside the

214

open window. Seven lamps stuck up on seven great tall sticks. I wondered what it meant. The footfalls went away together up the road, with laughter.

It seemed rather early for Christmas carols. One Christmas before, when I had been sitting in the same room, about twenty singers with lights had appeared outside the cottage, accompanied by another score of children and young people, and all I had in the house was a shilling. This I gave, withering internally at the comments, imagined and real, of those who turned out the bag into which I had dropped my struggling-author's all. So on this occasion, hearing the noises or sounds—the more one struggles for the precise word the more one struggles for the shilling—I began to search urgently in my pockets. Soon it was apparent that many people were coming down the lane, towards my cottage. I blew out the candle, turned off the radio which was now tuning up for the loveliest song of Delius, with the words of Dowson's poem *Cynara*, and with a curse knelt down on the floor, lest my face be visible in the blanching rays of the moon. Only my hair and narrow forehead would be visible; it might be mistaken for a piece of plaster fallen from the wall to the sill.

The seven lights, stack up on the seven girt tall sticks, bobbed down the road. They appeared to be hurricane lamps, of the type used to reveal dumps of gravel and holes in the road to motorists as night. On each globe was painted a red letter. As they came more or less to a standstill I read

NOISIMS

There was some shuffling of feet, accompanied by the wagging of lanterns. At length the combination of letters was changed to

ISSIMON

and then a hymn was started. To be precise, the familiar tune of a hymn was distinguishable among words that were bawled.

# THE FOX IN THE MOONLIGHT

The bawling was almost entirely caused by the treble shouting of boyish voices, which dominated the steady and serious but subdued bass voices belonging to the dark cluster of men in the moon-shadow of the thatch of Hole Farm. The trebles were led by a voice I recognized as belonging to a nice boy called Billy Tucker, the son of a mason, and nephew of Charlie Tucker the clerk of the Parish Council. Billy was one of the church choir boys. He had a sweet voice, but to-night he was bawling in a way which would have been described by a writer, no struggler after precisions, as ear-splitting.

After the hymn there was further adjustment of the girt tall sticks, and although the order of the lamps was "phonetical rather than educational" (as the Rector remarked afterwards), the meaning and purpose of the invasion was

MIISSON

A voice, earnest and careful, then cried:

"We have come out yurr among you to do you good. If there be anyone within sound of this voice who feels he is a sinner, let him come to the service in the chapel to-morrow night at half-past seven. This is the message we bring to you. The Lord Jesus Christ said: 'I come not to call the righteous, but the sinners, to repentance.' Let me tell you there is no one so far gone in sin that he cannot be saved by Jesus Christ. The Lord Jesus Christ can save to the uttermost. Every week this night at half-past seven there will be a service in the chapel. Come, and be saved. Welcome to all, in the name of our Lord Jesus Christ, who will wash away all sin."

While the earnest voice was turning in its address from the graveyard to Revvy and his wife in the open doorway—Ernie was carrying a lamp—to Bessie Carter hiding behind her half-open door, to Thunderbolt Willie her club-footed brother smoking contentedly on his threshold, thence towards me (crouching lower, in imitation of fallen plaster) and completing its orbit, to Farmer Stroyle George peering through the crack of his door reluctantly open, the lamp M was wagging about, until at the end of the exhortation, the order read again

ISSIMON

Afterwards I discovered that the bearer of lamp M was the boy called Tikey, who wanted to get nearer letter O—borne by his friend called Mustard. The lamp-bearing was not such fun as they had imagined when they volunteered to carry, and M was arranging with O to abandon their lights when next the Mission moved on.

Now during the earnest exhortation, while I crouched by the window sill, I heard the footfalls of someone coming down the road from the opposite direction. Darting to the other window, I saw the red glow from a cigarette, discreetly held in hand, showing against the wall of Hole Farm. It re-glowed every few moments. Was he waiting until they were gone, lest he be addressed personally, a dreaded ordeal?

When the voice ceased, the cigarette was dropped among the nettles. The figure moved down in the shadow of the corrugated iron roof and the wall. Another hymn was started by Billy Tucker leading off in his most piercing treble. The newcomer, a tall young dairy-farmer, who had recently taken a farm in the neighbourhood, stood and watched. A glint of moonlight showed that he was carrying a gun.

Apparently his arrival was expected, for immediately another figure attached itself to him and drew him apart from the scattered group near the lanterns. There was rapid talking in the shadow of the wall, words uttered in a low voice, and always by the shorter of the two men. The taller man, carrying the gun, seemed to nod occasionally. When the crowd went past my window they remained there, the low rapid voice pouring something into, or possibly against, the consciousness of the other. Was this other a genuine sinner who would be saved by the earnest young deacon? Another hymn began in the distance. After awhile, the two walked in its direction.

# THE FOX IN THE MOONLIGHT

I pulled out the switch of the wireless set. I pushed it back instantly, not wanting to hear the latest Fat Stock Prices. It was night once more, the moon merely a sister planet to our own, whose ways of ice and pallor our earth one day would share. Perhaps it was still Night for the sincere and gentle old men who had come to the village in hope and trust of their visions and beliefs, in the will to share their good tidings with their fellow-men. I hoped they had good overcoats, for it was growing chilly, and a mist was beginning to creep over the gardens in the hollow of the village.

I pulled the chair nearer the fire, put my feet up, and thought of nothing.

Stealthy footfalls outside. Whispered boyish voices came through the open silver window.

"My Gor, look at thaccy!"

"Gordarn, what be it?"

"I'm afraid."

"Let's tell Mis'r Wisson."

I looked down on the upturned faces of Tikey and Mustard.

"Look Mis'r Wisson, quick, look, what be thaccy up auver your steps?"

The garden of the cottage I had moved to, soon after my marriage, was a "made" garden, many hundreds of loads of soil being dumped on the slope of rock, and held in by a mortared wall of stone. The garden was level with the wall top, which was six or seven feet above the lane. Steps led up from the lane just under the window. At the top of the steps I had made a small rockery for Alpine plants; this was known locally as the Dog's Grave. Tikey and Mustard were pointing at the Dog's Grave. Moon-shadows from the lumps of rock made it look like a cubist picture; and staring at an unfamiliar halo of dimness at the top of the steps, I suddenly started: for there an animal stood, or rather crouched, its bushy tail half-curled about its hindquarters, its ears sharp as the fixed look of its eyes.

"Keep still! Don't move!" I hissed. "It's a fox!"

Mustard and Tikey stood obediently still in the lane below.

# THE FOX IN THE MOONLIGHT

For nearly half a minute I was as frozen as the fox in the moonlight.

"Now don't move, boys," I said quietly as I could. "Whatever you do, don't move. I want to get my wife to see it! Most
extraordinary! It thinks we haven't seen it—natural colour
protection—it will stay there so long as no one disturbs—now
don't make any sudden movement—keep still."

I fancied I saw a glint from one of the fox's eyes.

"Not a movement—keep very still—" I implored.

"Oh, sir," whispered Mustard.

"What?"

"Please, sir, will it hurt us?"

"No. Don't be frightened, boys. It's more scared than you
are. Please don't move."

"No, sir," whispered Tikey.

"No, sir," whispered Mustard.

Somehow I dragged my wife, holding a feeding bottle and
baby's napkins, and protesting that milk would boil over, to
the window. The fox had not moved. Other children were
below, about a score all standing still watching our window.
We stared at it. Tikey and Mustard and the children stared at
our moonlit faces. Momentarily they glanced at the fox; but
their interest was upon our faces. All the children were staring
at us, expectantly.

"It's not alive," said my wife. "The milk, I left it—"

The afore-referenced writer would have described what
followed as a merry burst of childish laughter; but actually a
devastating and united yell came upon me from below, like
many missiles. The only thing to do was to wait until it stopped,
and then to congratulate the promoters of the joke. Have you
ever been chased by a family of weasels, animals smaller than
rats? It is a disintegrating experience; you are actually hunted;
the world has turned upon you. And so when a group of children
is unanimous in laughing at you, the only thing to do, as with
any crowd, is to control it by keeping each individual separate
unto himself; and to do this, the individual must identify him-

self with you, and not against you. You must go with their mood. At least, this was my determined policy, following upon an experience of a few months before.

That was an occasion when the children, led by Tikey, had hunted me through the village. It began at my invitation, as a game, to ease the tears of one small boy; it developed into a terrifying, a humiliating experience, myself walking here and there with an increasing mass of shrill cries, taunts, jeers and shouts pursuing me. Nothing stopped them—rushes at them to scatter them like skittle pins only increased the massed shrillness. In smiling desperation I had invited some to go for a ride on my motor-cycle; they clambered in and on the side-car, the handlebars, the mudguards, on my back, clawing one another off amidst screams of exultation. Somehow we were in motion, moving, a swaying mass of humanity—sixteen souls, as I live, borne by the power of three and a half metallic horses on a swaying structure of hollow steel pipes and three-ply wood, moving on air imprisoned within rubber. Then a cunning thought came to my rescue. Up the long hill to Windwhistle Cross, a mile above the village, we went, pounding in low gear, bumping on the springs: there I scattered a few miserable copper coins into the road: thence I glided down the hill, free and alone. Now here they were again, below the window; and here was I again, wondering what to do.

"Please don't let them make such a noise," said a voice at my side, scarcely audible. "The baby—the milk—"

Another cunning idea came to me.

Below in the road, the children gathered round. I handed the stuffed fox—a sorry object when scrutinized, the abandoned nursery of many generations of moths—to Mustard, its owner. Mr. Taylor, landlord of the Lower House, had given it to Mustard, who was his grandson, that evening.

"Us put'n first by the stream," explained Mustard, "And when 'Champion' Hancock came by, he saw it, and cried, 'It be an otter—get me a stick, bigorr!' Then with the stick he ran to give it a dapp. That's why the head be broke."

# THE FOX IN THE MOONLIGHT

I learned that Champion had been angry—his tactics of avoiding the hunt. He had disappeared into the Lower House, where he would be able to laugh about it.

I invited Tikey and Mustard into my writing-room, first telling them to dismiss the children, which they did, with hard decisive voices.

"Listen," I said. "I wonder what would happen if the Mission saw the fox. They're down by Zeales. If you were to creep through Stroyle George's orchard, and through Gravedigger Clib's garden, through Oldmother Black's place, and put it on the stone wall beside Zeales. . . . Only be careful, for someone may shoot at it."

They disappeared into the shadow of Stroyle George's wall, and I hastily put on my boots.

In our dark little underground kitchen there was the smell of burnt milk. Other milk, or baby food, was being heated over the American blue-flame oil-stove, and so I went alone to the lane called Zeales.

### ISMONIS

"You will tell me that the harvest is over, but I will reply that God's Harvest is never over—"

The voice was now slightly hoarse.

I waited by the garden wall of Miss Black. The stream babbled gently as it disappeared in the culvert under the road. Against the wall of Billy Goldsworthy's cottage the deacon was pouring earnest words into, or possibly against, the consciousness of the young farmer.

During the singing of the hymn, many more children seemed to have come around.

Tikey touched my hand. "Look," he whispered. The hymn ceased. The young farmer was being led forward for introduction to an old man with a white beard.

"What is it, Tikey?" I said aloud.

"Please, sir, I don't know, sir. It looks like a fox, sir," he cried.

"A fox? Did you say a fox?" I called out.

"Yes, sir, a fox, sir, I'm almost sure it's a fox, sir." Suddenly Tikey threw up his nose like a puppy about to howl, and cried out "A FOX!"

ISMONIS became various combinations of letters, some leaning against the cottage wall, others waving perilously. Bang! Bang! and the fox fell over the wall.

"There he goes!" cried Tikey, pointing into the blur of apple trees.

"I hit him!" cried the farmer.

"Don't shoot!" I shouted, thinking of Mustard, and of myself in a police court unable to answer back the scathing condemnation of Foolishness by Justice.

"Here I am, sir," said Mustard, beside Tikey. "I threw it in the stream, sir, so they won't find it. Bigorr, but the shot whistled over my head, sir." He seemed delighted.

Led by the young farmer, the hangers on, including the lantern-bearers, disappeared into the orchard in pursuit of the quarry. The missioners were left alone, standing in a quiet, almost sad, group in the lane. They were middle-aged and elderly men, except the young deacon. Valiantly he addressed an invisible audience again.

Then to my alarm, I saw he was addressing his exhortation to me. It was too late to run with the others after the alleged fox.

" 'I come not to call the righteous, but sinners to repentance.' "

"An ironic remark of Jesus, obviously," I heard myself saying.

Explanations were vain. They had a scriptural quotation to counter every attempt to see the Nazarene as he lived, as his own personal vision drew the multitudes from organised religion to himself and his way of life. For the deacon, the spokesman of the forlorn and valiant band which had come in the night filled with hope for the Mission, it was all so simple; you accept all that is printed, literally; in time you believe it; you are baptized, completely put under water in white clothes—in olden days in the river Taw (at low tide), nowadays in the galvanised iron tank under the chapel floor; and you continue your human life in the same old way, except that you don't smoke or take alcoholic drink; but the business side of you, an eye for an eye, goes on as before. There are exceptions, whose human kindliness outshines their dogma. At least, that is what nearly ten years in the village (1919–1929) had shown me.

For it seemed to me in those days that the truth of the historical Jesus was not realised among them; that what the world needed was a fifth gospel to implement and explain the curious and naïve Jacobean prose in terms of human authenticity, so that the ordinary man would recognise instantly the truth of that great and grand person who gave all of his life to poor humanity —that authentic and revolutionary genius of civilisation, whose sayings had been inspired common sense. A truthful biography which would exclude all the falsehoods invented after the death of Jesus was needed, written by a modern clairvoyant poet: a biography exposing the idolatrous falsehoods of uninspired minds which could not see *plain and clear*, but like all second-rate literary minds must embellish and exaggerate because their eyes saw not the marvels of ordinary life, as the eyes of Jesus had seen them. Plan or perish—a new way of life, of intelligent benevolence, or die never having lived more than a tenth of your frustrated selves—that was what Jesus had cried with celestial truth: in vain, during his lifetime.

The mist was moving down the valley. Carrying the letter N, I followed the black-clothed men to their motor bus waiting by the Post Office to take them to the next village.

Looking forward as we walked, I saw that at last we were

MISSION

To my new acquaintances, whose sincerity was moving and kindly, I said good-bye; adding as I moved away in shadow that the thoughts of Jesus of Nazareth were the light of the world.

"Ah, 'tis what the world needs, my dear," said the leader,

who had a white beard. "There is no hope otherwise for us at all," and I walked home, serene in the white night, feeling the infinite beauty of life.